SUCCESSFUL
MIDLIFE
CAREER CHANGE

SUCCESSFUL MIDLIFE CAREER CHANGE

Self-Understanding and Strategies for Action

Paula I. Robbins

A Division of the American Management Associations

Library of Congress Cataloging in Publication Data

Robbins, Paula I
   Successful midlife career change.

   Bibliography: p.
   Includes index.
   1. Vocational guidance. 2. Occupational
mobility. I. Title.
HF5381.R64   650'.14   78-15805
ISBN 0-8144-5480-1

First Printing

Acknowledgments

MANY people helped make this book possible. My particular thanks go to Professor L. Eugene Thomas of the Department of Human Development and Family Relations of the University of Connecticut, who was a member of my doctoral committee and my co-researcher. I am also deeply grateful to the chairman of my committee, Professor William H. Roe, of the Department of Higher, Technical and Adult Education.

I also wish to thank the following people who contributed in one way or another to the research or to the book. David Harvey, Richard Mela, Robert Norris, Betty Roper, Dieter Paulus, Edward Iwanicki, David Palmer, John Viega, John Holland, Daniel Levinson, Seymour Sarason, Paula Goldman Leventman, John Donovan, Everett C. Hughes, Betty Holroyd Roberts, Alan D. Entine, Judd Adams, Jane Berry, A. Peter Fredrickson, Bill Stanley, Ernest Brown, Betty Hoffman, Clement Kerley, Pauline A. Russo, James A. Thomas, Carolyn C. Butler, Fred Holder, James Murdock, William Banis, Richard Dolliver, Patricia Moylan, James Brine, Betsy James, Linda Stantial Yenawine, Byron B. Aubrey, Mary Lou Powell, Ruth Bergengren, Rudite Robinson, Philip Rockwell, Robert B. Turnbull, Karen Hansen, Ivan

Backer, Andrew Gold, Alfred Burfeind, Tom Smith, Robbins Winslow, Joseph M. Cahalan, Chandler H. Stevens, Jerome Ellison, T. Joseph Sheehan, E. Weiss, Samuel R. Connor, Natalie Kass, T. Taylor Cahill, John Wiedenheft, William N. Goodwin, Robert G. Foulkes, Walter Truscinski, Anita Malone, William Olds, Hope Brothers, Robert Ellis, David M. Campbell, Beverly Clark, Harold A. Levey, Robin Clark, Charline Scott, Moira Birmingham, and Catherine Kandefer.

The University of Connecticut Research Foundation generously awarded a grant to Professor Thomas and a similar one to me to support the research. The people who were kind enough to comment on portions of the manuscript include Hal Pearson, Career Concepts, Inc.; Walter Storey, General Electric; Ted and Diane Youn, Mickey Neiditz, Cathy Kandefer, Paul Ferrini, and Barton Lloyd of the Mid-Atlantic Career Center; Lee Hammer, Mainstream; and Gene Thomas and Esther McCabe. I was fortunate to have so constructive and inspiring an editor as Eric Valentine of AMACOM. Gale Barrett was prompt and accurate in typing the manuscript. The library staff of the Hartford Graduate Center and Fitchburg State College were most helpful. Three good and dear friends, Betty Schlerman, Marcia Stern, and Sally Lewis, provided support when it was most needed. My children, Jeffery and Matthew Robbins, were uncomplaining while their mother worked.

To all the people mentioned above go my sincere thanks and appreciation. My special thanks go to the 91 men who so graciously cooperated in allowing me to study their careers.

THIS book is based on my ten years' experience as a career counselor in higher education and on my work with many adult clients, both individually and in groups, as well as on my doctoral work at the University of Connecticut. The research study was limited to upper-middle-class white male subjects. However, the how-to chapters are equally useful for women and men of other socioeconomic groups.

PAULA I. ROBBINS

Foreword

A near avalanche of books, articles, and media broadcasts devoted to the changing work and life-style patterns of American adults has been coming at us in the past few years. This onslaught reflects the very important social changes that are taking place in this country.

We are living longer and becoming better educated. Despite the crippling economic impact of recent recessions and continued inflation, the levels of real individual and national affluence have continued to rise. Contributing strongly to the maintenance of personal and family spending capacity has been the increasing numbers of women in the labor force. This increase, in turn, has provided both women and men with the economic freedom to make career and life-style choices that were unavailable to previous generations. National statistics document the heightened divorce and separation rate. Increased activity at hundreds of adult vocational counseling centers attests to the growing numbers of mature people seeking assistance to identify and pursue new careers at midlife.

To be sure, negative as well as positive factors have propelled people into midlife career changes. The economic downturn of the last few years adversely affected hundreds of thousands who lost jobs or found their careers dead-ended. Often, a marital disruption is accompanied by the unexpected need for a woman to enter the labor market at midlife without marketable skills or adequate training. Rapid technological change is causing many occupations to become obsolete. The younger person has probably had more recent training and can more readily understand new technological advances. The older worker, close to retirement and protected by seniority, can probably wait out the new methodologies. It is the middle-aged worker who feels the change most keenly; he must retrain or redirect just when family financial obligations are the greatest.

Whether the catalyst for career change at midlife is positive or negative, those facing this transition must deal with their own work objectives as well as with the economic realities of the job market. Passing through the middle years may cause some people to rethink and replace career goals for the second half of life. Awareness that you are aging, awareness that you now bear full responsibility for your actions (you can't go home for help; you are at home, and must carry the emotional burdens of parents as well as children), and awareness that death itself is a personal and identifiable issue may cause you to rechart your career and life-style plans. Recognizing that only so much time is left to reach your goals can cause a heightened sensitivity to the value of the hours in a day and the years in a life span. Thus, midlife awareness itself may become a stimulus for career and life-style change.

Paula Robbins has looked carefully at many of these issues by examining the midlife career-change patterns of 91 middle- and upper-class men. The core of her work is found in Chapters 3 and 4, where she profiles the career changes of individuals and then describes the processes by which these people changed careers and life-styles.

Among the most significant conclusions of Dr. Robbins' study was the fact that it took a fairly long time to change careers: more than 40 percent of those whose change did not mean further schooling took more than a year just to make the decision to leave their current jobs. Another relates to the direction of change: people generally left large, bureaucratic, profit-making institutions to pursue careers in which they would have a greater degree of autonomy and control over their lives.

The nature of work also changed as people moved from positions generally dealing with data and things to occupations and professions that brought them into contact with other people. Dr. Robbins makes it clear, however, that the helping professions do not attract only businessmen who become midlife career changers. In particular, there are examples of clergymen who became tired of the bureaucracy of the church and chose second careers in which autonomy and counseling skills combined to produce some innovative work roles.

Dr. Robbins has provided a lot of information in her book for those who seek career-change assistance. Although her study is limited to middle- and upper-class men, she discusses sources of help and guidance for both men and women from various economic and educational backgrounds. Her comparisons of selected profit and nonprofit counseling agencies should be particularly beneficial to the reader contemplating a career change.

This book is particularly timely for people facing retirement. The average retirement age is declining while life expectancy is increasing. A second career, especially a part-time one, may become the ideal work objective for those who retire at 55 and can look forward to at least 20 years of healthy, active life. Earnings from these jobs may very well be needed to supplement pension and Social Security income if current levels of inflation continue into the future. The suggestions and resources Dr. Robbins provides in the latter chapters of her book can be most helpful for those who begin to plan for postretirement second careers at midlife.

What Dr. Robbins has stated most succinctly is that midlife career change, although time consuming, arduous, and costly, can be achieved by middle- and upper-class men with enough motivation, dedication, and, most often, support from spouse and family. Changes from large organizations to small ones are generally the most successful. But what about those who don't have the resources and support of this sample? What about those who may need the security and structure of the large organization but have developed skills and abilities in smaller, and possibly unrelated, settings? Clearly, we need to know more about the nature of these career moves, but we suspect that midlife changes for these people will be more difficult than for the ones in Dr. Robbins' study.

But midlife career flexibility for all people will undoubtedly increase in the decades ahead as middle age becomes recognized as the time for significant new personal and work choices to be made. This book is most helpful as it charts the future direction of those changes and evaluates the resources available to people and to institutions facing those changes in future years.

Alan D. Entine
Director
Mid-Life Assessment Program
SUNY-Stony Brook

Contents

1

Introduction

A career is ". . . the moving perspective in which the person sees his life as a whole and interprets the meaning of his various attributes, actions, and the things which happen to him.[1]

UNTIL fairly recently most people assumed that a successful person was one who established himself in a career soon after completing his schooling, climbed up the ladder as far as he could go, and then stayed put in the same occupation or company until the time came for presentation of his gold watch. Implicit in this expectation were two perceptions of what a career is. The first was that of career as profession, the notion that certain occupations represent careers while others do not, and that these higher-order occupations represent stability. A doctor, lawyer, or clergyman has reached a pinnacle, and stays within that profession for as long as he or she is privileged to work in it. The other perception was that of career as advancement, of moving up in an organization, achieving higher status and remuneration—up is good, down is bad. Moving from one job or career to another was considered a sign of instability, if not failure, and, at the very least, caused raised eyebrows.

[1] Everett C. Hughes, "Institutional Office and the Person," *American Journal of Sociology*, **43**, 26 (1937).

Lately, the validity of this conventional wisdom has been challenged and, indeed, numerous articles in the popular press have described in positive terms the successful career changes of many men and women who in no sense could be considered failures. A real questioning of what Seymour Sarason calls "the one life–one career imperative" has begun. Some people are beginning to suggest that career change is a good thing, that we should all prepare for it, and that most of us are likely to experience it.

This new attitude represents a shift in our thinking about careers. We are beginning to place more value on the subjective idea of a career—its meaning for the individual and how it reflects the changing aspirations, satisfactions, self-conceptions, and other attitudes of the person toward his work and life—rather than its objective value, defined in terms of external symbols of success. We are shifting from a society in which most of us have what Donald E. Super and Martin J. Bohn, Jr., call "responsive" careers, those in which an individual meets the demands of his environment—the son takes over the family business or a young man pursues an occupation because it is there.

More of us are seeking "expressive" careers, those in which people can find outlets for their abilities and interests, in which the realization of self-concepts is possible, and which tend to be pursued because of the possibility of self-expression. As a result of this shift, we no longer look at a career as a choice. Rather, it is a lifelong sequence of work-related experiences. John Van Maanen goes so far as to say that "to study careers is to study change itself."

In the following pages we will be looking at the process of career change in the lives of a group of men who have reached middle age. We will try to analyze their motivation and to see how they went about changing their careers. We will see how their career change might reflect some of the normal psychological developmental stages we all pass through. We will look at how their career change related to their life-style, income, and family. One chapter will deal with education as a means for facilitating career change. We hope the examples of what others have done may be of use to people contemplating such a change. In Chapters 7 and 8, we will discuss how such a person might go about the process of career change and look for help. Last, we will try to see what the future may bring and determine what policy changes on the part of government, business, and higher education might facilitate career change.

FREQUENCY OF CAREER CHANGE

Despite the number of human interest stories in newspapers and magazines about the New York stockbroker who becomes an organic farmer in Maine, we actually know very little about career change, how frequent it is, who does it, why, and how. There is even some confusion as to exactly what it is. An engineer who moves up to being a manager in his firm is doing very different work every day, as is the teacher who becomes a principal, yet these people do not usually think of themselves as having made a career change. Their career progression is considered normal. Most people find that a change in work environment is necessary before they feel they have changed careers. In addition, new skills are needed, sometimes combined with a few of the old skills, but often with no carry-over from the old career.

A number of scholarly studies have indicated that career change is more common than was thought. A recent U.S. Department of Labor study compared males who were in the labor force in 1965 with those who were working in 1970. It found that 32.2 percent had transferred to a different detailed occupation.[2] Twenty-six percent of professional and technical workers and 24.6 percent of managers and administrators reported a change. In terms of age, 37.5 percent of men from 30 to 39, 31.6 percent of those from 40 to 49, and 25.5 percent of those from 50 to 59 switched occupations.

[2] Dixie Sommers and Alan Eck, "Occupational Mobility in the American Labor Force," *Monthly Labor Review* (U.S. Department of Labor), **100**, 3–19 (1977).

In another study based on Census Bureau data, 44 percent of a large sample of white males from 45 to 59 years of age were found to have changed their occupation over their working life.[3] A third study that investigated the career stability of a large sample of 21- to 70-year-old workers over a five-year period found that from 10 to 14 percent of them shifted to different kinds of work.[4] Obviously, the numbers depend on the criteria used for defining change. However, there is no doubt that many people are changing careers.

Many more are apparently thinking of changing careers. In a survey of middle managers belonging to the American Management Associations, Dale Tarnowieski found 55 percent claiming to have changed or to have considered changing their occupational field during the past five years. Forty-five percent said that there was an occupational field they preferred to the one they were in; three-quarters of these men expected to do something about it in the near future.

CHANGES IN DEMAND

The most obvious reason for this increase is the rapidity with which technological advances are taking place. As technology changes, requirements for skilled workers also change. We can think of many common categories of workers today that employ large numbers of people, but did not even exist 10, 20, or 40 years ago. Examples that come readily to mind are computer programmers, systems analysts, keypunch operators (themselves soon to become obsolete as microprocessors become more common), and physicians specializing in nuclear medicine or laser technology.

The demand for people trained in various fields rises and falls with changes in governmental and societal

[3] George E. Parsons and James V. Wigtil, "Occupational Mobility as Measured by Holland's Theory of Career Selection," *Journal of Vocational Behavior*, **5** 321–330 (1974).

[4] Gary D. Gottfredson, *Career Stability and Redirection in Adulthood* (Baltimore: The Johns Hopkins University Center for Social Organization of Schools, 1976), Report No. 219.

priorities and demographic trends. The post-Sputnik era brought about a tremendous demand for aerospace engineers and physicists. It ended with a crash in the early 1970s as governmental priorities changed. The same cycle occurred for social workers and other providers of community services, who found job opportunities plentiful during the Great Society period, but greatly decreased when a new administration took office. The post-World War II baby boom, which peaked in 1957, brought with it a greatly increased demand for teachers; the demand changed to a surfeit when the birthrate began to plummet.

There is no question that we will see a growing number of people employed in new technological fields emerging from the quest for alternative energy sources and the control of environmental pollution. The increase in the percentage of elderly people is bringing with it a demand for more people trained in gerontology and able to fill the needs of older people for health care, recreation, and housing.

The city of Danbury, Connecticut, is a very good example of how changing trends can influence the number and variety of available jobs. For at least a century, Danbury had been known as the hat city. (Students of occupational safety and health are familiar with the mad Danbury hatters, who slowly became insane from the ingestion of toxic materials used to prepare the felt for their hats.) After World War II, with a more casual way of life, American people stopped wearing hats, and this change in fashion closed many of Danbury's factories. For 25 years, Danbury was a depressed area, with high rates of unemployment.

Today, however, Danbury is again a boom town. This time, the city is the beneficiary of the trend of large companies to move their corporate headquarters out of New York City, but to remain in the metropolitan area so that they are close enough to keep in touch. Many companies moved to Stamford, Connecticut, to Westchester County, and to the surrounding areas, forcing real estate values to skyrocket. Corporations had to look farther afield. They found Danbury, only a little over an hour's drive from Manhattan, with plenty of reasonably priced land available. Several *Fortune* 500 companies are building their corporate headquarters there, and many smaller firms are moving in as well. While it is probably too late for the Danbury hatters, the area will now have a heavy demand for office workers, computer specialists, and all kinds of managerial support staff.

The effect of these kinds of changes in supply and demand have their greatest impact on young people. They may be unable to find employment in the field of their choice and be forced to turn to something else for which there is a greater demand. Or they may decide against preparing for a specific field when it seems likely that no job opportunities will be available, and instead seek training in another area. However, these trends do also have an impact on older workers, who are forced to look for new careers in different fields. We found many physicists and aeronautical engineers among the sample of career changers we studied, for instance.

CHANGES IN SOCIAL VALUES

Much more difficult to document, but having as important an effect on employment as changes in technology, demographic trends, and governmental priorities, is the role of changing societal values. Since World War II, we have seen a breakdown in the respect for authority and institutions that Americans once had. Instead, people have changed the direction of their definitions of right and wrong. The slogan of the 1960s and 1970s has been to "Do your own thing!"

Some people have had to expend vast amounts of psychic energy to try to discover what, indeed, *is* their "thing." No longer do they accept the definition of what one ought to be or do what is provided by parents, teachers, or employers; they must find out for themselves. As a result, vastly increased numbers engage in various kinds of psychotherapies, encounter groups, and human-potential movements; buy how-to books; and take courses describing how to find yourself, become more successful, be your own best friend, and have better orgasms.

Sarason, in his book, *Work, Aging, and Social Change,* describes what he sees as a marked increase in the extent to which individuals value personal growth and the search for an authentic self—what he calls a "sensitivity to authenticity." This desire for growth and personal development has marked implications for people's work lives. Since growth implies change, it is unlikely that the person looking for it will be satisfied to stay in the same job for years if there is no opportunity for change, learning, and development, no matter how large the paycheck or secure the situation. There is a direct conflict between this new growth ethic and the old "one life–one career imperative," with its traditional job stability in one career with one employer for the entire life span.

Douglas Hall says that there are no longer any absolute criteria for evaluating an individual's career because of these changes in societal values. Even the criterion of advancement, climbing up the ladder, is no longer valid, because people no longer place such weight on how they appear to others. Their concern is with how they appear to themselves. Each person measures his own life according to his internal criteria—what Daniel Levinson calls "the Dream."

Hall points out that a critical common element at the core of all the social movements we have witnessed in the past decades—civil rights, the lowering of the age of majority, consumer rights, women's liberation, reform of laws regarding privacy, sex, birth control, abortion, drugs—has been a movement in the direction of permitting people to define for themselves how they will live their lives and permitting them to make their own choices. As a result of these social changes, people have begun to examine their careers more carefully to define their own goals, rather than accepting the definitions of others, such as parents, employers, family, or friends.

Hall quotes the findings of Daniel Yankelovich in a

well-publicized poll of young people on their values and changing definitions of success and believes they indicate a trend throughout our society that will increase as these young people become a dominant element in the workforce. According to Yankelovich,

Since World War II most Americans have shaped their ideas of success around money, occupational status, possessions, and the social mobility of their children. Now, ideas about success are beginning to revolve around various forms of self-fulfillment. The emphasis is on self and its unrealized potential, a self that cries out for expression and demands satisfaction. If the key motif of the past was "keeping up with the Joneses," today it is "I have my own life to live, let Jones shift for himself."

As a result of these changes in values, Hall sees emerging what he calls the "protean career." This is a view of career as being self-satisfying, not necessarily complying with outward definitions of success or failure, but measured in terms of personal work satisfaction and intrinsic rewards from one's labors. It implies a decrease in organizational commitment and loyalty.

According to Hall, the old model was a passive one, in which the individual made only the initial choice of a career or of a company for which to work, then allowed circumstances or the decisions of higher-ups to propel him along, hopefully up the ladder. In this model, as long as the individual performed satisfactorily and found the monetary rewards sufficient, he didn't need to think much about career identity or fulfillment. The new model of the "protean career" provides for greater personal freedom of choice, but as is always the case with freedom, along with it go the problems and responsibilities for making choices and taking advantage of opportunities.

The increase in divorce that is taking place can be attributed partly to the increased value placed on self-fulfillment and personal definitions of what is right for oneself. Women, particularly, have a desire to escape from old role definitions to find self-identity and authenticity. They are even walking out on their families in order to "do their own thing." Some authors have suggested that rather than reflecting a devaluation of marriage, the increase in divorce rates reflects a heightened valuing of marriage. People want more from the marital relationship than they used to. They are not satisfied with the chance for regular sex—now commonly available without benefit of marriage—economic benefits, and the opportunity to raise a family. One of the things people hope to find in marriage is an opportunity for personal growth and fulfillment.

Sarason remarks on the parallels between divorce and career change. The motivation behind both is often the same. He finds it ironic that recent changes in laws regarding marriage, the institution of no-fault divorce, and the change in society's attitudes toward divorce have made it easier to change marital partners than to change careers. The parallel is in expectations. Just as people now expect more from marriage, they also expect more from their careers.

The changing nature of marriage and the family is also likely to affect the incidence of career change. Because of the impetus of the women's movement and the increased availability of reliable methods of birth control, a far greater percentage of married women is in the labor force. More women consider their careers as central to their lives rather than as peripheral jobs that fill time or earn money when family demands are not too great.

As a result, more families have two steady breadwinners. This gives one or the other of the marital partners more flexibility to take time off to go back to school, to raise children, or to try a new career. Specific sex roles in marriage are no longer sharply defined, so the partners have much greater leeway. Men are no longer so locked in to the role of provider. They don't have to take on the guilt of risking the whole family's security by giving up a well-paying but unsatisfying job to try something more interesting.

Increasing concern for self-fulfillment can be attributed to the amount of affluence most Americans have enjoyed since World War II. Many people still live in poverty, but the majority of Americans haven't had to worry about finding a job or getting money for the next meal. The memories of the Great Depression have faded; only a minority of the labor force is old enough to recall those hardships. Many of the changes initiated then, such as unemployment insurance and the Social Security system, have served the purposes for which they were designed so well that even the high unemployment rates of recent years have not caused widespread suffering or brought about the kinds of social protest movements that might have been expected. Most Americans have had enough disposable income to spend on leisure and self-improvement. Witness the phenomenal growth of recreation-related industries and all kinds of adult education courses—from yoga to macrame to furniture refinishing.

Most important, the concern with personal growth and fulfillment has come about because of the higher educational level of most Americans. "There is a clear and persistent positive correlation between educational attainment and rising expectations," according to James O'Toole. Sarason agrees, and he attributes the rise in job dissatisfaction that has been documented in recent years to the increase in educational level. He sees it not only as a phenomenon among blue-collar workers—the Lordstown strikers—but also among highly educated professionals. These people were taught to expect that if they invested heavily in years of difficult and expensive education, they would be rewarded with careers that would be exciting and stimulating and would engage all of their capacities and curiosities. When the educated professional finds himself in a dead-end position that gives him no satisfaction or feeling of personal growth, he will probably rebel and try to remedy the situation.

One of the career changers we interviewed, a man who runs a small publishing firm, seems to epitomize many of the new values toward work, marriage, and success we have discussed. He said,

This is an ideal business for someone my age (now 55); I can work at my own pace. I come in, and any morning there could be a manuscript on my desk that would make us a couple of million dollars. Of course, it isn't likely, but there is the excitement of not knowing what will turn up next. And there is flexibility in the work. You can drink a beer in the afternoon down at the local inn and maybe meet someone you will end up doing a project with. My basic change was realizing that I didn't really want to make a million dollars. That changed my attitude about many other things. Hell, the only ambition I have now is to do what I want to do, not what somebody else says is success. A couple of years ago I asked my partner if he wanted to see this become a multimillion-dollar business, and he said, "Hell, no." And I said, "I don't, either."

I think that we are living through a revolution, and we aren't even aware of it. It's the first time children can grow up without necessity. Without the necessity of doing what their parents want them to, of even having to work. Without people having to marry if they don't want to, or stay married. I think all the rules of the game have changed and we just don't realize it.

THE GROWTH OF BUREAUCRACIES

The desire for satisfaction and personal growth in the context of work comes in direct opposition to the fact that an increasingly large majority of American workers are employed by large organizations, not only in business but in the nonprofit and government sectors as well. Sociologists from Max Weber on have pointed out that bureaucracies, especially large ones, tend to be more rational, more bound by rules and regulations, more rigid, and less personal.

Chris Argyris formulated the basic conflict between individual growth and the demands of formal organizations some years ago in his book, *Personality and Organization*. In research of his own and in the examination of the work of others, he concluded that large bureaucracies make demands on healthy, mature individuals that are incongruent with their needs:

. . . the basic impact of the formal organizational structure is to make the employees feel dependent, submissive, and passive, and to require them to utilize only a few of their less important abilities.

Frederick Herzberg, in his research on work motivation, points up the conflict between the satisfaction of the individual's needs and the requirements of a bureaucracy. According to Herzberg, the two factors most likely to motivate performance are the recognition of individual achievement and a sense of personal growth, neither of which are likely to flourish in a large corporation. Not only are factory workers and middle managers subject to the constraints of the large bureaucracy, but more and more professionals now work for large organizations. Engineers, as a group, are increasingly alienated from their work, which is primarily for large companies. More and more physicians, lawyers, and other professionals, all of whom have been socialized to expect a high degree of autonomy in their work, are employed by large, impersonal, bureaucratized organizations. Even those who work on their own are caught up in the rules and red tape of government requirements.

Sarason suggests that if the bureaucratization of professional work continues, which he predicts it will, many professionals will place less importance on their work, and it will cease to be the central focus of their lives. They will concentrate on leisure-time activities to make up for their dissatisfactions in the office. The other alternative for those who experience a conflict between their desire for personal growth and the demands of the organization will be to leave the firm and change careers.

DEMOGRAPHIC TRENDS

Another factor that will encourage future career changes is the changing nature of the demographic profile of the United States. The fertility rate of American women has fallen dramatically, from 122.7 births per 1,000 women of childbearing age at the peak of the postwar "baby boom" in 1957 to 65.7 in 1976, which was even lower than the Depression rate.[5] Fewer children mean smaller families, and

[5] Robert Reinhold, "New Population Trends Transforming U.S.," *New York Sunday Times*, February 6, 1977, p. 42.

women with smaller families are more likely to be employed. As we have mentioned before, career change is easier in a two-salary family.

Even more significant is the fact that life expectancy is increasing dramatically. Girl babies born in 1977 can expect to live to 81 and boys to 72. The death rate of adults over 35 declined much more rapidly between 1973 and 1975 than for the previous ten years, which is explained largely by a decline in deaths due to cardiovascular disease. Apparently Americans are finally beginning to heed warnings about diet, smoking, and exercise. As a result, the median age of the population will continue to rise. In 1976 it was 29, and by the turn of the century it may be as high as 37.3.

Not only are Americans living longer, but they are remaining healthy and vigorous for a greater proportion of their lives, as a result of better health care and lifelong habits of nutrition and exercise. Consequently, forced retirement at age 65 is no longer legal. Many people are physically able and eager to continue working. With more people living longer, a severe strain has been put on the Social Security system. That strain would be eased if people were permitted to work longer. Secretary of Commerce Juanita Kreps has suggested that the age for obtaining Social Security benefits be raised from 65 to 68. However, many business leaders are concerned that if older workers do not retire, younger workers will feel frustrated by the lack of opportunities for advancement.

At the same time that pressure grew to eliminate forced retirement at 65, a concurrent trend toward early retirement has been evident in the United States. Many companies now permit their employees to retire with full pension benefits at 55 or even younger. These two trends may not be as contradictory as they seem. A third trend may provide a clue. Among part-time workers who are between the ages of 27 and 54, women outnumber men seven to one, but in the over-55 age group they outnumber men by only three to two.[6]

[6] Jerry Flint, "Early Retirement Is Growing," *New York Sunday Times*, July 10, 1977, p. 1.

Many men seem to be looking for a reduction in the intense work of their primary careers, but not complete idleness. They want a job with fewer hours per week, a slower pace, and fewer demands. A second career might be the answer for both the early retirees and those who want to continue working past 65 for as long as their health permits. The growing desire for a second career is obvious; we ought to make it easier for people who want it to find it.

A new movement in the United States has been toward the establishment of nonprofit employment agencies for senior citizens. One set up several years ago in West Hartford, Connecticut, called the West Hartford Seniors Job Bank, is funded partially by the town and partially by contributions. It has served thousands of men and women 55 and over, and hundreds of enthusiastic employers have been delighted with the steady and reliable older employees who fill their part-time or temporary employment needs. It has helped many people to supplement their Social Security checks or to fill idle hours with constructive employment.

The incidence of career change will increase in the future. The rapidity of technological change and the varying labor force demands of changing governmental and societal priorities, changes in social values regarding personal development and growth, the increased proportion of women in the labor force and the changing nature of the family, and, finally, demographic trends that will permit Americans to live longer and healthier lives are all contributing factors.

It seems important, therefore, that we learn as much as possible about career change. Government planners will need data to help them as they consider ways to improve employment possibilities for older workers. Educators, particularly in colleges and universities, will need to plan for older students who want training or retraining to further their career goals. Personnel officers in business and industry will need information to help them plan for more effective use of manpower resources. And people who are contemplating a career change will want to know as much as possible about what to expect.

PREVIOUS STUDIES OF CAREER CHANGERS

The few previous studies of career changers have begun to give us some information about who changes career, why, and how. Dale Hiestand, an economist working with Eli Ginzberg's Conservation of Human Resources project at Columbia University, published the first significant study of career changers in 1971, entitled *Changing Careers After Thirty-Five*. Using the enrollment records of a number of universities throughout the country, he contacted 70 people, 40 men and 30 women, who had returned to graduate school on a full-time basis. They ranged in age from 35 to 58, with a median age of 41. Nearly half were earning an advanced degree because of a significant change in ambitions or interest. Of the men, Hiestand found the following reasons for returning to school:

Entering a profession	4
Upward within a profession	11
Shift between closely related fields or within a broad field	14
Major change in occupation	11

The people Hiestand studied had a wide range of motives, but he found that the primary reasons were overwhelmingly positive; he saw little evidence that those who returned to school were unstable or unconventional. Sixty-five of the 70 said that they would do the same thing over again; only two had regrets. Hiestand's study had several limitations. Not everyone was actually changing careers. Since all the people Hiestand studied were students, his research sheds no light on what percentage of changers actually use further education in order to change.

Also in 1971, Harold Sheppard published an article describing 210 interviews with male workers at all occupational levels who were 40 and over about their job satisfaction. He compared those who were satisfied and wished to remain in their present jobs (91) with those who were dissatisfied and wished to change jobs or careers (49). The can-

didates for change were characterized by higher achievement values, lower degree of autonomy or independence in
their jobs, and lower chance for promotion in their jobs.
There was no difference in their financial motivation.

Lee D. Dyer reported on the experience of 115 unemployed blue- and white-collar men, 40 and over, who
were later able to find work. Of those, 10 percent shifted
from their original occupational classification, and 9 percent
became self-employed. Dyer reports that

those who expressed satisfaction emphasized the opportunities
their new jobs offered to advance and make worthwhile contributions to their organizations. Fifty-one percent of this group had
experienced salary decreases of more than 20%, but this impact was
apparently blunted by relatively favorable positions on other job
factors.

Will Clopton, in an unpublished doctoral dissertation,
studied 20 men who had returned to graduate school in
order to change careers and compared them with 20 controls
who did not. The small size of the sample tends to make any
findings questionable. Clopton reports that his changers had
financial support, were more likely than the controls to have
used personal counseling, and were more likely than the
controls to have changed marital status. He did not find that
the changers returned to an earlier interest that had been
dormant for a long time. He characterized his changers as
having a marked sense of personal self-esteem and a keen
awareness of personal mortality. All Clopton's changers, like
those of Hiestand, were obtained through university records,
and had used further schooling to help them make the
change.

Betty Holroyd Roberts, in an unpublished doctoral dissertation, reports on a study of 35 men and women who
dropped out, that is, who left conventional careers for significantly different and often counterculture life-styles. She
found most of these men through subscription listings for a
magazine for counterculture dropouts, *The Black Bart
Brigade*. She reports that the following frustrations generally
led to dropping out: value conflicts, boredom, oppressive-

ness, lack of autonomy, lack of meaning in work, and the detrimental impact of a successful career on family ties. The following factors aided the subjects in their decision to drop out:

1. The transitional practicality of having one foot in something else.
2. Being part of a dropout group (rap session or support group), which brought about a contagious effect.
3. The effect of their early socialization—influence of family in childhood.
4. Enough savings or income.
5. A lack of dependents.
6. The possibility of a pleasant living environment as a dropout.
7. A working spouse to provide financial support.

In her subjects' evaluations of their new situation, Roberts presents some interesting observations.

Their perception of quality of life included autonomy, independence, self-resourcefulness, freedom for creative expression, and for many of them a milieu of close personal interrelationships via community living.

She has some interesting insights into differences by age. Those who were 40 or over talked more of "plateauing," needing a challenge, wanting a change, and/or feeling it was time they did not delay personal gratification any longer. Roberts' research shares the limitations of the other studies in what we can learn about the general characteristics of career changers; her group was chosen because of their deviance, and the size of the sample was small.

THE PRESENT STUDY

My study was undertaken with colleagues at the University of Connecticut in order to learn more about career changers, their motivations, how they made the change, and what the outcome was. We were also interested in whether what we learned about career changers had any implications for the study of normal adult psychological development, particularly the issue of the "midlife crisis."

We decided to limit the study to men, because women's career patterns are often complicated by such additional factors as childbirth, moving because of husband's transfer, and the more restricted opportunities available to women. We sought subjects who were between 35 and 55 years old when they left their jobs to make the career change. They were people who had been reasonably successful in their previous careers, which were on a managerial or professional level. By the age of 35, most people are settled in a career and are no longer trying out various possibilities. Beyond 55, many men might be changing careers because of early retirement, and their motivation would be different. A detailed description of the sampling procedure used can be found in my doctoral dissertation. The final study included questionnaire data from 91 men ranging in age from 33 to 54, of whom 67 were interviewed.

The men we studied were all middle and upper-middle class, with high levels of educational achievement and above-average incomes. Although their lives are not typical of the majority of American working people, their values and behavior are significant far out of proportion to their numbers. As highly educated men in positions of responsibility, they may, in some ways, reflect the cutting edge of American society. Their views about their own careers and their feelings about the work they do are important because they may well represent what most Americans will aspire to in the near future.

Before we describe the findings of our study, we will present, in the next chapter, an overview of what is known about normal adult psychological development. This background is quite helpful in trying to understand the motivation of the men we studied. We will then be able to see if our findings lend support to some of the theories about how and why individuals change in middle adulthood.

2

Is There a
Midlife Crisis?

Though we would like to live without regrets, and sometimes proudly insist that we have none, this is not really possible, if only because we are mortal. When more time stretches behind than stretches before one, some assessments, however reluctantly and incompletely, begin to be made. Between what one wished to become and what one *has* become there is a momentous gap, which will now never be closed. And this gap seems to operate as one's final margin, one's last opportunity, for creation. And between the self as it is and the self as one sees it, there is also a distance, even harder to gauge. Some of us are compelled, around the middle of our lives, to make a study of this baffling geography, less in the hope of conquering these distances than in the determination that the distance shall not become any greater.[1]

UNTIL about ten years ago, almost no research had been done on psychological development in the years of middle adulthood. As one researcher put it, what happens to people in middle life was one of the best-kept secrets in the social sciences. Recently, however, this has changed. Several im-

[1] James Baldwin, quoted in Theodore Lidz, *The Person: His Development Throughout the Life Cycle* (New York: Basic Books, 1968), p. 458.

portant study councils have been set up, and many research projects are now investigating adult development. A number of researchers are paying specific attention to the interrelationship between adult psychology and the world of work. Along with the new scholarly interest in the area of adult psychological development has come a greatly increased popular concern, as evidenced by the publication of a large number of books on middle age, how to cope with the forties, and other subjects of the same genre. These seem to be divided about equally between the pessimistic and the optimistic, or perhaps what could be called "The Midlife Crisis" school and "The Life Begins at Forty" school. Each school has its points, as we shall see. In this chapter we will investigate what the social sciences have learned about middle adulthood and what implications the findings have for midlife career change.

Since the scientific study of human behavior originated in the nineteenth century with the diagnosis of mental illness and investigation into its causes, it is understandable that social scientists did not get around to studying normal human development until recently. Most of this study focused on the more obvious developmental changes of infancy, childhood, and adolescence, which are apparent to all of us.

Even the idea that there are differences in the psychology of people at different life stages is fairly new. Until the late eighteenth century, for example, children were considered smaller replicas of adults and were treated accordingly. Since so few survived infancy and early childhood, little emotional investment was made in them until they did. Adolescence viewed as a separate psychological stage is a recent phenomenon. In the days when children started to work in factories by the age of ten, there was no time for the luxury of an "adolescent identity crisis." In ancient times, 90 percent of the population was dead by 40. Old age was considered to begin very early.

In modern American society, our standard of living has

enabled large numbers of people to live physically healthy lives through middle adulthood and well into old age. Problems of health and survival are not all-consuming for most middle-class Americans, and they have time and energy left to be curious about their emotional state. So now we have the luxury of being able to think about the psychological events of normal adulthood. We are beginning to be able to differentiate various periods of adult life. The current focus is concern with middle age.

Interest in the next stage is already close at hand. Bernice Neugarten of the University of Chicago has coined a new term, "the young old," referring to those approximately between the ages of 60 and 75, who are often retired but still in good health and involved in life. They are concerned with productive use of their new-found leisure. A new group in American society, they are different from the old old, those who are 80 and beyond and show signs of serious mental and physical decline. As the proportion of our population in "the young old" stage increases over the next decades, we shall see increasing attention paid to the psychology of this age group as well.

THEORIES OF ADULT PSYCHOLOGICAL DEVELOPMENT

Charlotte Buhler was one of the first psychologists to study adult development systematically, and her pioneering work in the early 1930s has strongly influenced subsequent efforts. Analyzing a large number of biographies, she showed that there was a clear pattern in psychological development. It parallels the expansion and growth that take place physically, after which come 20 to 30 years of stability, followed inevitably by decline. She said that a similar pattern occurred in the role of work in people's lives. By 30, people have chosen a vocation; at 45 they are concerned with testing the results and determining whether they have realized their desired goals.

In 1933, Carl Jung wrote a short article entitled "The Stages of Life," which very forcefully identified many of the characteristics of midlife that are only now, 45 years later being confirmed through empirical research. Jung found a rise in the frequency of mental depressions in men about 40 and in women a little younger, and believed that they were indicative of important changes in the human psyche that take place at about this age.

Jung noted that both physical attributes and a person's values tend to change into their opposites. For example, men and women begin to look and act more like each other. Men's bodies become softer and flabbier; women's features become coarser and they develop facial hair. These are the result of hormonal changes. Jung suggested that all of us have a mixture of the masculine and the feminine—and, indeed, both sexes have both male and female hormones. In youth and early adulthood, we use up the quality that predominates. At midlife we begin to dip into the supply of the opposite.

Often, Jung pointed out, women over 40 begin to go out into the world and become masculine and tough-minded, using their new-found sharpness of mind, whereas men slowly begin to discover their tender feelings. My own grandmother became a sharp businesswoman in her later years. We all know older men who love to tend their roses or irises, but wouldn't have revealed such a hobby when they were younger. As we shall see, a number of the men who changed careers moved into such fields as teaching, nursing, and social work, where they would be able to express feelings of warmth and caring for other people.

Jung did not attribute the changes of midlife to fear of death, which he thought at this stage was still seen as distant and abstract. He characterized the change as follows:

Often it is something like a slow change in a person's character; in another case certain traits may come to light which had disappeared since childhood; or again, one's previous inclinations and interests begin to weaken and others take their place.

He warns that we must be willing to change. Many people find a way of life they believe is right and stick to it at all cost, fearful of changing, but he says that such rigidity, while it may help to ward off fear of the unknown, is paid for dearly at the cost of diminution in personality. Such people have hidden away in dark and dusty closets many aspects of their lives that should have been experienced.

The first half of life has specific goals of expansion, procreation, and establishment, but when these purposes have been attained, Jung argues, we should stop striving after our earlier worldly and material goals and turn to other things. Change becomes necessary, and the individual should turn to introspection and concern with culture and wisdom. In primitive societies, it was always the elderly, no longer concerned with hunting or reaping, who preserved the culture and the mores. Jung sums up his conclusions concerning the changes that take place in midlife in beautifully poetic terms.

But we cannot live the afternoon of life according to the programme of life's morning; for what was great in the morning will be little at evening, and what in the morning was true will at evening become a lie.

The next major work in the literature of adult development was Erik Erikson's *Childhood and Society,* in which he postulated eight developmental life stages through which all individuals go. Each stage has specific tasks that must be accomplished if the normal human being is to progress to the next. The first of the adult stages takes place primarily in the twenties and requires the individual to leave home and establish himself in the adult world by finding an occupation and by developing intimate ties with significant others, usually a spouse of the opposite sex, in order to create a new family unit. The next stage, which covers most of middle adulthood, Erikson calls "generativity vs. stagnation." It begins in the early thirties and is concerned with generativity in a very broad sense, not only as a parent, but more broadly still as a creative worker in one's occupation or profession and as a mentor for younger members of one's field. The last stage, called "ego integrity vs. despair," takes place before and during senescence, when the individual sums up the meaning of his life.

The University of Chicago has been a fruitful source of much research on adult development. R. J. Havighurst developed the concept of "life tasks" that had been mentioned by Erikson—that is, that each stage of life has certain characteristic psychic work that must be done if one is to proceed normally to the next stage of development. For example, if the young adult does not succeed in cutting the apron strings to his parents by his early twenties and entering into a new and much looser relationship with them, it is unlikely that he will be able to go on to more mature tasks such as marrying and establishing a family. We all are familiar with the middle-aged son or daughter who has dutifully stayed on to live with and care for aging parents, still maintaining the role of the child.

For the past 20 years, another University of Chicago professor, Bernice Neugarten, and her associates have conducted far-ranging studies of middle-aged and aging populations, most notably their Kansas City study of a large population of normal older adults. They have exploded many of the myths about the nature of the aging process. They have shown, for instance, that aging per se in middle adulthood and beyond does not result in decreasing mental or emotional flexibility.

Neugarten and others have discovered that one of the changes that occur at midlife is in the individual's time perspective. She found that

A particularly conspicuous feature of middle age is that life is restructured in terms of time left to live rather than time since birth. Not only is there a reversal in directionality, but also an awareness that time is finite.

This attitude toward time results in a significant change in one's orientation and motivation. There is a feeling that time s running out, that if you are to accomplish your goals, you must do it now.

For a number of the men to whom we talked, their realization of the press of time came about as a result of the death of someone close to them. For two of them, it was the death of their father. One man had surgery on his back a few months after the death of his father. He recalled what had happened:

i idolized my Dad, and his death was a real blow to me. During the two weeks that I was lying in bed in the hospital, I kept thinking about him and about my own life and what I had accomplished. I had just completed a major project for my firm that had taken almost five years of my life. I was proud of it because I had done a good job, and it was a success. But I knew that in that company it was highly unlikely that there would ever be a similar opportunity. I could foresee that my job would be quite routine in the future by comparison. When I went back to work after my convalescence, my heart just wasn't in it. Soon after, I learned of this new opportunity to go into business for myself, and I just grabbed it.

Another man had been having difficulty with his superiors. He was scheduled to give a presentation to the board of directors. His superiors warned him to leave out a certain section of the report; they thought it would meet with disapproval from the chairman of the board. In recalling that event, he said,

I had reluctantly agreed to leave it out, but just before the presentation I was looking out the window and I saw a hearse followed by a funeral procession driving down the road. I wondered to myself whether that guy had been told to do something that he didn't want to do, and, if so, what difference it made to him now. When I got up to speak, I decided to include the material I was supposed to leave out. That was the beginning of my decision to leave the company and look for a job in which I could be my own boss.

Along with the change in time perspective comes an increase in introspection, stock taking, and the structuring and restructuring of past experience. There is a good deal of measuring of self and accomplishments against mental yardsticks. For the two men mentioned above, the yardsticks were their fathers' lives. Would they be able to accomplish as much or live as fully as their fathers had?

Neugarten believes that this heightened introspection reflects certain normal internal psychological processes as well as the individual's response to his changing role with age, which comes about when children leave home, parents become dependent or die, and so on. She found it measurable in well-functioning adults by the mid-forties, long before the social losses of aging, such as the death of friends occurred and long before there was any measurable change in competency of performance in adult social roles.

Neugarten and her associates also found an increased control over impulse life. They found that the successful middle-aged person often describes himself as no longer "driven" but the "driver"—in short, as being in command. Biological needs are less important, and the actions directed by our conscience and philosophy of life as well as practical demands become more central. This is in contrast to the view some other writers have of the middle-aged, particularly men, claiming they are driven by impulse, especially in the area of sex, for a last fling to assert their potency and to try to recapture their youth. On reflection, however, the middle-aged man having an affair with a young "chick" is cause for comment simply because he is going against expected behavior. After all, the middle-aged are the ones who usually maintain the standards and mores of any society.

Other characteristics of healthy middle-aged people found by the University of Chicago researchers include a seeming reversal of value priorities, much as was suggested by Jung. The career-oriented individual who has achieved economic security and success may put aside his need to get ahead and turn to family or community activities for gratification. Conversely, the woman who has been content to focus on children and the home may become thoroughly involved in the demands of a new job.

Peck asserts that

. . . it has been my impression that those people who age most "successfully" in this stage [midlife transition] with little psychic discomfort and with no less affectiveness, are those who calmly invert their previous value hierarchy, now putting the use of their "heads" above the use of their "hands," both as their standard for self-evaluation and as their chief resource for solving life problems.

Perhaps a good example of someone who has found a need to reverse his values and roles, if only on a periodic basis, is the former president of Haverford College, John Coleman, who took a sabbatical to try his hand at garbage collecting and other menial jobs in order to get back in touch with reality.

One man in the study presented a very dramatic example of this kind of complete reversal. John went to the state university, where he studied business administration, but majored in girls and sports. A superb athlete, he was picked up by a Yankee scout and played major league baseball for several years after graduation. During the off season, he began to work in construction for his father in Florida. Business was booming, and he left baseball to devote himself full time to contracting.

In the ten years that he was in the business, it grew, and he made a great deal of money. He had not been inside a church for many years, but he began to get involved because of his children, first in the activities of the youth group, then in other aspects. He found himself becoming less interested in his business and more concerned with spiritual values. "Making money was not the answer. It was just not that important to me. I was looking for something else."

The rector's wife suggested that he go into the ministry. John thought he was too old, but he talked to the bishop, who thought it was a great idea. He decided to enroll in seminary a year later and was surprised to discover that his age, 35, was the average age of his classmates. He sold his home and his business. He has had no regrets. His goals and values have changed 180 degrees. He firmly believes that "You cannot serve two gods." It bothers him that everything is measured in terms of money. His definition of success has changed. His present goal is to continue in the ministry and try to find a position in which he can work with people making decisions about changing their lives.

Marjorie Fiske Lowenthal and her associates, in a study of 216 men and women in a middle- and lower-class community approaching four different periods of life changes, found the same shifting of value priorities that Jung and the University of Chicago researchers commented on. This study again suggests that the values that were useful to provide structure and meaning for one stage of life may not be functional for the next.

Lowenthal found that among the middle-aged men she studied, the values associated with either family or work were the most important in determining their feelings of well-being or dissatisfaction with life. Those who seemed to be satisfied were the ones whose values were concerned with relationships with other people, primarily within their family. Those who were mainly concerned with money, possessions, status, and work seemed much less happy. This was certainly true among the men we interviewed.

According to Lowenthal, the men who were unhappier felt that way either because they realized that their original occupation and material goals could never be met or because they were increasingly concerned with whether or not they would be able to achieve certain occupational goals before it was too late. The character of Scrooge in Dickens' *A Christmas Carol* is perhaps the best-known example of a man who has lost touch with any human relationships, concentrating on business, to his own ultimate despair. He is fortunate enough to be able to learn, before it is too late, of the rewards of family relationships and the fact that they are more valuable than gold.

Although not directly related to research in developmental psychology, the work of John B. Miner on the issue of conformity gives us some interesting input into the psychology of middle age and perhaps some clues as to what causes the value changes of midlife. It may be that we no longer worry so much about how others see us; we feel freer to be ourselves and live by our own standards. Miner found that at about the age of 40,

. . . the rewards to be gained by inhibiting one's individuality begin to pale. There appears to be less and less to be gained by conforming, as a man's ambitions are satisfied or as he sees that they never will be satisfied, . . . one's place in life is pretty well set.

MIDLIFE TRANSITION

In studying the question as to whether there is, indeed, a "midlife crisis" or transition period, Roger Gould, a psychiatrist, and his associates at UCLA collected questionnaire data from 524 people of all ages who were attending group therapy clinics. The questionnaire probed their attitudes toward life. Those who were between 40 and 43 years old seemed to be going through an acutely unstable period with a great deal of personal discomfort, much more so than those from other age groups. The people who were between 35 and 43 were asking themselves, "Have I done the right thing?" "Is there time to change?"

Another view of the midlife crisis is given by two Harvard psychiatrists, George Vaillant and Charles McArthur, who are the present custodians of the long-term Grant Study of a group of men who were chosen when they were Harvard undergraduates and showed high potential for achievement as well as mental and physical health. These men, now in their fifties, have been studied at regular intervals.

A recent report shows that they changed markedly at about 40, undergoing a stormy period that resembled a second adolescence. Vaillant and McArthur found their group went through the same themes of reassessment and reordering of the past at that age that other groups had been found to go through. In summation, they write,

Perhaps the most important conclusion of the Grant Study has been that the agonizing self-reappraisal and instinctual reawakening at age 40—the so-called "mid-life crisis"—does not appear to portend decay. However marred by depression and turmoil middle life may be, it often heralds a new stage of man.

The psychoanalytic view of midlife is, in contrast, a rather pessimistic one. Elliot Jaques, who represents this point of view, sees the psychic changes at midlife as caused by the realization of the inevitability of one's eventual death. He calls the midlife crisis a "period of purgatory—of anguish and depression," of mourning for the loss of youth. Jaques finds the same change in the perception of time that Neugarten and her associates discovered. There is a sense that one's life can no longer be changed, that it is set. Important things that we would like to have done or to have become are now out of the question. A race against time begins. According to Jaques, this is reflected in the compulsive attempts of many middle-aged people to try to remain young, in their increasing concern with health and appearance, and in the emergence of sexual promiscuity in order to prove youth and potency.

Jaques says that the midlife crisis may be expressed in three different ways with regard to creative output in one's profession. The creative career may come to an end, either by drying up or by actual death. The creative capacity may begin to show and express itself for the first time. Or a decisive change in quality and content of creativeness may take place.

In a random sample of 310 artists, Jaques found that the death rate jumped suddenly much above normal in the period between 35 and 39, made a large drop below normal between 40 and 44, and then returned to normal. He saw a change in the mode of work at the time of the midlife crisis from the impulsive, quick creativity of early adulthood to a sculpted, slower creativity of mature adulthood.

There seemed to be a change in quality and content of creativity from the lyrical and descriptive in early adulthood to the tragic and philosophic in midlife, leading later toward serenity in middle and later adulthood.

Harvey C. Lehman found trends indicating a midlife crisis in the research described in his remarkable work, *Age and Achievement*. The book documents his life work, examining the accomplishments of hundreds of people in a broad spectrum of fields. He clearly found that in creative fields, whether scientific research or musical composition, the most fruitful years for production are those between 30 and 39. He documents a marked drop at about 40.

Donald C. Pelz and F. M. Andrews, in a study of scientific researchers, found the same peak of creativity in the late thirties, with a sharp drop at about 40, followed by a rise again in the late forties, but not as high as the earlier peak. These studies imply that something takes place at about the age of 40 that diminishes the individual's creative capacities, and would be indirect proof of a midlife crisis.[2]

SEASONS OF A MAN'S LIFE

Perhaps the most exciting and definitive research on adult psychosocial development has been under way at the Yale Medical School for the past ten years under the direction of a thoughtful and wise psychologist named Daniel Levinson. Despite the fact that the findings of his group were not published for some time and then only in rather out-of-the-way volumes, word got out that they were on to something. Long before the publication of his book, *Seasons of a Man's Life*, there were articles on his work in *Time*, and his theories became the basis for a long-time best seller, *Passages*, by Gail Sheehy.

Levinson and his colleagues are a multidisciplinary group, combining the insights of psychology, sociology, and psychiatry. They carried out an intensive study of 40 men between the ages of 35 and 45, each of whom was interviewed for a total of 10 to 20 hours. The subjects were from four occupational categories: hourly workers in industry, business executives, academic biologists, and novelists. The aim of the interviews was to develop a biography of the person to get at all the aspects of his life and their

[2] In another study, however, no midcareer drop in performance was found, but this study was based on self-ratings of performance. See Douglas T. Hall and Roger Mansfield, "Relationships of Age and Seniority with Career Variables of Engineers and Scientists," *Journal of Applied Psychology*, **60**, 202 (1975).

interconnection, and to determine the course of the man's individual life structure. In addition to studying the men in depth, the researchers used materials from biographies, autobiographies, poetry, plays, and novels that dealt with men's adult lives.

For Levinson, the concept of "life structure" is central; adult development is seen as the evolution of the life structure, which is composed of the outside sociocultural world in which man lives and his participation in this world in all his various roles—as worker, husband, father, and self—both as it appears to the world in his behavior and as he experiences it internally or even in his subconscious.

The life structure does not remain static, but changes according to a sequence of alternating stable and transitional periods. According to Levinson, the stable periods tend to last from six to eight years, while the transitional periods last from four to five years. In an article in *Psychiatry*, he says,

The primary developmental task of a stable period is to make certain crucial choices, build a life structure around them, and seek to attain particular goals and values within this structure. Each stable period also has its own distinctive tasks, which reflect the requirements of that time in the life cycle. Many changes may occur during a stable period, but the basic life structure remains relatively intact.

The primary developmental task of a transitional period is to terminate the existing structure and to work toward the initiation of a new structure. This requires a man to reappraise the existing life structure, to explore various possibilities for change in the world and in the self, and to move toward the crucial choices that will form the basis for a new life structure in the ensuing stable period. Each transitional period also has its own distinctive tasks reflecting its place in the life cycle.

Levinson's description of the task of a transitional period is exactly the process that was undertaken by the men whose career change was most successful. Those who did not take the time to reappraise themselves and to explore the possibilities open to them were much more likely to find themselves unhappy in their new position.

Levinson has found in his study that there are specific developmental periods in adult life. His journal article describes them as follows:

DEVELOPMENTAL PERIODS IN EARLY ADULTHOOD

As indicated, my main emphasis here is on one of the major transitional periods in adult development, the Mid-Life Transition. This period ordinarily starts at age 40, give or take two years, and lasts some 4–6 years. In the mid-40s a new life structure emerges and persists for several years until a new transition gets under way. The Mid-Life Transition serves as a developmental link between two eras in the life cycle: early adulthood and middle adulthood. I cannot present here our overall conception of the life cycle and its component eras (cf. Levinson, 1977; Levinson et al., 1977). Each era contains a series of developmental periods (see below), but it also has an overall character of its own. It must suffice merely to identify the eras and their approximate age spans:

> Pre-Adulthood: Age 0–22
> Early Adulthood: Age 17–45
> Middle Adulthood: Age 40–65
> Late Adulthood: Age 60–85
> Late Late Adulthood: Age 80+

The shift from one era to the next is a massive development step and requires a transitional period of several years. Every transition is both an ending and a beginning, a departure and arrival, a death and rebirth, a meeting of past and future. The basic task of a cross-era transition is to terminate the era just ending and to create a basis for the next. Thus, the Early Adult Transition, which lasts from roughly age 17 to 22, is part of both pre-adulthood and early adulthood. It is equally correct to say that pre-adulthood extends into the early twenties, and that early adulthood begins in the late teens. The Early Adult Transition is of special developmental importance precisely because it contains and bridges the two eras. Likewise, the midlife transition, from roughly age 40 to 45, serves as a boundary region linking early and middle adulthood.

In order to provide a context for discussion of the Mid-life Transition I shall first review briefly the preceding periods in early adulthood. I shall give a modal age for the onset of each period; there is a range of about two years above and below this modal figure. We did not start the research with the expectation of finding age-linked periods; they are an empirical finding rather than an *a priori* assumption.

THE EARLY ADULT TRANSITION

This period ordinarily lasts from age 17 until 22. Its twin developmental tasks are to terminate pre-adulthood and to initiate early adulthood. The first task is to start moving out of the pre-adult world: to question the nature of that world and one's place in it; to modify or terminate existing relationships with important persons, groups and institutions; to reappraise and modify the self that had formed in it. Various kinds of separation, ending, and transformation must be made as one completes an entire phase of life. The second task is to make a preliminary step into the adult world: to explore its possibilities, to imagine oneself as a participant in it, to consolidate an initial adult identity, to make and test some preliminary choices for adult living.

ENTERING THE ADULT WORLD: THE FIRST
ADULT LIFE STRUCTURE

The period extends from about 22 to 28. The underlying developmental task is to fashion and test out a structure that provides a viable link between the valued self and the adult society. The young man must shift the center of gravity of his life from the position of child in his family of origin to the position of novice adult, with a new home base that is more truly his own. He must make and live with initial choices regarding occupation, love relationships (usually including marriage and family), values, and life style.

In this period a man has two major yet antithetical tasks: (a) He needs to explore the possibilities for adult living: to keep his options open, to avoid strong commitments, and to maximize the alternatives. This task is reflected in a sense of adventure and wonderment, a wish to seek out all the treasures of the new world he is entering. (b) The contrasting task is to create a stable life structure: to settle down, become responsible, and "make something of my life." Each task has sources and supports in the external world and in the self. There is usually moderate or great discontinuity between the pre-adult world in which a man grew up and the adult world in which he forms his first life structure. Exploring this new world and building a life within it is an exciting yet often confusing and painful process.

Each man works out his own balance of exploration-openness and stability-commitment during this period. Some men go through it on a highly tentative basis, leading transient lives and capriciously changing jobs, residences, relationships. They create a loose structure without stability or rootedness—not investing much of the self in the world nor taking much of the world into the self. Others have some mixture of stability and change, making some commitments but feeling open to change. Or they initially "keep loose" and then at perhaps 25 or 26 get more serious about forming a stable life. A man may make a strong commitment in one sector of his life, such as work or marriage, and not in others.

Still other men make strong commitments at the outset and build what they hope will be an enduring life structure. These men usually make their key choices regarding marriage and occupation in the Early Adult Transition and maintain great continuity with the pre-adult world, without exploring new options or questioning their values and goals.

In the late 20's, as this period draws to a close, the seemingly firm structure comes into question. The man wonders: Did I commit myself prematurely? Do I want to keep this way of life forever? Shall I seek new possibilities more suitable for the person I am now? Likewise, the young man who had created a loose or fragmented structure comes now to recognize its limitations and to seek a life of greater order and more stable attachments.

THE AGE THIRTY TRANSITION

This transition, which lasts from about 28–33, is another of nature's ingenious devices for permitting growth and redirection in our lives. It provides an opportunity to work on the flaws and limitations of the first adult life structure and to create the basis for a new and more satisfactory structure with which to complete the era of early adulthood.

At about 28 the provisional, exploratory quality of the 20s is ending and life is becoming more serious, more restrictive, more "for real." A voice from deep within the self says: "If I want to change my life—if there are things in it I want to modify or exclude, or things missing I want to add—I must now make a start, for soon it will be too late." Men differ in the kinds of changes they make, but the life structure is always different at the end of the Age Thirty Transition than it was at the start.

Some men have a rather smooth transition, without overt disruption or sense of crisis. They may use this period to modify and enrich their lives in certain respects, but they build directly upon the past and do not make fundamental changes. It is a time of reform, not revolution.

For other men the Age Thirty Transition takes a more stressful form, the age 30 crisis. A truly developmental crisis occurs when a man is having difficulty with the developmental tasks of this period; he finds his present life structure is intolerable, yet seems unable to form a better one. In a severe crisis he experiences a threat to life itself, the danger of chaos and dissolution, the loss of hope for the future. Most of the men in our study went through a moderate or severe crisis during this period.

There is a peaking of marital problems and divorce in the Age Thirty Transition. It is also a time for various kinds of occupational change: a shift in occupational category or kind of work; a settling down after a period of transient or multiple jobs; a promotion or advancement that brings one into a new occupational world; and, apart from the external aspects, a change in the internal meanings and goals of work. Many men hit "rock bottom" in this period before discovering a new path. There is a higher frequency of psychotherapy. For some men the Age Thirty Transition is a period of excitement, of growth, of "getting oneself together" for the first time.

These first three periods—the Early Adult Transition, Entering the Adult World, and the Age Thirty Transition—generally last about 15 years, from age 17–18 until 32–33. Together they constitute the preparatory, "novice" phase of early adulthood. This is not an extended adolescence but a highly formative, evolving phase of adult life (White, 1952).

The shift from the end of the Age Thirty Transition to the start of the next period is one of the crucial steps in adult development. At this time a man may make important new choices. If these choices are congruent with his dreams, values, talents, and possibilities, they provide the basis for a relatively satisfactory life structure. If the choices are poorly made and the new structure seriously flawed, however, he will pay a heavy price in the next period. But even the best structure has its contradictions and must in time be changed.

SETTLING DOWN: THE SECOND
ADULT LIFE STRUCTURE

The second life structure takes shape at 32 or 33 and persists until 39 or 40. A young man now tries to build a life structure for the culmination of early adulthood. He seeks to invest himself in the primary components of this structure (work, family, friendships, leisure, community—whatever is most central for him) and to realize his youthful aspirations.

In this period a man has two major tasks: (a) to establish a niche in society: to dig in, anchor his life more firmly, develop competence in a chosen craft, become a valued member of a valued world; (b) to work at "making it": planning, striving to advance, progressing along a timetable. One version of "making it" is the American Success Dream of getting rich, powerful, and famous. I use the term more broadly to include all efforts to build a better life, to attain valued goals, to contribute to the tribe and be affirmed by it. The artist and intellectual, like the worker, businessman, cleric, and revolutionary, normally use the Settling Down period toward these aims.

Until the early 30s, a young man has been a "novice" adult, forming an adult life and seeking a more established place in adult society. His task in the Settling Down period is to become a full-fledged adult within his own world. He defines a personal enterprise, a direction in which to strive, a sense of the future, a life plan, a "project," as Sartre (1953) has termed it. The enterprise may be precisely defined from the start (to become a successful middle manager or corporation executive, to become a great scientist or artist, to have some financial security and a happy family life in the suburbs) or it may take shape only gradually over the course of this period.

The imagery of the *ladder* is central to the Settling Down enterprise. The ladder is psychosocial: it reflects the realities of the external social world, but it is defined by the person in terms of his own meanings, motives, and strivings. By "ladder" I mean all dimensions of advancement—social rank, income, power, fame, creativity, quality of family life, social contribution—as these are important for the man and his world.

At the start of this period, a man is on the bottom rung of his ladder and is entering a world in which he is a junior member. His aims are to advance in the enterprise, to climb the ladder and become a senior member in that world. His sense of self-being during this period depends strongly on his own and others' evaluation of his progress toward these aims.

Toward the end of the Settling Down period, starting ordinarily at age 36–37, there is a phase so distinctive that we have given it a name: Becoming One's Own Man. The acronym BOOM connotes an important aspect of what man wants in this phase, though not necessarily what he gets. The major developmental tasks of BOOM are to accomplish the goals of the Settling Down enterprise, to become a senior member in that world, to speak more strongly with one's own voice, and to have a greater measure of authority. A crucial dilemma here is that a man wants to be more independent, more true to his own wishes even if they run counter to external demands, but he also wants affirmation, respect, and reward from his world.

This is a fateful time in a man's life. Attaining seniority and approaching the top rung of his ladder are signs to him that he is becoming more fully a man (not just a person, but a male adult). However, his progress not only brings new rewards, it also carries the burden of greater responsibilities and pressures. It means that he must give up even more of the little boy within himself—an internal figure who is never completely outgrown, and certainly not in early adulthood—and this intensifies the inner struggle between the little boy and the evolving man.

The activation of the pre-adult self during BOOM is a part of normal psychosocial development. It represents a step forward in that it brings out the boy–man polarity and creates the possibility of resolving it at a higher level. For a time, however, the conflicts may contribute to difficulties in the man's relationships with wife, children, lover, boss, friends, co-workers. He often feels that others regard him as a little boy to be deprived, exploited, and controlled. He may experience his boss as a tyrannical, corrupt, or inept authority, his wife as a depriving or smothering mother, his critics as jealous rivals who cannot tolerate his success. There is usually some mixture of reality and distortion in these apperceptions; it takes time to deal with the inner conflicts and to gain a more realistic view of self and others.

The life course can evolve in many ways during the Settling Down period. We have found three main sequences, each with countless variations on its themes:

Sequence A: Advancement within a stable life structure. As the Settling Down period begins, primary commitments are made, an enterprise is defined, and the initial structure is gradually enriched and elaborated. During the BOOM phase the man defines more precisely the last few rungs on his ladder and intensifies his efforts to advance. Often, he works toward a key event that brings him to the top rung of his ladder and carries the ultimate message of his affirmation and disaffirmation by society. This "culminating event" typically occurs at about age 39–41. It serves as an external marker for the conclusion of Settling Down and the beginning of the next period, the Mid-life Transition. It may take myriad forms: promotion to a certain rank in his work organization; producing a book, scientific discovery, or other product that establishes his reputation and inner identity at the desired stature; attaining a certain position in the extended family or community. His life structure is relatively stable over the course of this period and he does moderately or spectacularly well in reaching his goals. The top of this ladder becomes the bottom of the next: he takes his place now as a newcomer in a more senior generation and a more established world, qualitatively different from the past.

Sequence B: Failure–decline within a stable structure. As in Sequence A, these men form a relatively integrated life structure early in the Settling Down period. During BOOM, however, their aspirations are not realized. Some of them fail in gross and obvious ways. Others achieve a good deal of external success but fail in certain crucial respects which vitiate the entire enterprise in their own eyes. There is usually a "culminating event" that carries the ultimate message of failure; but we can understand the meaning and impact of this event only by placing it within the unfolding developmental process. The distinction between Sequences A and B is primarily one of degree; many men advance in some ways (external and internal) and fail or do poorly in others.

Sequence C: Changing structure. These men do not maintain a stable life structure over the course of Settling Down. Some men have an unstable structure that remains in flux through this entire period. They try to commit themselves to a flawed marriage or occupation or life style, and then make recurrent changes that work no better. Being unable (for internal as well as external reasons) to launch an enterprise that serves as a vehicle for advancement and Becoming One's Own Man, they face serious problems in middle adulthood. To make use of this creativity during the 30s, a man needs a flexible but relatively stable structure within which he can work toward a disciplined freedom.

In some cases, Settling Down begins with a seemingly stable structure, but as BOOM gets under way, the man experiences more acutely the flaws in this structure and his life becomes intolerable. The locus of difficulty may be in one sector such as work or marriage, or he may feel profoundly alienated from his entire world—suffocated, oppressed, and without space in which to be himself and to do what matters most. He decides in BOOM that he must change his life. Our name for this sequence is Breaking Out. He seeks a radical change in life structure. No matter how well his enterprise succeeds, the success will not provide what he really wants: he is in the wrong enterprise, involved in the wrong relationships, violating his most cherished dreams and aspirations. He decides to build a new life within which he can truly become his own man and live out the most important aspects of his self.

The breaking out may be dramatized by a decisive act such as quitting his job, leaving his wife, or moving to "another part of the country." However, this event is but one step in a developmental process that began earlier and will continue for some years. It is part of a "BOOM crisis" that is as fundamental as the other, more documented crises in human development. This crisis involves a terrible dilemma. The man fears that if he stays put, he faces a living death, a future without promise, a self-betrayal. Yet to make a major change at this point may be hurtful to his loved ones as well as himself; his hopes for a better life may be only a pipe dream that will soon end in failure, disappointment, and remorse.

Breaking out does, indeed, exact great costs. A man who attempts a major change at 36 or 38 is not likely to establish a new structure and gain some stability in his life in less than 8–10 years. It takes time to break away, to sever or modify old relationships and commitments. It takes time, also, to "break in," to enter a new world and create a new life. The new enterprise is hardly under way when the Mid-life Transition begins and, with it, a new effort to question and improve one's life.

For every man who attempts to break out, there are several who, after great inner struggle, decide to stay put. The long-term costs of remaining in an oppressive life structure may also be very large. It is a task for Solomon—to say, in any individual case, what the wise decision is.

THE MIDLIFE TRANSITION

During his 30s, a man's primary developmental task is to build a satisfactory life structure. Within it, he tries to establish his place in society, to pursue his youthful aspirations, and to live out important aspects of the self. The late 30s mark the culmination of early adulthood. The Mid-life Transition, which lasts from roughly 40 to 45, provides a bridge from early to middle adulthood.

The start of the Mid-life Transition brings a new set of developmental tasks. Now the life structure itself comes into question and cannot be taken for granted. It becomes important to ask: What have I done with my life? What do I really get from and give to my wife, children, friends, work, community—and self? What is it I truly want for myself and others? What are my real values and how are they reflected in my life? What are my greatest talents and how am I using—or wasting—them? What have I done with my early dreams and what do I want with them now? Can I live in a way that best combines my current desires, values, talents, and aspirations?

Some men—but very few, according to our study—do very little questioning or searching during the Mid-life Transition. They are apparently untroubled by difficult questions regarding the meaning, value, and direction of their lives. They may be working on these questions in implicit or unconscious ways that will become evident later. If not, they will pay the price in a later developmental crisis or a life structure minimally connected to the self. Other men, again not a large number, realize that the character of their lives is changing, but the process is not a painful one. They are, so to say, in a manageable transition without crisis.

For the great majority—about 80% of our subjects—this period evokes tumultuous struggles within the self and with the external world. Their Mid-life Transition is a time of moderate or severe crisis. They question virtually every aspect of their lives and are horrified by what they find. They cannot go on as before, but it will take several years to form a new path or to modify the old one.

Because a man in this crisis is often somewhat irrational, others may regard him as "upset" or "sick." It is therefore important to recognize that he is working on a normal mid-life task and that the desire to question and enrich his life stems from the most healthy part of the self. The doubting and searching are "normal"; the real question is how best to make use of them. The difficulty is compounded by the fact that the process of reappraisal activates neurotic problems (the unconscious baggage carried forward from hard times in the past) which hinder the effort to change. The pathology is not in the desire to improve one's life but in the inner obstacles to pursuing this aim. The pathological anxiety and guilt, the ancient dependencies, animosities, and vanities of earlier years, keep one from examining the real issues at mid-life. They make it difficult for a man to free himself from an oppressive life structure.

A profound reappraisal of this kind cannot be a cool, intellectual process. It must also involve emotional turmoil, despair, the sense of not knowing where to turn or of being stagnant and unable to move at all. A man in this state often makes false starts. He tentatively tests a variety of new choices, not only out of confusion or impulsiveness but also out of a need to explore, to learn how it feels to engage in a particular love relationship, occupation, or solitary pursuit. Every genuine reappraisal must be agonizing, because it challenges the assumptions, illusions, and vested interests on which the existing structure is based.

The life structure of the 30s was initiated and stabilized by powerful forces within the person and his environment. These forces continue to make their claim for preserving the status quo. The man who attempts a radical critique of his life at 40 will be up against the parts of himself that have a strong investment in the present structure. He will often be opposed by other persons and institutions—his wife, children, boss, parents, colleagues, the organization and the broader occupational system in which he works, the implicit web of social conformity—that seek to maintain order and prevent change. With luck he will also find support in himself and others for the effort to examine and improve his life.

Why do we go through this painful process? We need developmental transitions in adulthood partly because no life structure can permit the living out of all aspects of the self. To create a life structure I must make choices and set priorities. In making a choice, I select one option and reject many others. Committing myself to a structure, I try over a span of time to realize its potential, to bear the responsibilities and tolerate the costs it entails.

The life structure of the 30s necessarily gives high priority to certain aspects of the self and neglects or minimizes other aspects. With the onset of MLT these neglected parts of the self urgently seek expression and stimulate a man to reappraise his life. He experiences them as "other voices in other rooms" (to build on Truman Capote's evocative phrase), as internal voices that have been silent or muted for years and now clamor to be heard. He may hear only a vague whispering, the content unclear but the tone indicating grief over lost opportunities, outrage over betrayal by others, or guilt over betrayal by himself. Or the voices may come through as a thunderous roar, the content all too clear, stating names and times and places and demanding that something be done to right the balance. He hears the voice of an identity prematurely rejected; of a love lost or not pursued; of a valued interest or relationship given up in acquiescence to parental or other authority; of an internal figure who wants to be an athlete or nomad or artist, to marry for love or remain a bachelor, to get rich or enter the clergy or live a sensual carefree life—possibilities set aside earlier to become what he now is. During the Mid-life Transition, he must learn to listen more attentively to these voices and, in the end, to decide what part he will give them in his life.

I have quoted so extensively from Daniel Levinson's writing because he seems to have synthesized perfectly all the previous work on adult psychological development and to have made such sense out of it. As we go on in the next chapter to examine the career changes of the men we studied, it will be clear that Levinson's theory helps to explain and give meaning to their actions.

MEN AND WOMEN

Few researchers on adult psychological development have looked at women; almost all the studies done thus far have concentrated on men. From my own experience, I think that there are many similarities. However, the content of the stages is probably somewhat different for women. I would guess that the Age Thirty Transition Levinson describes is usually more severe and traumatic for women in American culture than it is for men, because society so clearly defines for men what they should be doing at that time in their life.

Women wait until later in life to deal with the question of identity, since that question is connected with their choice of a marital partner. It is at 30 that women usually deal with the issue of what being a woman means in our society in terms of how she will live her own life. A single woman may come to the realization at 30 that she may never marry and must therefore concentrate on developing a meaningful career that will provide a central focus. A married woman will have fairly young children, and while her husband is out making his way in the world, she may feel trapped in the home with a sense that there is nothing ahead for her but endless piles of dirty dishes.

I have known several women who, while married, concentrated their energies on developing a career during their twenties but at the Age Thirty Transition suddenly decided that their lives would not be fulfilled without children. They then had to cope with balancing their energies between work and family. No matter what their situation, it seems to me that women at the Age Thirty Transition must deal with the realization that despite what society has taught them, they must establish an identity of their own, independent of whether or not they have an identity connected to a man.

For men, the Mid-life Transition at 40 is the more difficult. By that age, a woman can begin to feel less need to prove her femininity. A woman's task at the Mid-life Transition is to move out into the world, whereas a man's is usually to deal with the interior, with the feelings and emotions he has so carefully ignored during all those years of "making it." For him, the life tasks he must deal with tend to go counter to the conventional wisdom of continuing to climb the ladder to success; therefore he has fewer outside resources to help him in his struggle.

There is a paradox in our society. When he is young, a man must struggle to develop a career and a strong attachment to work, by which he is identified and gains status. A woman, on the other hand, has traditionally been expected to find a husband and raise a family, from whom she gains her identity and status. The women's movement, beginning with Betty Friedan's *The Feminine Mystique*, has made us realize that, in today's society, identification through their husbands and families is simply not enough for most women. Women need to go out in the world to develop other interests and other sources of satisfaction in order to be fulfilled.

What developmental psychologists and such observers of the corporate world as Michael Maccoby are telling us is that a man cannot gain all of his identification from one source alone—his work—without becoming as narrow and dried up as the wife and mother when her nest empties and there is nothing to replace it. Men who have invested themselves exclusively in their jobs, to the neglect of family and other outside ties, find themselves at midlife losing their satisfaction from work, but having nothing to replace it. Freud's famous dictum, *lieben und arbeiten,* was correct. The healthy person must have a balance between love and work to make a whole and satisfying life.

IS THERE A MIDLIFE CRISIS?

Do most people go through a midlife crisis? Students of the question disagree on how severe the experience is and what percentage of the population experiences it. My preference is for the term "midlife transition" rather than "crisis." A crisis implies both a rapid and a substantial change in personality dynamics, probably causing significant pain. Some people do experience pain, but the term "transition" would probably be more accurate for most people.

The severity of the transition often depends on external events as well as, of course, the individual's overall emotional health and stability. Some men can make the changes of middle adulthood gradually and with no trouble. However, if a man's father dies, if he doesn't gain a long-hoped-for promotion at work, if his youngest son beats him at tennis, and if his wife takes on a demanding new job all in one year, the likelihood is quite strong that he will have a midlife crisis. It may be that for the men in our study, luck was on their side, and external circumstances were such that they were able to resolve the midlife transition favorably through action before it could become a crisis.

Perhaps another factor that will affect the severity of the transition is a person's lifelong habits of introspection and reassessment. A man who has always assumed that his life plan was engraved in stone at age 21 and has followed it implicitly for 20 years may well have a major crisis when he is about 40 if things don't work out. As columnist Ellen Goodman points out, it is a "profound misconception that the best armament against uncertainty is a life plan that reads like a Piece of the Rock." If we have learned from youth onward to be able to face life with flexibility and a fairly continuous reassessment of goals and means for reaching them, we may not hit midlife with such a crash.

There is a contradiction in society. Most people agree that the pace of external change is inexorably increasing. It is only reasonable to think that people living in such a changing world will themselves change. Yet the status expectations we face and the institutions in which we live are not programmed to allow us to change. We are taught to expect life to be neat and orderly, and we are caught by surprise when it is not.

One value of the research on adult development may

well be that more people will become aware that their symptoms of transition are not indicative of mental aberration, but are simply signs of normal life processes. It may be that fewer people would have a midlife crisis if they were better prepared to cope with the inevitability of change in themselves.

3

The Career Changers

WE will now describe the general findings of our study of 91 successful men of managerial and professional level who changed their careers between the ages of 35 and 54. Collecting the information was fun. As a group, these people were interesting, intelligent, dynamic, and alive. They were generally proud of their accomplishments and pleased at the way they had handled their lives. The cooperation they gave the interviewers was surprisingly generous. They gave up several hours of valuable time.

The interviews usually lasted between one and two hours, and the respondents spent several additional hours completing questionnaires and tests. By and large, they were open, frank, and honest in their answers to the interviewers' questions. A number of the men indicated that they found the opportunity to review and summarize their careers a valuable one.

Most of the men were interviewed in their homes or offices, where they could be seen on their own turf; they were quite hospitable. In general, they were very sympathetic with the aims of the study. Since they had experienced positive effects in their own lives as a result of career change, they wanted others to know about it and share the experience.

We will begin by looking at some generalizations that

can be made about the group as a whole. Then, in subsequent chapters, we will look more closely at specific aspects of their career change and its effects.

AGE AT CAREER CHANGE

As we saw in Chapter 2, most developmental psychologists seem to agree that some changes take place at about the age of 40, whether they are called "midlife crisis" or not. It was natural, then, to assume that a change of career might well be a symptom of these psychological changes. A distinct clustering of time of career change around the early forties would suggest that some upheaval was going on in the men's lives at that period that could be attributed to a midlife crisis or transition.

Figure 1 shows the distribution of ages at which career change took place among the men in the study. This is defined as when they left their former jobs, either to begin new ones or to attend school full time. A slightly greater number of the men changed careers during the early forties than at other times between the ages of 35 and 54, with the changes occurring between the ages of 40 and 44 amounting to 33 percent of the total distribution, as against the approximately 25 percent that would be expected by chance alone.

More of the men changed careers at the age of 40 than at any other age in the 20-year range. However, it was not *quite* a statistically significant number, and, therefore, no significant relationship was shown to exist between age and time of career change. On the other hand, the findings certainly do not rule out the likelihood that midlife transition was a factor in the career change for many of the men.

The reported motivation of many of the men who changed careers was concern with the meaning of their work, values, life-style, and other issues that, as we know, are central concerns of the midlife transition. Nothing in our findings would serve as evidence against the theories of midlife discussed in the last chapter.

Figure 1. Distribution of age at career change among the sample studied.

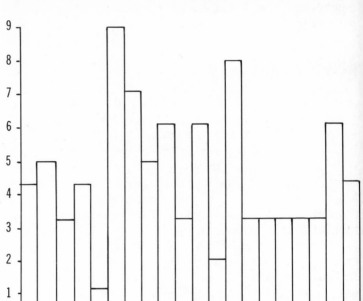

Probably the reason a more conclusive and statistical result was not obtained was that career change can also be prompted by other, more purely economic reasons. The decade before the men were studied saw drastic changes in the employment picture for well-educated managerial and professional men. From a time of expansion in research, engineering, and education in the late 1960s, the United States went to a time of dramatic decline in defense and space-related industries and education as well as the worst recession this nation has seen since the Great Depression.

It is natural to assume that for many of the men we talked to, economic issues figured in their decision to change careers. As we shall see, a number of the physicists and engineers we studied were motivated primarily because the demand for people with their backgrounds was declining so drastically that they could see no future for themselves. They had either been laid off or were in dead-end jobs with tenuous security.

Of course, human behavior is amazingly complex, and we seldom make any important decisions in our lives from only one motive. For most of the men we studied, the psychological changes of the midlife transition certainly played a part in their decisions to change career.

It was interesting to note that younger men were more likely to have taken a longer time to change their career. Older men moved more quickly, perhaps pushed by the thought that time was running out. As might have been anticipated, younger men also went back to school more frequently as a means toward changing their careers. Of course, there are always exceptions. One man in his early fifties started law school. He had the financial resources to do so without sacrifice. In addition, he came from a long-lived family and was positive that he had a long life ahead of him. Indeed, he looked and acted much younger than his years.

FAMILY AND EDUCATIONAL BACKGROUND

Of the 91 men, 20 reported their childhood family socioeconomic status as being "well above average," 26 "a little above average," 22 "average," 12 "a little below average," and 7 as "poor"; 4 did not respond. The majority of the men were raised as members of the middle class or higher, and they all have that status now.

An interesting correlation, which may reflect upon problems of inital career choice, is between socioeconomic status of childhood family and pressure to leave the former job as a factor in career change. Those from families of average or lower socioeconomic status were more likely to have had to leave their jobs; they had either been fired or laid off.

Men from poorer families generally have far fewer options in their initial job choices than men from more well-to-do homes. Therefore, they are more likely to enter a field that does not suit them. Also, men from middle- or upper-class families have greater feelings of economic security and are more apt to make a voluntary change rather than wait to be forced by circumstances. Not having experienced poverty, they are not as afraid of failure.

In terms of educational background of the men in the study, 12 reported no college degree, although all had had some college, 34 had a bachelor's degree, 31 had a master's degree, 3 had a professional degree, and 11 had a Ph.D.

CATEGORIES OF CHANGERS

We divided the men into categories according to the radicalness of their change. Eight did not have to learn new skills or obtain new knowledge. Typical of these were men who had held important staff or line positions for large corporations and had substantial knowledge of a particular area, such as marketing or data processing, and who then went into business for themselves or became outside consultants.

Fred worked for many years for a major insurance firm, starting in at the beginning of the computer revolution. He had worked himself up to head of data processing for the company. We spoke to him when he was in his mid-fifties, several years after he had started his own consulting business. A heavy-set, distinguished-looking man with an air of confidence and success, he said,

Over the years I became disenchanted with company policies. I disliked several major new policies that were initiated and, as a result, I finally decided to leave. The parting was amicable, and I still do some work as a consultant for the firm. However, I do a great deal of consulting across the country. I travel a lot, giving lectures and training sessions and consulting with a variety of clients. I'm in the middle of writing a book that will explain the programs I have developed.

The knowledge and skills Fred draws on in his new career are the same as in his old job. But he has had to adjust to the complexities of running his own business, with an office in his home. He ruefully admits that he misses the amenities and support services of a large corporation. "The one thing I miss most is having a secretary on hand to relieve me of details. But I do relish my independence, and my business is doing well."

Forty-seven men combined old skills and knowledge with newly acquired learning to embark on their new careers. Don, in his early forties, had had a successful career in personnel, culminating with a position as director of training and manpower development in a medium-sized corporation. He suddenly found himself put on the shelf with a bleak future as the result of a corporate merger and takeover. He described what happened.

The previous year had been the happiest of my life. I was setting up the companywide training program. I was given a free hand, with almost unlimited resources for audiovisuals and personnel. I was going around the country interviewing trainees. And then the takeover by [Company X], and the whole tone of the place changed. Their philosophy was strictly cost accounting, the fiscal, with no attention to personal and human elements. I became a glorified accountant, even though I had the same job title. I could see that there wasn't much future for me there, so I left.

Don had been active on his community's school board and at that time was interviewing candidates for superintendent. He began to think that he could probably do educational administration as well as anyone else and would enjoy it. He had already taught an occasional course at the local university, so he had a chat with the dean, who offered him an assistantship while he completed his master's degree. According to Don, "It was only a couple of thousand, but it was the greatest news in the world when I learned I got it."

Don went back to school and obtained a master's degree in adult education. Luckily, when he finished, he was able to find a position as director of that university's continuing education program. He enjoys the change to the academic

world, and his past experiences in business have helped him
to develop many clients for the university's programs among
area firms.

Thirty-two men made a complete change—that is, the
knowledge and skills required in their new occupation had
no relationship to the old. In this last category were men like
Bob, a victim of the decline in the aerospace industry. A
successful aeronautical engineer who was a group leader
supervising a number of engineers for a large aerospace firm
he was given two weeks' notice when the company's contracts were not renewed.

Bob decided fairly soon that he would not look for
another engineering job, but instead would try to make a
lifelong avocation into a paying vocation. He had always
been interested in books, and whenever he traveled, he spent
much time haunting second-hand bookstores. He thought
this might be a good time to see if he could get into the
business himself. He received some good advice from the
Small Business Administration and the American Booksell-
ers Association. Bob looked into franchises, but rejected that
idea because there were too many strings attached. He didn't
have enough capital to start a new bookstore from scratch.
Fortunately, by chance, he saw an advertisement in the
newspaper for a used bookstore for sale in his area, and he
bought it.

Shortly before his layoff, Bob's wife had gone back to
work on a part-time basis to help with the college expenses
for their children. She has since shifted to a full-time job,
which she enjoys, and the kids are almost finished with
school. The business broke even after six months and is now
showing a profit. Between Bob's wife's income and the growing profit from the bookstore, the couple is beginning to
rebuild the large chunk of savings they drew upon to buy the
bookstore and to tide them over during the first year of operation.

Bob reports that he is much happier in his new occupation than he had ever been as an engineer. People warned
him that he might feel cooped up and tied to his shop, since
it is basically a one-man operation, but this doesn't bother

im. He is clearly comfortable in the organized clutter of the
hop, which is packed from floor to ceiling with books. He
resses casually in an old sweater and loafers. He does get
ut to examine and purchase collections. He has also built
p a group of steady customers who either write in or phone
heir requests for particular titles; thus he has developed a
vide network of friends and acquaintances who share his
nterest.

Those men who, like Bob, were forced to leave their
revious jobs because they were laid off or fired, were more
ikely to make radical career changes, requiring the learning
f entirely new skills, than those for whom external pressure
vas not a factor.

NTERNAL VERSUS EXTERNAL PRESSURE TO LEAVE

When we decided on our study, our initial decision was
o limit it only to men whose change of career had been
ntirely voluntary. The more we began to talk to people
bout career change, the more difficult we realized it would
e to separate out the voluntary from the involuntary.

We talked with the personnel director of a large com-
)any who was interested in the study. In the course of the
:onversation, he gave us the names of several people he
:new who had left his firm to make a career change. He
nentioned one man we had already interviewed. He said,

t was really a relief that Mike left; his work had deteriorated during
he last few years he was with the company, and we had come to the
lecision that he would have to be terminated.

)ne of us who had interviewed Mike said,

)h, no, that's not the picture I got at all. Mike told me that he had
)een losing interest in the company for several years and had been
)lanning to leave. He had been devoting all of his energy to prepar-
ng for the move to open up his own business.

:learly, it depends on your point of view. Many men, of
:ourse, left their old positions entirely voluntarily and were

urged not to go. In fact, several had the option of returning t
their jobs if things didn't work out. Other men were laid o
because contracts had been terminated or their firms ha
gone out of business. Others, however, were in the middl
They did not have to leave, but then, things were not goin
all that well, and those for whom they worked may hav
been relieved to see them go. In some cases, the terminatio
was the "kick in the pants" the person had secretly bee
hoping for, because he was too afraid to risk changing
clearly unpleasant situation on his own initiative.

In reality, the success or failure is not in losing a job, bu
in whether or not the person turns it into an opportunity
Some of the most successful career changes were made b
men who were dismissed from their previous jobs.

The following scale shows how the men ranked the ex
ternal pressures to leave their former jobs. Fifteen of the me
reported that they had received strong encouragement from
their former employers to stay. Eleven were fired or laid of
The rest are distributed fairly evenly along the scale.

External pressure to leave former job:

Numbers:	15	4	8	2	14	6	5	3	5	1

1	2	3	4	5	6	7	8	9	1
Strong			Neutral: not encouraged					Strong	
encouragement			or discouraged					pressur	
to stay			or balanced out					to leav	

(No data: 18)

Personal desire to make career change:

Numbers:	0	4	2	1	4	1	4	11	15	32

1	2	3	4	5	6	7	8	9	1
Strong			Neutral: desire to					Strong	
desire to			change balanced by					desire t	
remain			desire to stay					make a	
									change	

The second scale shows the men's personal desire to make the career change. A few men really would have preferred to stay in their old jobs, but the majority felt a strong desire to change.

As is evident, our final decision was to study men who had changed careers whether or not the change was voluntary. Our concern was to discover as much as we could about career changers in general and particularly about the process they used. We found distinct differences between voluntary and involuntary changers. The outcome of the career change was clearly correlated with whether or not the change was their own choice. Those for whom pressure to leave was a factor were much less likely to experience a very rewarding outcome. By and large, they also took less time to make the change than those who did not feel any external pressures to leave.

My impression is that although involuntary changers are less likely to end up happily, a lot depends on how they go about looking for a new position. Bob, whose story is given above, was able to turn a forced layoff into a most successful transition to a new career. He did have several things going for him: a supportive wife, a financial cushion of savings plus her salary, and a long-standing hobby that he could turn into a business. In addition, he went about his investigation in a thorough and methodical way.

REASONS FOR CHANGING

We found the following categories of reasons for changing careers:

1. *Laid off or fired.* Many of these men were victims of the crash of the aerospace industry in the early 1970s. A variant on this theme occurs when someone sees that the field or profession he is in is contracting. Although his present job tenure may not be in imminent danger, the future potential in that field is slight. Several of the men we studied were physicists who decided to go in a new direction. Most of them enjoyed research physics and would have liked to

remain in the field, but realized that the demand for physi
cists had contracted drastically. We will be seeing more an
more educators changing careers for this reason in the com
ing years.

2. *Put on the shelf* (job remains, but no further advance
ment or growth possible). Some of the men found them
selves in this position through company mergers. It wa
clear that the managers of the acquiring firm were takin
over, and although the staff of the original firm would not b
fired, it was no longer in the political mainstream of opera
tions. In other cases, some of the men found that age had
caught up with them: competition for the same top manage
ment level jobs was the same age or younger. Looking at the
situation realistically, they saw no possibility for further ad
vancement.

"Topping out" is what William R. Stanley, Director o
Personnel Planning and Development at the Connecticu
General Life Insurance Company, calls this phenomenon. In
his experience, dealing with it is one of the most difficul
adjustments people have to make at midlife. He finds that i
occurs when a person realizes he or she has gone as far as he
or she is likely to go in that organization in terms of advancement and professional development.

Stanley says, "It is very hard to watch first your peers
and then younger people go past you; I have seen many men
in such a situation grow bitter and become rigid." He is an
advocate of job rotation or career change for people in mid-
career. When that time arrives, it is much more productive to
accept the inevitable with grace and turn our ambitions and
energies to new pursuits. For many, this would be an ideal
time for a second career, if not within our current company,
then outside the corporation, but people are shackled by
what Stanley calls "the golden handcuffs" of company pensions, high salaries, and health benefits.

Rosabeth Moss Kanter, in her book, *Men and Women of
the Corporation*, observes that in a large, hierarchical corporation success is too often defined in terms of mobility.

When you cease to climb the ladder and are stuck in a dead end or have lost out to the competition, you can either turn to other means of satisfaction or become frustrated and hostile. According to Kanter,

Such people could constitute a considerable problem for the organization, for they could occupy key positions and be relatively highly paid. They were often people with seniority who had been valued performers in the past; their dissaffection represented a real cost.

Thus, leaving the company for a career change can be a productive way of coping both for the individual and for his former employer.

3. *Growth of a hobby or outside interest* to the point of becoming a full-time vocation. For example, one man took a course in weaving. He spent more and more of his spare time on it, and began to win prizes at crafts shows. Finally, he and his wife made a conscious decision to go into the field on a full-time basis. They planned their finances over a period of several years until they were in a position to purchase and stock a store in which they could sell their fabrics and other crafts. She concentrates on running the store while he spends most of his time weaving and teaching.

4. The *"How Many Times Do You Climb Mt. Everest?"* phenomenon. Although few in number, the men in this category (so named by Seymour Sarason) were fascinating individuals who could be labeled superachievers. Some of them had a history of several career changes, in each of which they were highly successful. After achieving as much success as was likely, they simply got bored and were ready to go on to find new worlds to conquer.

Brian became a full professor of physics at a midwestern university when he was 37 and chairman of his department a year later. When faculty unionization and collective bargaining became an issue, he got deeply involved in the struggle. He was elected by his fellow professors to head the local chapter of the American Association of University Professors in its bargaining efforts with the university administration and worked closely with the lawyers in drawing up the final agreement. It changed his life:

After two years of political battles, going back to the classroom just seemed very anticlimactic. In addition, I know that great discoveries in physics are made by the young. Here I was pushing 40; I was over the hill. I thought about going into academic administration, but those people had been my adversaries for two years, and I wasn't very eager to join them.

Ironically, after I had left and started law school the president called me up and asked if I would come back as dean. At any rate on impulse, I took the Law School Admissions Test, primarily, I guess, to see if I was as smart as the lawyers I had been working with. I thought I was. I had almost forgotten about it and had become involved in other things when the score came in the mail. It was very high. I decided to apply to Harvard, Stamford, and Yale, and if I could get accepted, I would go.

Brian was accepted by one of these schools. Fortunately, he was able to take advantage of the offer of a year's salary for tenured professors who choose to retire early. He also had enough savings so that he and his wife and son could live frugally. He was interviewed a few months before his graduation, and was looking forward to his new job with a Washington law firm.

5. *Change in values* leading to a different vocational direction. Some of these men were influenced by the peace movement of the late 1960s. Their civil rights and antiwar activities made them question the moral value of what they were doing, particularly if they were working in defense-related industries. They then left their former jobs to enter fields—such as education or social work—in which they could be of more direct service to others.

Bruce, a soft-spoken, bearded man in his mid-forties, was typical of this type of career changer. The whole change process took five years for him, beginning in 1967. He had been brought up a Catholic, and while the seeds of doubt were probably planted during college, they came to a head at this time. He searched around for other religions, and finally joined and became very active in the Unitarian Church, where he became involved in anti-Vietnam War activities along with many other members. He began to question the meaning of his job, which was as an operations analyst doing cost-benefit analysis for military systems.

I figured that if I wasn't doing anything overtly evil, I really wasn't doing much that was positive. My job had long since stopped being exciting or challenging, and I began to question a lot of things.

As part of his new activity in the church, Bruce was asked to serve on the religious education committee. The religious education director asked him to teach. He had never thought about it before, but agreed to try. He started by leading a discussion group with junior high school students, and it proved successful. He then tried younger groups, which he liked better. He ended up by taking care of the nursery, which he enjoyed most of all.

At one meeting of the religious education committee, Bruce remembers talking to a woman who had raised her children and was returning to school for a degree in early childhood education. She suggested that he take one course and see how he liked it. He loved it and decided to continue. Both the university and his employer were flexible in terms of his schedule. Most of the courses were in the evenings, and he was able to take a summer leave of absence in order to do the practice teaching.

When Bruce obtained his master's degree, he applied for jobs in the area. He found one as a kindergarten teacher in a local school, left his job at the end of August, and started as a teacher in September. He found the reaction to a male kindergarten teacher somewhat mixed. "Some systems just weren't interested in a man, but in others, it was clear that I had an advantage." He enjoys his new work very much. The only serious drawback is the low salary level of elementary school teachers. He is earning half his former salary, which causes problems, since his children are approaching college age.

Table 1. Subjects' ranking of motivation for career change

Motivation	Very Impor- tant	Impor- tant	Of Slight Impor- tance	Not a Factor
Chance for greater achievement	33	17	8	33
Better salary	2	8	12	69
More meaningful work	48	21	3	19
More congenial colleagues	7	13	18	53
Greater responsibility	15	9	11	56
More time with family	13	11	15	52
Better fit of values and work	44	19	6	22
Time for recreation, hobbies	9	12	18	52
Live in better locality	11	7	5	68
Less hectic pace	12	11	13	55
Greater security	3	9	5	74
Felt pressure to leave	6	7	8	70
Laid off or terminated	7	2	3	79
Health reasons	5	3	5	78

Most subjects listed a number of motivations.

MOTIVATION

Table 1 shows how the men ranked their reasons for changing careers. We find it striking that the reason given most often was a desire for work that was more meaningful; next was a better fit of values and work, and third was a chance for greater achievement. In other words, these men were concerned with the *intrinsic* rewards and satisfactions of what they were doing; money and financial security were the least important reasons for most of them. These findings contradict the popular view that Americans are only concerned with money, material values, and status.

However, the concern for values and the intrinsic re-
vards of the work is quite consistent with what we learned
1 the last chapter about adult psychological development.
t midlife, according to the developmental psychologists,
1en tend to become less interested in material things and
onventional measures of success and turn inward for their
atisfactions. This seemed to be true for many of the men
rith whom we spoke. They spent a great deal of time in
1trospection and in reevaluating their accomplishments
1nd measuring them against a dream of what they would like
2 do or be.

In addition to being consistent with the predictions of
evelopmental psychologists on what happens at midlife,
1e men's reasons for changing careers are also consistent
vith the theories of psychologists who have worked in the
rea of motivation. The late Abraham Maslow would have
ategorized the men who changed careers as primarily
self-actualizers." He suggested that people have what he
alled a "hierarchy of needs," beginning with the purely
hysiological survival needs for food, sleep, and so on, and
scending through safety, belongingness and love, to es-
2em. When all other needs are basically satisfied, people
an deal with the higher order needs, such as enjoyment of
rt and music, learning, and, finally, self-actualization,
. . . the desire to become more and more what one is, to
ecome everything that one is capable of becoming."

By and large, these men had achieved comfortable stan-
ards of living, so that they could live in pleasant suburban
omes, eat well, send their children to college—in short,
ealize the American Dream. They didn't have to worry un-
uly about finances, so they could concentrate on the satis-
1ction and value to themselves of the work they were doing.
'hey could concern themselves with making their careers
1eaningful, with doing work that was intrinsically satisfy-
ng.

The motivation of the career changers is also consistent
vith the findings of Frederick Herzberg and his associates in
he research they conducted on the motivation to work. They

found that the strongest motivation to work comes from one's sense of pride in one's accomplishments and the rec ognition by others of one's achievements, as well as th sense of growth and development in the work one is doing In their research they were able to isolate aspects of a job tha they called "motivators." These lead to job satisfaction Other factors, which they called "hygiene factors," lead t job dissatisfaction if they are not attended to. Hygiene factor include such things as salary, work environment, and hours

According to Herzberg, "The factors that lead to positiv job attitudes do so because they satisfy the individual's nee for self-actualization in his work." Motivators relate to

. . . the need to develop in one's occupation as a source of per sonal growth. The second group operates as an essential base to th first and is associated with fair treatment in compensation, supervi sion, working conditions, and administrative practices.

Most of the men in the study were not dissatisfied with th "hygiene factors" in their previous jobs, although they ma have played a minor role. More importantly, they were look ing for better "motivators," work environments in which they could find personal meaning and growth. As one man who changed from being a stockbroker to running a countr inn, put it, "I grew increasingly tired of working with peopl who were only after money for money's sake."

In a Rand Corporation study on career change and it policy implications, the authors found from their review o many national cross-sectional studies on job satisfaction tha salary seems to be important as an indication of job satisfac tion only in lower paid occupations, and that meaningful ness and creativity become much more important in highe level occupations where the salary is perceived to b adequate. This finding agrees with Maslow's theory of th "hierarchy of needs" and with the results of this study.

The comments of many of the men when we inter viewed them clearly illustrate their motivation. A number o the men expressed their realization that making money di not buy them happiness. One said, "I realized that I reall didn't want to make a million dollars. I wanted to do what I wanted to do, not what someone else says leads to success." Another reported that he and his family were now living on a quarter of their former income. He said, "We really didn't need all those things we used to buy. After all, you can only eat one steak at a time."

Several of the men who were successful in corporate life said that they had originally wanted to get to the top, but they soon discovered that "presidents of corporations are unhappy people." This comment was such a frequent one—it was made by at least half a dozen of the men we talked to—that we began to wonder if it is really true. More probably this belief was a useful mechanism that helped these men to readjust their sights when it became apparent that they were not ever going to get to the top. Far healthier to harbor such a belief than to blame yourself for failure.

Michael Maccoby, in his study of top corporate managers, describes them thus:

Yet they are not a particularly happy group. They lack passion and compassion. They are cool or lukewarm. Intellectually open and interested, they are emotionally cautious, protected against intense experience.

This, presumably, was the quality that many of the career changers observed and opted against. Many of the men Maccoby describes report having thought seriously of changing their careers.

Fred, a tall, handsome man in his mid-forties who looked younger, was typical of those who opted against climbing up the corporate ladder. He attended an Ivy League college on an NROTC scholarship. After his tour of duty in the navy he joined the staff of a large insurance company, where he worked for 14 years, making steady progress. He became an officer of the firm at a relatively young age. He had always been interested in law and was active in local politics, envying several fellow employees who had been able to attend the local law school at night.

Fred thought about his future in the company and the

possibility of law school for about three years. He had a
promising future ahead in the company, but he had lost
interest. He didn't enjoy supervision, preferring to do things
by himself. He said,

The further up the corporate ladder you go, the less independence
you have. I didn't like the direction the company was going in
either. It underwent a financial crunch, and the reaction was too
panicky, too tough. Many people were fired who should have been
able to stay.

A family inheritance enabled Fred to go to law school full
time He continued to do some consulting for his old firm for
a while, then began to work part-time for the small firm
where he is now happily employed.

A man who left a high position with an auto manufac-
turer to teach in a university reported that he seriously began
to consider leaving the corporate world when his son, who
was then a senior in high school, told him that he would
never lead the kind of life his father did.

Several of the men expressed their motivation in terms
of changed values. One, who had become involved in civil
rights and anti-Vietnam War activities, said that these had
changed him so that he now had "less interest in material
success, getting up the organization, making money."
Another said that he was "dissatisfied with the wheeling and
dealing of the business world" and "wanted to do something
useful. There is more to life than making money." Another
reported that his goals and values had broadened; he is more
concerned with ethics, and not just Sunday religion.

Despite some of the comments listed above, it would be
false to think of these men as antibusiness or antiestablish-
ment. We had actually begun the study thinking that we
would find many men with this point of view, and called it a
study of "corporate dropouts." We found, however, that this
was not the case and changed our title. Many of the career
changers did leave big corporations, but they were not
necessarily *against* big business as such. Actually, their
views were generally quite traditional, and their political

outlook was typical of that of any cross section of middle-aged American men, ranging from fairly radical to quite conservative. A good number of them were actually old-fashioned entrepreneurs who wanted to establish businesses for themselves.

A theme that recurs throughout is a desire for autonomy. Thirty of the men changed careers in order to start their own businesses. Their feelings were quite similar to those of the "dropouts" Betty Roberts studied. She commented on how much they needed to control the structure of their lives; they wanted to create it rather than have the structure imposed on them.

In a study by Douglas T. Hall and Roger Mansfield of scientists and engineers, they found that the need for autonomy of the men they interviewed seemed to peak in the midcareer years (40–49), which agrees with our findings. Maccoby also found that on middle and lower levels, the managers and engineers he interviewed felt that if they had the option, they would prefer running a small company of their own to reaching a high level in a large company.

Ken's story almost exactly fits the theories we have discussed. A quiet, serious man, he had a degree in electrical engineering from Rensselaer Polytechnic Institute and served in the army for two years in World War II. After his discharge, he worked his way up rapidly to high managerial positions in several firms engaged in aeronautical engineering. His last job, as manager of production, he admits was

a terrible mistake. I was not suited for it or for the company. I was also becoming disenchanted with what we and similar companies were doing—80 percent military projects, many boondoggles. It was not satisfying.

Ken thought hard about leaving for six months, but had thought vaguely about it much longer. He had always been a book lover and had often thought that running a bookstore would be very satisfying. He read a great deal about bookstores and obtained some information from the Small Business Administration in preparation. He discussed the change with his wife a great deal. She had some misgivings, but was mostly positive. They both disliked the direction in which their suburban town seemed to be going, with a rapid influx of new developments, and both wanted to live in a more rural atmosphere.

Ken left the company in November and took a trip through northern New England to see if he might find any bookstores for sale. He found one in a lovely resort town in New Hampshire. He and his wife looked at it, liked it, and made an offer. They bought it in early January, sold their suburban Boston house for a good profit, and moved to New Hampshire with their two school-aged children at the end of March. The bookstore came with an attached house and three acres of land in a beautiful valley with views of the mountains beyond. The children love it. Ken's present goal is to lead a "good life."

Money has no bearing on the good life, so long as minimal wants are provided for. For me it involves a happy family life, lots of good books to read, and a minimum of outside interference.

KINDS OF JOBS THEY ENTERED AND LEFT

It is possible to make some broad generalizations about the kinds of fields the men left and the ones they entered. By and large, they left large, bureaucratic, usually profit-making organizations and jobs in which they were dealing with data and things. They entered smaller organizations, businesses of their own or professions in which they would have a great deal of personal autonomy, such as law or college teaching. Their new occupations tended to be ones in which they were much more involved with helping other people; they were positions that allowed them to be able to see some specific value or result from their work.

We have already given some examples of men who left large companies in order to find more autonomy; there is a fairly sizable number of these people. Another man who felt strongly that he was a victim of bureaucracies was Ned, who made his career change in his early forties. He had gotten in on the ground floor of the computer era right after his discharge from the army. He worked his way up in data processing, attending courses and workshops and earning an M.B.A. by attending school part-time in the evenings. Working at progressively better paying jobs as a systems analyst, he eventually became a data processing manager.

Describing his history, Ned said,

I enjoyed my work, I worked hard, and I was good at it. I decided to leave not because I was basically unhappy with what I was doing—because I was not—but because I got caught in the cross fire of top management decisions three times, and I simply refused to be put in such a position again.

In listening to his story, I agreed that he was probably a victim, being a middle management person responsible for supervising others by carrying out orders from above. However, he admits that he is not a very political person, so his own personal style may have been partially responsible for his problems. In observing him in his shop for a few minutes before the last customer left, I found him a very capable and positive kind of person—one who would not be likely to take any nonsense from anyone.

Ned explained:

In my first job, I was asked to fire someone, which I felt was grossly unfair to that individual. I simply refused and resigned rather than do so. In the second job, I was reporting to two bosses, and when the one with whom I was siding in terms of policy lost out, I was fired. In the third job, I was given the task of being the hatchet man in an intolerable situation. The top management were apparently guilty about the difficult situation they had put me in, so that, when I quit in disgust after nine months, they gave me three months' severance pay.

Fortunately, Ned was able to start his own business, with help from his father, based on a hobby they both had shared for many years. His two sons now help him after school. His competence has enabled him to match his last salary within just a few years of starting the shop.

Some of the men left large companies because they were not able to see any tangible results from what they were doing. One, who had been an advertising executive, and now, in his early forties, runs his own business, said,

I didn't enjoy my work. I was either bored or driven by external requirements. Advertising was highly competitive, but there was no intrinsic reward. It was like a giant game of Monopoly— overstimulating.

Another man described his situation thus:

There was no external pressure. I could have stayed with the company. I was vice-president, one of the top group of management. The reason I left was that I realized I had lost my commitment to business. It occurred to me that here we were beating our brains out trying to sell [product Y], competing with three other companies, any one of which could supply what was needed. I reacted to the waste of all this talent doing these relatively useless things. I was undergoing a value change. I wanted to express myself, to get away from the manipulation of customers, the whole competitive thing.

In retrospect, several of the men said that they had never really felt a part of the large companies for which they worked. The man who became a kindergarten teacher said that he had never joined the company retirement program because even ten years before, he felt that he didn't want to be tied to the company. We found many other men who had similar comments: "I never was the engineering type." "I was never really part of the steel business." "I shouldn't have gone into insurance anyway." "I never thought of myself as a hotel man." Why were these men unable to identify themselves with the companies for which they had worked so long?

Eight of the men had initially been in family-owned businesses and were persuaded to join the company by either their father or father-in-law. For most of them, the job was not really right from the beginning, but they fell into it because of a lack of anything better to do to earn a living and because of the appeal to their family loyalties. Once they were in, they were bound by all sorts of emotional ties, and getting out was a long and painful process; for several, it involved psychotherapy.

Phil was a typical example. Now in his early fifties, he grew up in a poor immigrant family very much involved in Socialist and labor causes. He was lucky enough to be able to go to college on a full scholarship and part-time work. After graduation, he spent three years in the navy.

When I was discharged, I returned to my hometown and soon met a girl from a well-to-do family there whom I had not known before. We fell in love and were married. I began job hunting in the summer of 1948, which was a time of a mild recession when jobs were scarce. My father-in-law offered me a job in his insurance firm, which I gladly accepted for the security. I worked there for 26 years, selling insurance and doing reasonably well financially, but I hated every minute of it.

I lived my life primarily after five. My wife and I had four children, and we were a close family, participating in a lot of outdoor sports together. I was very active in civic affairs; I must have run practically every fund-raising campaign in that town at one time or another. I tried to get out of the business several times, but I didn't quite make it. Finally, my partner bought me out, and I looked for another job.

Phil is now an executive in a nonprofit agency, which he enjoys, although his future is somewhat tenuous. He seems quite sad at the thought of all those years wasted. In retrospect, he wishes he had gone to law school, as he had once hoped to do.

ENGINEERS AND CAREER CHANGE

In the Rand Corporation study of career change, much of the research that has been done on job dissatisfaction and its causes was reviewed. The consensus was that dissatisfaction with employment increases with lower socioeconomic status, except that engineers are even more alienated from their jobs than many lower white-collar or blue-collar groups. The study also found the obvious—that people who are dissatisfied with their work are often interested in a job change or career redirection. The authors suggest that it may be possible to predict which groups of workers are most likely to pursue midlife career redirection—older people in technical, data-oriented, or materials-oriented professions, of which engineers would be a major segment.

Both Cyril Sofer and Richard R. Ritti also reported that among all the professional employees of the large corporations they studied, the engineers were the least satisfied with their job prospects, hours, opportunity for travel, and working conditions, the extent to which they would use their skills, and the amount of responsibility they were given. Sofer states that

. . . a proportion (of the engineers) seemed as alienated from their work as assembly-line workers are reported to be from theirs. Nearly half the respondents felt they were "under-used" in the sense of possessing abilities they were not called upon to exercise. They seemed to feel partially redundant in the sense of their full potential not being drawn on or realized.

We found that many of the men we studied had been engineers.

Ron's story is typical of the dissatisfaction felt by many engineers who work for giant firms.

There wasn't that much external pressure for me to leave. I could have stayed on at the same level with no prospect for advancement and only some increments in salary until retirement. It was the political infighting that turned me off. Men below you and ones at the same level would cut you down to try to get to your position. I was extremely unhappy, had stomach troubles, and was often depressed. I enjoyed the work for the first ten years or so, but when it became clear that I would be doing the same thing as long as I stayed at [Company Z], then it got to be terrible.

I would have to commute an hour in, spend the day working at this job, and then spend an hour commuting home. When I got home, I just wanted to crawl into a hole and watch television. It goes deeper than boredom with the work I was doing. With that size company there can be a phenomenal waste of manpower. They would stick me on things that could be done by a lesser level guy because they knew I would get it done. Then when they had a project they wanted me on, but which wasn't ready to begin just then, I would have to wait around for it to start. You'd have to kind of dissolve into the woodwork until it was ready to start.

Ron now runs his own small business. He says, "The change has had a tremendous benefit for the family. We feel much closer now, do more things together."

Why are engineers like Ron so likely to be dissatisfied with their work? Engineering is the single largest occupational group categorized as a profession in the United States. Most engineers are employed by very large organizations. Three-fourths of all engineers work in one percent of the firms that employ engineers. Thirty-five percent work in organizations with more than 10,000 employees, and 75 percent in organizations with more than 1,000 employees.[1]

Engineering has long been seen as a route to upward mobility in American society. It is not as difficult to become an engineer as it is to enter some of the other professions, such as law and medicine, because the amount of training required is less. As a result, engineers tend to come from families of lower socioeconomic status than those of any other professional group. Technical training in engineering provides an avenue of upward social mobility for the intelligent sons of working-class families.[2] They have high expectations of both professional prestige and satisfaction and financial security.

Many studies have been done of the indoctrination process people undergo during professional training. They all show quite clearly that during the course of professional

[1] Robert Perrucci and Joel E. Gerstl, *The Engineers and the Social System* (New York: John Wiley, 1969), pp. 1–2.
[2] Jay M. Gould, *The Technical Elite* (New York: Kelly, 1966), p. 83.

education students become "socialized" to the values and goals of the profession. A medical student, for example, learns how to behave and act like a doctor. In schools of engineering, students are encouraged to aspire to positions in management; indeed, part of the curriculum includes courses in management. Therefore, the technical aspects of engineering itself are seen by many as merely a means to an end, which actually involves leaving the profession. That is, the message aspiring engineers are given during their training is that being an engineer all their lives would be a sign of failure. The successful graduate engineer is the one who, in effect, leaves the field.

What the engineering student aspires to does take place. Ritti reports on a survey he did of engineers who had been with their companies for 11 to 15 years. Of these, one-half were in management positions, one-third in staff positions equivalent to management, and 15 percent in nonmanagerial positions. Not only do the training and socialization of engineers lead them to desire to become managers, but there is also pressure from the nature of their work. Most engineers work for giant companies on vast projects taking long periods of time to complete. A typical example would be a NASA space shuttle. Hundreds of engineers would be involved, and completion might take years.

Large engineering enterprises are organized as bureaucracies, and their first priority is efficiency and predictability rather than the creativity and self-actualization of their employees. Work is divided into small, formatted segments and doled out in such a way that no one engineer has much say about what he is doing. Thus, there is a strong motivation to become a manager of a project group. It is one way to move from being a small cog working on a minor part of a large whole of which one is kept ignorant to being in a position to see and contribute to the larger picture. There are, therefore, both internal and external pushes to move from the purely technical side of engineering into management—for status and for greater job satisfaction.

Many engineers make the transition from engineering to

management without difficulty and with satisfaction. But what happens to those who don't? Presumably, people who are attracted to the field initially are those with an interest and ability in mathematics and science and a desire to work on their own to solve technical problems involving data and things. Some of them will also have an aptitude and interest in the organizational and people-related skills of a manager, but many will not.

Initially, these technically oriented men will be satisfied with their work, since young engineers tend to be paid well at first and given challenging assignments. However, as time goes on, the typical engineer becomes less and less challenged by his work. If he goes on for further study and maintains a "scientific" view of himself in his profession, he may maintain his involvement. He may, however, come to see it as just a job, and find that his allegiance is to the company rather than to the science and expansion of knowledge in his field. He will become less involved in his work, and his knowledge will become obsolete. This likelihood is increased by the fact that engineering is often extremely specialized work. If a man works on one project for five years, when it ends, there may no longer be a need for that particular technology, and he is caught in a bind.

In a study of Massachusetts Institute of Technology graduates of the classes of 1951, 1955, and 1959, Lotte Bailyn found that those who were in applied engineering fields and had not gone on for further study or had not become managers were the least involved in their work:

Hence the professionally oriented and technically most competent engineers are the ones most able to retain their involvement with work. In other words, though it has sometimes been stated that only a move to management can satisfy the engineer, these results indicate that for some engineers, those whose orientation is more scientifically professional, technical work can continue to be involving. These are the people, presumably, who are more interested in working with things than with people. . . . Their orientation was and remains technical, and, given the right conditions, they remain involved with their technical duties even many years into their careers.

In contrast, those engineers in staff positions who are less technically oriented and more interested in working with people have a more problematic relation in their work. Whether they have always had these inclinations and hence would have been better off in a different field from the beginning, or whether these tendencies represent new developmental stages which point to the desirability of a mid-career change after an involving initial decade or so of technical work, we do not know. At this point in their careers, however, this group, as opposed to the more professionally oriented one referred to before, would benefit less from opportunities for technical up-dating than from training that would help them make a mid-career transition—training in management, for example.

Thus the "plight" of the engineer at mid-career is a complex phenomenon, and there is no one "solution" for it. It requires diagnosis on the level of the individual and flexibility in response to his (or her) needs: there must be not one kind of arrangement between engineers and their employing organizations regarding their future careers but several, and a discriminating approach to selecting these paths.

Abraham Zaleznik and his associates studied a group of engineers in a large corporation and found

That the path of upward mobility and increased reward seemed to be in the managerial hierarchy was the most significant problem confronting the technical specialist. The professional employee, gifted in technical work and with little inclination for management, could anticipate a real limitation on his earnings, status and recognition if he remained outside of a managerial career. However, to move gifted professional specialists into management, apart from real ability in this direction, often resulted in poor management and the loss of technical expertise.

The company they studied experimented with a two-track system, in which top-performing technical specialists were given salaries and status on a nonmanagement track that were rewarding enough to keep them from opting for management.

For many engineers, however, there is neither the option of moving happily into management or of gaining status and rewards through scientific achievement: The salary curve flattens with age; they are no longer likely to get significant increases or promotions. Hall and Mansfield, in their study of a group of engineers and scientists, reported that the importance to them of self-actualization seemed to decrease with age. However, they imply that this was not a result of normal adult developmental trends, but of increasing dependency on the bureaucratic organizations for which they worked. As the men grew older, their need for security seemed to increase. Thus, they apparently sublimated their desires for autonomy and self-actualization in favor of retaining the security provided by the corporation.

Sofer reported that among the engineers he studied, those who were in their forties were markedly the least satisfied with their career progress. Thus, for many engineers and their employing companies, career change may be a welcome solution if finances and desire for security are not too great a barrier. Many companies who employ large numbers of engineers have become increasingly concerned with the problem of technical obsolescence and are spending large sums for training programs to update the knowledge of their older engineers. It might be as cost-effective for them in the long run if they also developed programs of career counseling and training that might help older engineers to move out of the company into other fields. These men could then be replaced by younger, more recent graduate engineers at lower salary levels.

The company would not be encumbered by a highly paid employee with seniority who is no longer very productive, and that employee would have the stimulation of a new and potentially more satisfying career. At any rate, engineers, engineering schools, and employers need to recognize that engineering may be, like professional sports and airline piloting, a field for the young, one that is likely to end by the time a man is in his forties.

CAREERS THEY ENTERED

Some intriguing trends are observed in the kinds of careers into which the men moved. Many chose areas that are less traditionally masculine than their former fields—education, nursing or social work, or generally helping kinds of professions. This choice would confirm the theories of a number of the psychologists, beginning with Jung, who believe that at midlife men become more feminine and women more masculine.

Jean Lipman-Blumen and Harold J. Leavitt express it quite specifically:

. . . we have begun to think about moving males into roles which can meet their stifled social needs and women into roles in which they can express more directly their egoistic needs. Perhaps it is not untenable to begin to talk in terms of different achievement orienta- tions being suitable to males and females at different stages in the life cycle.

What they are referring to is the fact that the man, in his early career years, must put aside his concern for others and con- centrate on the demands of getting ahead. Concurrently, his wife is often totally immersed in nurturing and caring. At middle age, each finds that they have had their fill of their particular roles and would like the opportunity to concen- trate on the activities they have been forced to put aside. Thus, the man is newly interested in cultivating personal relationships, while the wife is eager to go out in the world and establish a career.

Ted was one of these men. He attended college for two years, then left to marry and to help his father manage the family's businesses, including real estate and a store. His wife was a student nurse when he met her. She stopped working when the children were small, but soon went back on a part-time basis because she enjoyed nursing so much. He had thought about leaving the family business on and off for five years, but the final decision came on the spur of the moment during an argument with his father.

Years before, Ted's wife had suggested to him that he go into nursing. He decided to try, and spent the spring taking a chemistry course at a local community college. He took the National League of Nursing tests in July and was accepted by a nursing school for September, primarily because he was male, as their classes were actually already filled. Once he got used to the routine of studying, he enjoyed it. Ted's wife worked full time as a nurse, as their three children were all in school. He found a job weekends and during vacations at the local hospital as an emergency room technician; he was able to get a full-time job there as a nurse after graduation. They managed financially without dipping into savings, although they lived somewhat more frugally.

Ted seems to be about as "masculine" a person as one is likely to find. Until he started nursing school he played hockey in the winter; he still plays basketball and softball and swims. He is in excellent physical condition and looks much younger than his 40 years. One of the drawbacks of going back to school was that he no longer had the time to "go out drinking with the boys." As a result of his new career, he says, "I value people's feelings much more now, I am a more caring person. I also feel that education is more important." He plans to return to school to earn a B.S. in nursing.

Quite a number of the men (19) went into higher education, either as teachers or administrators. With the rapid expansion of community colleges in the late 1960s and early 1970s, there was a need for teachers, and with their practical emphasis, they welcomed older people who had had experience in the business world as teachers. One man, who had earned an M.B.A. at Harvard Business School directly after college and then worked for 20 years in various positions in retailing, went directly into teaching business at a community college. He enjoys it tremendously, and wishes that he had made the change much sooner.

Tony also became a college teacher, on the university level. He had received an undergraduate degree in accounting and worked for several companies in that capacity. After his marriage in his early thirties he took over the management of a small manufacturing company, which became very successful. I interviewed Tony in his beautiful contemporary home in an expensive suburb. His wife stayed with us for the first few minutes. They were an extremely attractive couple, obviously devoted to each other.

Tony described the evolution of his career change to me.

I went to [X] University to take a course in computers to prepare myself for the installation of a small computer in our firm. I enjoyed the course so much that I stayed to earn an M.B.A. I had always liked school and did well. Soon after I finished the M.B.A., the owner of the company I was running decided that he wanted to sell, and he pressured me to buy it. I knew that if I did, I would become committed to the business, and I just didn't want to.

Elaine was very encouraging, and really pushed me to leave the business and return to graduate school. I had been very lucky and had done well financially, both from my earnings in the company and on the stock market. I also had inherited some money when my father died. I had always wanted to teach, but when I was younger, there wasn't enough money in it. When I told my mother of my decision to leave the business and go back to school to prepare to teach, she wasn't at all surprised. In fact, she, too, was very encouraging. My father had worked very hard all his life, and had died before he had a chance to enjoy the fruits of his labors. She didn't want that to happen to me. In fact, my whole family, which is very close knit, was very supportive and enthusiastic.

I went back to the university where I had earned my M.B.A. and talked to some of the professors whom I had gotten to know; they were encouraging. I applied and was accepted by a university in a neighboring state. I really enjoyed going back to school; I had a ball. It made me feel ten years younger. After I finished my Ph.D. I was able to find a teaching position at a nearby university. I really love teaching. The change has had a positive effect on my family. I now have more time to spend with my wife and children, and I've become very active in the community.

Tony summarized his experience by saying,

My career change came about because I wanted to do something useful. There is more to life than just making money. My goals are still the same, but I am coming closer to attaining them. I want a happy family life, and I want to contribute something.

At the time many of the men made their career change, in the late 1960s and early 1970s, education was still expanding, and there were many opportunities for men who had been in business to take up teaching. However, the subsequent decline in the birthrate has caused schools to close, and there is a marked surplus of teachers. The same is true for such fields as social work, which expanded greatly in the Great Society days but have since been cut back. Career changers will no longer be able to move easily into these fields unless they have unusual combinations of background and experience to offer.

However, one emerging field that is likely to expand greatly in the foreseeable future is that of care of the elderly, providing all sorts of services, including health care, housing, recreation, and both voluntary and paid employment offers. This would seem to be a natural opportunity for mid-career changers. Already, many universities are offering master's level graduate programs dealing with the delivery of services to the elderly.

THE MEN WHO DIDN'T LEAVE

When we first decided to do a study of men who changed careers we thought seriously about matching them with a control group of men who had thought about changing but had decided against it. Obviously, this would be the best way to find out what made the career changers different. But how could you possibly find the men who had been afraid to do it? No one else would know about them, certainly not the personnel officers, alumni directors, or career counselors who had referred the names of career changers to us. Many of the men would be reluctant to admit their decision to anyone. Because of this apparent impasse, we decided to drop that phase of our research.

I had several counseling sessions with one man who was going through the agony of deciding whether or not to make a change. I suspect he won't. Luke was born to a poor farm family in the South, and worked his way through a nearby state college. He still retains his soft-spoken Southern accent and manners, which add charm to his good looks and Madison Avenue tailoring. By chance, he went to work for a branch of a large insurance company in his native town. He was bright and worked hard, soon advancing to the corporate headquarters. Here he met and married a woman who also worked in the company, but who had grown up in a well-to-do Eastern suburb and gone to Smith. They have three children, 8, 11, and 13, whom Luke adores.

Luke was spotted by one of the top men in the company as a comer. This man took him under his wing, and Luke rose rapidly to a supervisory position in a division providing corporate services. Luke's success has brought him nationwide recognition and requests for speaking engagements and training sessions. Unfortunately, two years ago, Luke's mentor lost out in a power struggle and is no longer with the company. While Luke's job is secure, he is unlikely to go any farther, and he is only 42.

Ideally, what Luke would like to do is to develop a consulting practice of his own and perhaps teach at a business school. But he has only a B.A. from Podunk State College. Several people who know him well have urged him to apply for a doctoral program at a top business school, and he would like to go. But he is afraid of giving up the security of his high salary. He and his family have a lovely home in an expensive suburb; his wife is unwilling to move. She is fearful of the financial risk involved and worried that they won't have enough savings left to send their children to college.

Luke seems to have two choices. The first is to stay

where he is in the company and take an early retirement. If he chooses this route, I would expect that he will lessen his commitment to work and devote much more time to his family and community. The other choice is to take the risk and go back to school. This would put heavy strains on his marriage, which might not survive if his wife remains adamantly opposed to the change. Even if she goes along, he would have much less time to devote to his children while he is going to school, and they are at an age when he would really like to spend time with them. I think he will choose his family over a career change.

However, it is interesting to speculate why some men change careers while others only think about it. Psychologist David McClelland talks about the ability to take risks, and says that those who take moderate risks are likely to be the most successful. Others are immobilized by fear of failure. Judging by the things the successful career changers had going for them, one can only guess that those who didn't dare may have lacked the financial resources, the self-confidence, or the support of their wives; perhaps they were unable to think of anything else they really wanted to do. Many of the career changers remarked that the hardest part of the process was coming to the final decision. Several gave us their parting advice to others, "Do it!"

4

Process and Outcomes

WE have taken a general look at the men who changed careers, their background, their age when they left their previous jobs, their outward reasons and motivation for change, and the kinds of work they left and entered. Now we will look more closely at how they accomplished their career change, the process they used, and the outcome in terms of personal satisfaction. We will also want to see if the process can be related in any way to the success of the outcome.

PROCESS OF CHANGE

Most of the men we talked to decided fairly early not to look for another position in the same field. The following scale shows that 48, or more than half, did not try at all. The rest of the men are spread out along the scale, although none of them tried exhaustively to find another job in the same field.

Numbers:	48	3	6	5	2	0	3	5	1	
	1	2	3	4	5	6	7	8	9	10
	Did not try at all								Tried every way possible	

(No data: 18)

Most of the men took a fairly long time between the point at which they first thought of leaving their old jobs and the time they actually left. Eight of the men took only one month or less, 21 took one to six months, 21 took seven to twelve months, 33 took one to five years, and 6 took five years or more. The men who went back to school to prepare themselves for their new careers took even longer, some as many as three or four years additional. The studies of career changers already cited in Chapter 1 also found that it took a long time to change. The dropouts Roberts interviewed averaged three years from the time they first thought of leaving until they actually did it. Hiestand reports that ten of the people he talked to took one month or less to decide to return to school. Eleven took one to six months, 8 took seven to twelve months, 19 took one to five years, and 4 took five years or more.

Most of the men did not discuss the change very much with people outside of their immediate families; most relied primarily on their wives for discussion. Almost none of the men discussed the change with parents or brothers and sisters. A few consulted business associates or friends. Many were careful to keep their plans secret until they had become definite for fear that things wouldn't work out.

The fact that so few of the career changers consulted with other people is not surprising. As any professional in the business of providing help—counseling, medical, or any other kind of help—knows, men are much less likely to ask for help or discuss their problems with other people than women. They only ask for help after a situation becomes untenable. Upper-class, "successful" men like those in our study would be even more reluctant to seek help than other men because of their self-image of independence and competence.

Men's friendship patterns are such that they do not use their friends for advice, reality testing, and support in the way women do. Even close men friends must keep up the image of competence, of being in control, with each other. One of the benefits of the breakdown in sex-role stereotypes now going on in our society may be a loosening of this attitude about masculinity. Men ought to learn to be able to ask for help and advice when problems are relatively simple, before they develop into crises.

Bernie was more articulate about the suffering he went through and more active in seeking help, but his story is still quite typical of many of the others. At 42, he was vice-president for marketing of a large manufacturing company. He was becoming bored with the work, and he felt that staying on was intolerable.

I had the feeling that I had lost control of my own life and wanted to regain it. All my life I had had a strong desire for material achievement, but when I got it, it was a hollow victory. I tried psychotherapy, which was useful, but mainly concentrated on my relationships with my wife and children. I tried to adjust to the business, to find ways to refresh myself. I went to a week-long meeting of other marketing executives in Hawaii, but the enthusiasm was worn off in six months. I attended one meeting in which some psychologists spoke; they advised that if you're unhappy you should do something else. That laid the groundwork.

Later that year I had a bad experience. I went to a party, drank too much, made a fool of myself, and then got very sick. When I woke up the next day I was so disgusted with myself that I drove out in the country and walked around in the woods for a long time thinking. I decided that I had to do something about it. I went to a vocational counselor, had tests, and five or six sessions of counseling. The counselor played the role of the devil's advocate and really helped me to sort out my thinking. It was his idea that I consider law school based upon my involvement in local politics and other interests, but it seemed to click. I went to talk to the dean of admissions, who was encouraging, then took the Law School Admissions Test.

We interviewed him on a Saturday morning, while he enjoyed a leisurely late breakfast in the sunny kitchen of his attractive suburban home. Bernie was in the second year of law school, and enjoying it immensely. He missed the skiing vacations and the fancy restaurants that were part of his ormer life, but he felt much happier in his new existence. His wife had gone back to work after earning a master's degree, and was enjoying her new job. With savings and investments plus her earnings, they were able to make ends meet. I sensed a feeling of excitement and purpose in both of them.

Unlike Bernie, 72 of the 91 men we studied used no formal counseling to help them before or during their change of career. Five of the men had been in psycho-therapy, although most did not think it was relevant to their career concerns.Two of the men who were trying to break away from family businesses found it useful to help resolve some family-related emotional entanglements so they could deal with the issue of finding a new career. Five of the men used formal career counseling, although most went for only one or two sessions. Bernie's experience was the most posi-tive.

One man luckily landed just the job he wanted through his college placement office, but the six others who used that resource or an employment agency or executive search firm found them to be unproductive. Two used a self-help group of unemployed professionals, and three men received assis-ance from the Small Business Administration. These helped as far as they went; the information provided was useful but somewhat elementary and superficial.

None of the men used the counseling or job placement services of the state employment service. Despite the fact that managerial and professional jobs are listed with the branches of the U.S. Employment Service in each state, few people of that level think of using it. There is still too close a link with recipients of unemployment compensation and the aura of low-level dead-end jobs. Professional and managerial men don't even go into these offices unless they are in severe difficulty, because they carry the stigma of failure.

Our findings are similar to those of Hiestand, who re-ported that only five of the 70 men and women with whom he talked sought guidance from another person about going back to school. Clopton, however, reported that many of the

men he studied had had personal counseling or psychc
therapy. Roberts did not report on counseling per se, but di
indicate that the people she interviewed valued the suppoı
of groups of like-minded individuals.

One reason the men did not use career counseling is the
it is not that available to most adults. Eli Ginzberg, directc
of Columbia University's Conservation of Human Resource
Project, deplores the maldistribution of career guidance
Two-thirds of all guidance counselors are employed in sec
ondary schools, and the next largest group works in vc
cational rehabilitation agencies or for the state employmer
service. Few are available to the adults who need the seı
vices, such as returning veterans, mature women returnin
to the labor force after a period of work in the home, mid
career changers, and people planning for retirement. Ac
cording to Ginzberg, "Guidance today is preoccupied wit
youth to the neglect of adults; it is overly concerned wit
educational goals and underinvolved with the problems c
the workplace."

Of course, it may well be that most of the men had
rather low opinion of the kind of help that might be availabl
to them from career counselors. Unfortunately, the level c
services offered by most high-school guidance counselors i
low. They are burdened by large case loads, and must spreaı
themselves very thin. No one student can receive much c
their time. They also have a heavy load of paperwork, paı
ticularly in connection with helping students apply to col
lege. In addition, they spend a lot of time with students witl
discipline problems and with severe emotional difficultie
All this puts career counseling in last place.

Furthermore, as the traditional route to guidance couπ
seling is via teaching, few counselors in high schools knov
very much about the world of work. They are therefore ill
equipped to give any but the most superficial advice to stu
dents. Most of them have a background in psychology, bu
little if any knowledge of economics or business. Finally
many of the student clients they see are there because the
have to be, rather than in a voluntary capacity. If the latte

were true they might be more willing to work *with* the counselor rather than expect to be *given* to. None of this creates a high opinion of the field on the part of potential clients.

Bill *did* have a positive experience with an organization providing help in career planning. He had been a research physicist working for a large company dealing with defense contracts.

The company was shrinking from over 5,000 people when I joined them 12 years ago to a little over 1,000 when I left. Toward the end I could see the handwriting on the wall. I enjoyed my work and had no desire to make a change, but there were no jobs in physics. My two children were in their junior and senior years in high school, and my wife and I decided that we just couldn't uproot them to move geographically until they had both graduated. I went to a state employment service special project for unemployed professionals. The people there went over my resume with me, helped me redo it. Also, I participated in a group with other unemployed people, where we talked about our situation to help break down the embarrassment of being unemployed. We did role playing and some things like that. We would also volunteer four hours a week there to help them keep their records up to date. This gave us a chance to see the inside of the job market and keep to a regular schedule at least one day a week. It gave us a chance to exchange leads with other guys.

I decided to look into computer programming, since I had done some of that in my former job. I discussed it in the group somewhat, but I made the decision largely by myself. I found myself looking at ads in the paper for the computer field. Fortunately, one lead came through, and I found the job I am in, which I enjoy, as it has much more people contact than I had ever had before.

Most of the men who moved into a new field spent a good deal of time and energy investigating it beforehand. For example, Bob, a business school professor who became an architect, first thought about his change when he and his wife had a beautiful contemporary home built for them at the end of a wooded road.

I enjoyed the whole process of design and building and was fasci
nated by watching the architect and the builders at work. The same
thing happened several years later when we built our summer
home on Cape Cod. I really thought vaguely about becoming an
architect for about five years, then more specifically for one year.
must have talked with about 20 professors at the School of Ar
chitecture and at least a half dozen practicing architects. They were
encouraging. In order to test out my ability, I took a tutorial in
drawing with a graphics instructor. This was lots of fun, and i
whetted my desire to go back to school. Fortunately, the dean of the
School of Architecture, knowing my background, asked me to work
part-time for him as an administrative assistant while I attended
school, so this financed my tuition and gave me a small salary.

Bob is now working for a consulting firm that advises on
space and facilities. In addition, he teaches one course at the
School of Architecture on management in architecture.

Some of the men who were less successful in their
career change did not really take the time to investigate pos
sibilities or to analyze themselves and their own potential as
they should have. Jim was one of those. After a stint as a
newspaperman, he became director of public relations for a
company in his hometown. He said,

I had grown up in this town and was part of a large family, so I have
strong roots here. My wife and our five children are very much a
part of the community; we belong here. After the old president of
the firm who had known my father and grandfather died, a new
man came in. I never got along with him. His ideas were very
different, and I could see almost from the beginning that things
were not going to work out. I wasn't actually fired, but I finally left
by mutual agreement.

I was really in a bind; we were so tied to this town that I couldn't
see leaving. The nearest big city is almost an hour's drive away, and
opportunities here are limited. My wife encouraged me to take my
time and look around for another job, but I panicked about being
able to support the family. We could have managed to live for six
months or so on my wife's teaching salary with no problems, but I
was too scared.

I should have taken more time and discussed possibilities with someone who could really help me. But the local sporting goods store was up for sale. I had been an athlete in college and had coached Little League, so I knew something about sports equipment. I borrowed enough capital from a friend and bought the business. The first few years were a real struggle. My wife and kids helped out in the store, but that didn't work out very well; they don't anymore.

I'm doing pretty well now, but the hours are long, and I don't enjoy the business aspects of the job—keeping the books and managing the accounts. Learning the business end was grubbing. There were always bills to be paid—like running in place. While it has worked out pretty well, I regret that my writing talents are being wasted. In retrospect, I didn't prepare properly, which was a big mistake. I should have talked to people, looked for help. I had no idea of what possibilities there might have been.

Actually, as a result of our interview, Jim is again thinking of a change. He is looking around for a job that would involve writing and is thinking of a partner to help him run the store.

Some men do not really deal with the personal issues involved, but shove them under the table and attempt to go on, Tom was this kind of man. He had gone to business school directly after the service and done very well, graduating at the top of his class. He went to work for a large insurance company, became an actuary, and worked his way up to becoming a highly placed officer of the firm. He supervised a major section of the company, comprising several thousand people.

The year Tom was 52, the company decided to split his division into several parts. He naturally hoped to get the top job, but lost out to someone younger. In effect, he was demoted. His new job involved a lot of traveling, but he felt "like an ambassador without much portfolio." "I realized that at (Company A) there was a ceiling over my head." He had been very happy in the company until he failed to get the promotion, and he had never thought of leaving. The other man was given the job in October. A power struggle ensued for the next six or seven months. Tom started looking for a new job July 1 and left in October.

My impression of Tom was that he had had a severe blow, but that he had not dealt with it adequately. He kept inserting remarks into our interview about his high I.Q., his great ability at tests, the fact that he is well known across the country—as if to prove his worth to me. Was he questioning it himself? I also sensed that his marriage was not a happy one. In the initial questionnaire, he had answered the question about number of children with "none," yet I discovered that he had three. When I rang the doorbell of his home for our scheduled interview, his wife answered and was very puzzled about who I was. He had neglected to tell her about my coming. He said that he had consulted with his wife before leaving his former company, and she had told him that it was up to him. I had the feeling that they lived in the same house but didn't communicate. Unfortunately, Tom, like many successful men, had never before had to ask for help, and when he needed it, he didn't know how to ask.

Tom has had two jobs in the two years since he left the company. They haven't worked out, although he tried to give the impression that he was doing well. Tom really needs to sit down and sort out his life. At his stage of panic, he needs some help, someone to assure him that he is not a failure. He needs to reestablish lines of communication with his wife and family. He may discover, to his surprise, that his worth in their eyes is not necessarily measured by the size of his salary or the number of people he supervises.

THE CLERGY

Men who either entered or left the clergy had the benefit of a good deal of counseling from others, often on a fairly formalized basis. Interestingly enough, some of the best work on how to counsel career changers has been done by church-related groups or individuals. This has come about as an outgrowth of the vast upheaval among clergy of all denominations during the 1960s, when many questioned their vocations and quite a number left them. Former Catholic priests and nuns have set up self-help counseling groups for others considering leaving or looking for employment.

Many Protestant denominations now offer the possibility of an intensive counseling experience to their clergy on a fairly routine basis. During the course of the counseling they may reevaluate their career goals and commitment to their calling. Many, of course, return to their parishes with renewed commitment, but some choose to leave, and this decision is accepted without censure on the part of the sponsoring religious group.

A typical counseling agency that deals with clergy sees each individual with his or her spouse over a period of several days of intensive discussion and testing, paid for by the denomination. Concern about the whole area of career counseling is so strong among Protestant denominations that they sponsor The National Career Development Project of United Ministries in Higher Education, whose director, Richard N. Bolles, an ordained minister, has written several of the best and most creative works in this field.

Pierre, who left the Catholic priesthood, discussed his change a great deal with fellow priests, many of whom were also leaving. In retrospect, he says,

I found it to be a very difficult adjustment to leave a situation of total security and move out into the world. It has been a very long process. It took me about five years to work my way free emotionally of the bureaucracy of the church, while working in various interim jobs for small companies during my transition.

Pierre is now in his own business and, he says, "It took me four years to make my way in to working on my own, to develop independence." He is a tall, handsome man in his mid-forties whose exterior manner is warm, pleasant, and light-hearted. He is given to much bantering, and people are immediately drawn to him. It is difficult to realize the extent of the turmoil that has gone on underneath his happy-go-lucky exterior.

I used to think that ideas were important. I taught philosophy and religion in a Catholic college. I never liked myself very much, and it was a big surprise to me after I left the priesthood that so many people were so kind and helpful to me. Now I believe that people are most important. My life is totally centered in my family. My wife and I share an equal partnership in our business, and I have a real relationship with my children. I haven't formally left the church, but I am impatient with all its trappings and structure. We worship with a small group of like-minded people for whom the essence of religion is most important.

They have bought a lovely old farmhouse with several acres of land, where Pierre enjoys tinkering and growing a huge vegetable garden.

The first position Larry, another former clergyman, held after graduating from seminary was as rector of a small dying parish in Rhode Island, which he was able to revitalize. He then went to Pennsylvania, where he started a new parish from scratch, again very successfully. After a number of years, he became more and more involved in problems of mental health. He realized that he didn't like the everyday running of the parish. He also realized that "I needed formal training in counseling if I was really going to be effective in dealing with the people who were coming to me for help." The parish recognized his involvement and changed his job so that 50 percent of his time would be devoted to community work in civil rights and mental health.

About that time Larry received a call to become the bishop's assistant, but he turned it down, thinking that it would mean even more administration.

I saw an advertisement in a journal describing a one-year grant for clinical pastoral counseling at a mental hospital. I decided to apply for it and was accepted. When I finished the training, I knew I could not go back into the parish ministry.

Larry has had jobs in counseling ever since. In retrospect, he says, "I made a commitment to the ministry at too early an age. I should have been more honest with myself about my dissatisfaction earlier and done something about it sooner." He discussed his move a great deal with his wife and children, who were very supportive. He also talked at length with a few close friends among the clergy who were also dissatisfied and leaving.

In adjusting to his change, Larry has had financial problems and has missed the status of being a rector. But for the first time in years, he has had free time; he had to learn how to use it. The effect on his family is good. He has more time to spend with them, and they are relieved of the heavy burden of being clergy family. Through the process of change, he has learned that he must focus on his personal impact rather than hope to accomplish things on a broad scale.

The career changers in the study who considered entering the ministry went through a fairly formalized series of intensive conversations and counseling sessions conducted by clergy in their denomination before they made their decisions to enter the seminary. One of these men is now a member of a committee involved in helping other people who are thinking of finding late vocations in ministry.

Military retirees, too, had more counseling available to them, both from within the formal structure of the military and from outside organizations specifically set up to help them. For example, one of the men in the study found a course given by Stanley D. Hyman at Catholic University in Washington, D.C., very helpful. Hyman has offered this career transition course for four years and has served some 2,000 students, primarily military retirees.

OUTCOME

In the interviews, the men were asked if, in retrospect, they wished that they had prepared themselves differently. Forty-three said that if they were to do it over again they would do it in exactly the same way. Twenty said that they would have done it somewhat differently. Several said they wished they had had access to career counseling before making their decision. Financial worries were usually the catalyst that made them rush to a quick decision. Only three claimed that they would have done things very differently. The majority of those who said they would have made some changes stated that they wished they had made the career change much earlier or had never even gone into the first career. Many said that the hardest part of the career change was coming to the decision; once the decision was firm, the rest was easy.

On the questionnaire, the men were asked to describe the outcome of their job change in terms of personal satisfaction. Fifty-six checked "very rewarding," 26 checked "on the whole, favorable," and only three indicated that the change had been "unfavorable." Of course, one wonders how honest these men were. Through the interviews, however, we came to the conclusion that most of the men who said they were happy really were well adjusted and enjoying their new life.

Some half dozen didn't seem to have made a success of it. Some, like Tom, tried to cover up their unhappiness. From what information we could gather and from our own perceptions of these men, most of the failures stemmed from difficulties in dealing with other people and in developing satisfactory relationships with those who were important to them. They may have had the technical knowledge and know-how to do their jobs well and have worked hard, but their relationships with other people were faulty. Some of them had left their former jobs because of disagreements with the boss or fellow workers, and they were unable to work well in any team situation. They had abrasive qualities and tended to rub people the wrong way. Their marriages were empty, and they were unable to communicate with their wives.

Besides the few who were not able to make a satisfactory career change, possibly because their previous careers had ended traumatically, there were four or five others who adjusted to the career change but whose lives remained under tension. They have still not found the right place for themselves, or stressful problems in their lives continue to need resolution. Of the 91 men, we would estimate that 10 to 15 percent had made unsatisfactory adjustments to their career changes.

Phil was one of these. He had earned a Ph.D. in psychology and became dean of students at a California college. He said,

The year 1968 was a critical one for me. I needed a sabbatical. The president wasn't committed to anything; he went with the political winds. Groups could make him do anything if they put enough pressure on him. There was the unrest of the students—the Dow Chemical demonstrations. The faculty had made a decision, and then some wouldn't abide by it. I made a public statement on it, which contradicted the president, and I guess I put him in an untenable position. He called me in and said I was going to have to leave. It came like a bolt out of the blue. I started sending out feelers to other colleges, but nothing was available. All of a sudden, no one was interested in me. I suspect the president put the word out.

Phil has had a number of jobs since leaving the college, but nothing has worked out very well. He is now running a franchise business, but his income is small, and his wife has had to go back to work to help support the family. He has all sorts of excuses to explain his predicament—the college president, the poor academic job market, the recession, the stock market going sour, the Birchers and the left-wingers, his age, his color, his sex—everything but himself.

The questionnaire, aiming to discover the level of job satisfaction, also asked the men what they would like to be doing five years from now. Forty-eight said that they would like to be doing essentially what they were doing now. Twenty-six said that they would like to be doing the same type of work, but would make some changes.

We talked to one man who has returned to his original career. Curtis was an engineer who had had a succession of increasingly responsible management positions with man-

ufacturing firms that made electronic equipment. His last job
was as vice-president of a division.

The president died suddenly of a heart attack. The new president
was the former treasurer, and was very cost conscious. He was not
willing to support the research for which I had been responsible,
and it was clear that I didn't have much of a future there. Shortly
before that, my wife and I had bought a house in a rural area to get
away from the pressures of suburban living.

For about a month Curtis thought about setting up a business
there. He negotiated with the president of his company for a
license to produce the instruments he had been designing
for them. He agreed, since the company had nothing to lose
if he failed and a percentage of his earnings if he succeeded.
He secured two bank loans and bought a building. He left the
old company in March and started manufacturing on May 1.
The new role involved a good deal of traveling, selling and
providing technical services. Customers were people he had
known before. His wife became involved with the business
and worked as treasurer. "It was the happiest period of my
life, until the economy ruined the business. It was a job
situation I controlled."

The sharply rising inflation caught him off guard. His
material costs rose astronomically over a short period of
time, and he lost money on orders that had been placed only
six months before. He finally had to close the business. He
has been able to get back into his old field in a responsible
position, although he does have a long commute. He is
slowly recovering his financial losses, but despite the set-
back he says, "Money is less important to me now. What I
value is living in a happy environment." If he could, he
would go back to having his own company. "I was happiest
then."

We ended each of the interviews with a provocative
question: "If you had open options—if money and other
practical considerations were of no concern—what would
you most like to do in the future?" An amazing number of
people said, "Exactly what I am doing now." Several en-

visioned ways in which they could do their present job better if they were not constrained by finances. For example, the curator of a museum would go back to school for a Ph.D. in American history in order to be able to understand the background for his present job better. Another man, who is a management consultant said,

. . . what I am doing now, but I would be more selective. I would develop a sense of the kinds of contributions I am most capable of making. Now I have to spend too much time building situations in which I can be effective. I would be more direct, take more risks, be less patient with garbage.

A man who owns his own business in the computer field said,

I have become more and more concerned about how little opportunity most people have for individual initiative. This philosophy has partially influenced me in the decision not to expand my business further, although it would be relatively easy to do so. Instead, I have decided to look around for new businesses I might help other people to start. In this way, I would be able to create additional opportunities.

One or two, of course, mentioned that they wanted to sail around the world or do other extensive traveling. Two, surprisingly, had exactly the same dual interest—teaching and owning a hardware store. One would hold classes in the back room to show youngsters how to use tools. Most concurred with one man who said, "I need to be working to be happy." One man has already planned his third career; he wants to open a homemade ice-cream business on Cape Cod or a craft shop where he could also do some teaching.

Clarence was one of the few men I felt had failed. His answer to this last question was very revealing. He said, "I can't possibly conceive of having enough money. I wouldn't know what to do—buy a sports car, fishing rods, or other things." Of all the men, he was the only one who mentioned buying anything. His was one of the few career changes that had been motivated by making money.

Clarence had started life quite successfully. He earned a Ph.D. in engineering and worked his way up to high management levels in a large firm. Along with it came a large home for his wife and three children, and membership in the country club. In his early forties, Clarence began to have difficulties. There was a succession of jobs that didn't work out. He and his wife had problems, and she was a patient in a mental hospital for awhile. One of his jobs took him out of state, but his wife refused to move, and he lived there in a small apartment, returning to spend weekends with the family. At this point he began to have affairs with other women. When he lost his job again, he was unable to find anything else in his salary bracket. He blamed his age, which may well have been a factor. In desperation, Clarence turned to life insurance sales. Although financial circumstances had forced him to drop the country club membership, he still had a wide circle of acquaintances, and he was a good salesman. His success is based on an approach that is outwardly smooth, pleasant, and deferential, but inwardly ruthless. He is in good physical condition and very well dressed; he is a master at small talk.

Clarence has no professional pride in what he does. His only measure is in terms of dollars and cents. He feels himself to be a failure in comparison to his old professional self. He and his wife continue to live together, although they barely communicate. Their children are grown and married, but still come to him for support, which he gives, as if to buy their favor. He said, "I think they only value me for my money." He used to be very active in the church, but no longer goes, since "they got involved in all sorts of left-wing causes."

Often the career change itself was the last stage in a midlife transition, but sometimes it was only a midpoint that left the career changers still searching. Bob, who became an architect, said,

I am now in the middle of sorting out my values. I find that architects are not very socially conscious, and it bothers me that I am not doing anything socially useful now. I would like to do something with how to use space educationally, but I can't see any market for it. I am less sure of my goals now than when I started. I began life being very religious, then became an agnostic, and am now an active Unitarian.

For Carl, a distinguished-looking man with gray hair in his late fifties, the change of career came as a surprise, but it fit into a transition that was going on anyway. He had a Ph.D. in economics, and became dean of the business school of the university at which he was teaching. He had developed their M.B.A. program. Although he hadn't been actively looking for another position, he was approached to take a management post in business. The salary was attractive, and he had been going through a time of reappraisal.

The offer came during the upheavals in higher education of the late 1960s. He said,

The character of universities was changing. I had read the predictions of declining enrollments and resources, and it seemed like a good time to get out. I had done my "thing" in setting up the M.B.A. program, and it was challenging to think of being involved in a totally new experience. So I decided to accept the offer. . . . there have been no fundamental changes in my goals and values except that I am somewhat more conservative, but this may be due to the aging process. My goal is to make some contribution, have a sense of achievement. My personal goals are now tied up with the goals of the organization, to make it viable. I am convinced that being able to take on new challenges keeps one mentally young. It is stimulating.

Alden, who is now 60, has been a perpetual career changer. He has never stayed in one position for longer than eight years and often for much shorter periods. All the jobs have been quite successful. He fully intends to keep on switching. His story is a long but fascinating one.

I started out to be a college teacher. I went from law to English. At that time, in the late 1930s, a college teacher could expect to start out at $1,800 a year. And after he had worked his way up in his profession, he would make less than half the income of a lawyer.

My family disapproved of this plan and thought that it was a departure from the family heritage. They had been in banking in Oklahoma since my grandfather came out and claimed the land and started the town. He was the only educated man in the town, and actually organized it, setting up the first bank, which has been run by my family ever since. They have been the town elite.

My doctoral studies in English were interrupted by the war. I went into the army and did writing and editing. I was on the staff of Eisenhower's command, and toward the end of the war was writing material that went to some 8 million men every two weeks. When I got out of the army, I was approached to go into academic publishing for a university press. I decided to take the job instead of finishing my doctorate. I had three wonderful years there writing and editing.

Then family considerations led me back to Oklahoma. The family wanted me to come back, since I was the last male heir, so to speak. My father was aging, and he told me that I could be president of the bank in four or five years. My wife wanted to go back to our hometown. All the temptations led me back, like Satan talking to Jesus. So I went back to be loan manager. I knew the business, since I had worked there summers for four years.

By the third day I knew I had made a horrible mistake. I couldn't work for my father. I loved him, but in his eyes I would never grow up. After the first week I told my wife that I had to find a new career. I couldn't arrest my development for 20 years waiting to take over the bank. From then on I treated the work as a school to learn all that I could. And I began exploring ways to escape, to find work that would give me the freedom I needed.

I made a list of all the good places to live. I needed something new for my own growth and development. I needed to be in charge of my life. I had to get command of my situation. I studied the banking laws in a number of states and looked for the right location. I decided on Colorado because it had the most favorable banking laws. And I was looking for a place with a college or university. I liked the academic atmosphere, and the friends I wanted were in that kind of place. Boulder, Colorado, was my choice of an ideal place.

I had $13,000 capital, profits from several homes we had bought and sold. I took a month getting to know the state banking commissioner, and sold stock to friends. I ended up with a goddamn controlling interest, although I had put up only a fraction of the capital. I told the other stockholders that I was offering my time and expertise in working for the bank, and that I was risking everything. To make a long story short, I was in the right place at the right time. Colorado boomed; people were bringing their life savings from their home states and putting them into the bank. Everything we touched turned to money; it was that kind of time and place. It didn't take a lot of skill or work. After three years, I realized that I was doing the same thing every day. I had mastered the job; there was nothing else to learn. And I felt I would be condemned to spend the rest of my life doing the same thing every day. I could stay and make a pile of money. I figure I could have stayed to retirement and been worth something like $14 or $15 million.

I had a friend in New York who was involved in a large bond house there that was having all kinds of trouble. He kept after me to come and help them iron out their problems. I think he felt that because I had made the bank go in Colorado, I could do anything. I can honestly say I had no regard for money and money making. They meant nothing to me, beyond the needs of the family. I was interested in problem solving, and the bond house sure had problems. And there was also the attraction of being in the major leagues in terms of finance. So I decided to try it; that was the year I turned 40.

Within four months I was made executive vice-president. After four years of trying everything, I came to the conclusion that the firm would never make money; the times weren't favorable for private banking firms like that. I went and told the stockholders that I thought the firm should be liquidated while it still had its capital intact. This created an uproar, of course. It took a lot of work, but I won the decision. The company was closed in 1965.

I was able to get a job for every employee. If we had waited five years to liquidate, we would have been lucky to get jobs for 10 percent of them. As it turned out, we were lucky to get out when we did, because the bottom fell out of the investment banking field soon after. Even now, when I meet friends from Wall Street, they ask me how I knew when to get out when I did. It wasn't just making a shrewd move in beating the economic changes. I really was ready to get into something else myself—the five- or six- or seven-year itch.

I had been active in education, and was considering something in that area. I had a number of offers from other banking firms and was offered partnerships. But I was approached by the Ford and Carnegie foundations to start an institute to evaluate new developments in education. It would be small, but it could have a large impact. I would be the only officer at first, and thus would be able to hire people and set the directions for the institute. I discussed it with all kinds of people in education, and decided to take it. By educational standards I was well paid, but it was about half my former salary. And the new job required twice as much work. They thought I was crazy on the Street for making the change. It was a tremendous learning experience, very rewarding. The work with this organization was great. We were doing $1.5 million in research contracts a year.

After six or seven years I got the itch to change. During this time I had been divorced and remarried. My new wife and I wanted a life outside of New York City; we wanted to put down roots in another place. We spent two years looking for the most interesting place to live. We studied every place and developed 50 criteria with weights of one to six for each. At that point I didn't pay attention to what occupation I would go into. I kept a file cabinet of "adventures," things I would be interested in doing. I had 50 of them in my file at the time. I figured I could dip into one of them when we decided where we would live.

I never believed that you have to do one thing at a time. In Colorado I had a construction company, an insurance agency, an appraisal company. They all fed into each other. That way I felt that I wasn't trapped in one kind of work. In deciding what I would do after leaving the education job, I knew that if I got a job in a major institution I would lose my options, my freedom and independence.

We moved to a lovely old New England town, where I've been able to develop my tennis and golf games, play the piano, write poetry, and do all the other things I never had time for in New York. I'm doing a variety of consulting jobs in between adventures. Last month we came back from a six-week trip to Africa that we took after one consulting job ended.

I feel I'm still in a developmental process, and my concern is to maintain this process. The most powerful value I have is self-interest, in that I want the rest of my life to continue this process. My enjoyment varies with the amount of learning that happens. That is the criterion I have for selecting careers and friends—the opportunity they give for learning. There are 50 lines of work I would be interested in. I measure them by criteria in four categories: the managerial burden or amount of supervision you have to do; the disposable time left over for enjoyment; the skills needed for the job—I want something that draws on my skills. And the last criterion is related to the importance of the work. Is it consequential by my values?

I am familiar with the theorists of middle age, Levinson and others. But I know something that Levinson doesn't know. I am off his scale, past the midlife transition. And I am still developing. And I believe that there is the opportunity to continue developing up through the sixties. At least I certainly plan to keep at it.

All of us may not have had Alden's good fortune, but his life story is certainly a testimonial to career change. He may have something in common with Peter Drucker, who is quoted as having said, "Here I am 58, and I still don't know what I am going to do when I grow up." [1]

[1] Mary Harrington Hall, "A Conversation with Peter Drucker," *Psychology Today* (March 1968), p. 21.

5

Family, Income, and Life-style

LIFE-STYLE

A significant number of the men we talked to changed their careers in order to improve their life-style. They seemed to recognize that they could not separate their career or occupation from the rest of their lives. For many, the ideal life-style is one in which all aspects of life are integrated and contribute to one another.

We all know people who have happily given up the battle of the crabgrass and forsaken suburbia to return to the city, especially after the children have grown. This was not the case with any of the men we talked to. All of them who changed careers in order to move went from a city or suburb to a small town or rural area.

Many wanted to get away from what they thought of as the epitome of the disjointed life-style of the New York City commuter, the man whose career life in the workplace is separated by several hours a day of nonexistence in the unreal environment of the subway and the commuter train from the play world of family, hobbies, pleasure, and relaxation. They felt that they never had time to put down roots in the uburban communities in which they lived, and they could nly spend time with their children on weekends.

One man's decision came very abruptly, although it had een brewing for a long time. He had been with a major New 'ork investment firm for 14 years, working up to a vice-residency. Five years before his change, he had bought an ld farmhouse in the Berkshires, which he fixed up. During he intervening time he went through a divorce and a serious eart attack, followed by cardiac surgery. He found himself pending more and more of his weekends in Massachusetts.

was almost as if I was submerged all week, and I needed to get to he farm every weekend to come up for air and breathe. One morn-ng in August of 1971, I was listening to the news on the radio while I was shaving. I heard a report that a youth gang had attacked nd thrown rocks at a team of firefighters trying to put out a blaze in he South Bronx. That did it! I decided then and there that New ork City was beyond civilization, and I could no longer live there.

The man dressed and went to work that morning and tunned his boss by telling him that he was leaving his job to love to his farm permanently. He was able to live on in-estment income and savings for a while, restored an old armhouse that he sold for a profit, and now is involved in a ew job somewhat related to his old field. He has remarried nd has become very active in civic affairs in their small wn, plays tennis, and skis cross country.

Another man had been an executive for a large computer rm. He and his wife had often driven through a lovely town 1 southern Vermont and talked of some day buying an old olonial house and retiring there. They were then living in Vestchester, and he was commuting to his job in New York .ity. They were unhappy with the town—with air pollution, rugs in the schools, muggings in their neighborhood.

On one drive through the Vermont town they asked each ther, "Why wait 25 years to move here? Let's do it now." 'hey had some income in addition to that from his job. They

bought a house built in 1790 and spent a lot of time workin
on it. He took courses for teacher certification and now er
joys teaching mathematics in the local high school, while hi
wife runs a gift shop. They are both very active in the com
munity, in civic organizations, their children's school PTA
and the church.

This former executive commented:

When I grew up in a small town I resented it and wanted to get t
the anonymous city. And it was great at first. But I got tired of it an
wanted to get to a small place where you could put down roots, ge
to know people. We fell in love with this place. We figured peopl
who could keep up such a beautiful town must be pretty nice then
selves. Like I said, we decided not to wait until we were 60 to retir
here, so we made the break. And we've loved it here ever since. La
summer when we were having supper out on the lawn, I leane
back and told my wife I had never been happier in my life.

The concern for location and life-style we saw in thes
two men and other career changers we studied is not uniqu
Richard Beckhard, a member of the faculty of the Sloa
School of Management at MIT and an active consultant t
many businesses, has written about this increasing phenom
enon. He tells of the amazement of the top management of
company with which he was familiar when two of their mos
highly valued middle managers turned down offers of posi
tions in its top-level marketing management. The new job
carried substantial increases both in salary and opportunit
for advancement, but a move would be necessary.

One man said that he did not want to live in that cit
and the other would not move until his youngest child ha
finished high school. According to Beckhard, similar situa
tions are increasing in frequency. Men in their forties ar
under a variety of pressures when they make caree
decisions—from personal needs and aspirations; family, so
cial, and cultural environment; and the demands of the or
ganization for which they work. Beckhard believes that th

pressures from outside the company are becoming increas-
ngly important for more men.

The crucial change is that the organizational pressures are becom-
ng weaker. Not that management is less demanding today; on the
contrary, it is perhaps more demanding. However, the penalties for
resisting its demands have become less severe. For a manager to
step off the corporate treadmill at 45, say, no longer carries the risk
of near-catastrophe or at least the same form of deprivation, as it did
20 years ago. Naturally, as this risk has decreased, managers have
become more willing to reevaluate the organizational demands on
them in the light of conflicting nonorganizational demands. The
strongest of these are likely to come from the manager's family.

Beckhard goes further. We have all read about and experienced among our friends and acquaintances the increase
in divorce among couples in the forties, but he feels that
notoriety has obscured something else that is going on in
marriages of people at midlife. He believes that for every
divorce among managers who are in their forties, there are
several other men who change their life-style in order to
spend more time with their wives, even if it means spending
less time on the job. It may be that both situations are
symptomatic of a greater concern with the quality of marital
life.

Beckhard sees such changes in individual outlook as
symptoms of important changes in the broader social cli-
mate. "I do not think I have to document that the Horatio
Alger ideal of single-mindedly amassing wealth no longer
attracts many people." With pension and Social Security
payments plus the likelihood of national health insurance, it
is no longer necessary for a manager to be worried about
survival during retirement. Nor are people concerned any
longer with amassing an estate to leave for their children.

Again, Beckhard's comments jibe with the replies of our
career changers regarding money and financial security.
More managers, Beckhard finds, are interested in the opportunity to do some teaching, devote themselves to public ser-

vice, or pursue sports or hobbies. Usually these men are willing to stay with their companies if it does not interfere with the other pursuits.

But if his top management confronts him with an all-or-nothing choice, he may well quit and look for work somewhere else, where he will be able to spend part of his time teaching or studying or taking color pictures of hummingbirds.

Beckhard also sees a trend, which is documented among our career changers, for managers to value the intrinsic rewards of the work they are doing over the compensation.

Several of the men we interviewed said they wanted to spend more time with their families and help bring up their children. Peter, who changed from being a New York City advertising executive to weaving and selling fabrics in a small New England town, reported that his family is now happier and more relaxed. The children enjoy the country town, and the family is much closer. He and his wife run the business together, which consumes a great deal of time and energy for both of them. They also have a large vegetable garden and grow most of their own vegetables.

Another man who now runs a management consulting firm says that his goal within five years is to cut his work time in half while maintaining his income at the same level so that he can spend the time gained at home with his wife and children and work on their small farm in southern New Hampshire. The manager of a country inn says that he feels much closer to his children now than he did when he commuted to his New York City office as a stockbroker. He is able to do a great deal of fathering, as his wife also works in the business, and he finds that work, leisure, and family all intertwine.

In the study of MIT graduate engineers and their attachment to work, which was discussed in Chapter 3, Lotte Bailyn also looks at their degree of involvement with their families. From the data she presents, engineers whose primary life satisfaction is derived from family seem to be less involved in their careers and less confident of their professional ability. It is difficult to determine what is cause and what is effect, but it may be that men who have found their technical careers to be unsatisfying and do not attain the success they had hoped for turn to their families for satisfaction. The picture she presents indicates that we cannot expect the same degree of work involvement from everyone, not even from such high-level professionals as MIT alumni. Some will prefer to obtain their primary gratification from their life away from the office or laboratory.

MARRIAGE

When we began to study men who had changed careers, we tried to be as scientific and unbiased as possible in our approach. However, being human, we did have some initial stereotypical ideas of what career changers would be like. They all proved wrong! One of these was a strong preconception about the marriages of career changers. We thought that they would probably be divorced and have gone through a great deal of family upheaval along with their career change. Gail Sheehy's *Passages* gives a strong impression that this would be the case. In addition, a previous study had suggested that career change might occur along with change in marital status. Willard Clopton reported a better than average probability that his subjects had changed their marital status along with their careers.

Much to our surprise, this was not true for the men we studied. Seventy-eight of the 91 men had been married only once and were still married at the time of the study. Three were unmarried at the time of the career change; one was a priest and another had been widowed. Two of them subsequently married quite happily. Five of the men had been divorced at some time unrelated to the career change. Only five obtained a divorce at the time of the career change or as a direct result of it. Actually, one man changed career as a result of his divorce; he had been the headmaster of a private school, and was forced to leave his position.

These findings compare quite favorably with those of the Grant study of outstanding Harvard graduates. George E. Vaillant and Charles C. McArthur report that 25 years out of college, 95 percent of their subjects were married, and 15 percent had been divorced. Betty Roberts' dropouts were less likely to be married, which is logical for a nonconformist group. Two-thirds of the people she studied were married when they dropped out.

Much to our suprise, the interviews uncovered a group of men who were, on the whole, remarkably happily married. Many of them spoke of their career change in direct relationship with their wives, speaking of "we" rather than "I." In some cases, it seemed to have brought the couple closer together, since they were working toward a joint goal. This was often the case with those who started their own businesses; in several instances the wife took on an important role in the business enterprise. One couple ran a country inn; they each had talents vital to the operation. She was a good cook, had been responsible for the redecoration of the inn, enjoyed arranging flowers on the tables, and was good at keeping the books. He was a natural handyman and enjoyed doing the repairs; he was also the more gregarious of the two and acted as host.

For another couple, in the lowest age bracket we studied (they were both 35), the career change provided an opportunity for the husband and wife to come to a more satisfactory mix of responsibility for earning a living, keeping the home, and raising the children. Alan, a soft-spoken, bearded, tall man, had a master's degree in landscape architectuce and city planning, and had worked successfully in those fields for ten years both for a large city and for a private consulting firm. When his job with a consulting firm ended, he was almost immediately offered another good city position.

Alan considered it briefly, but decided not to take it. He and his wife, Jill, had three young children. Jill had taught school early in their marriage, but stayed home when the children came. She was becoming itchy, feeling herself tied to the house and kids, and was eagerly awaiting the time the youngest would be in school all day so that she could get out of the house and back to work. Her irritability had its effect on the family; she was especially impatient in her dealings with the youngest boy.

Alan had developed a hobby of building fine contemporary furniture and had displayed and sold a number of pieces. His job prevented him from spending as much time on this hobby as he would have liked. Both Alan and Jill were also involved in a committee dedicated to saving the city and rebuilding some urban neighborhoods. Alan had done some consulting on renovating and restoring old houses, which had been sold for a good profit.

The couple sat down and had a long talk about their joint future. Out of their long discussions came a plan. Jill would go back to work on a full-time basis. Alan calculated that they had enough savings so that with only a modest salary from Jill, they could live for a year without reducing their standard of living. Jill had some initial misgivings and anxieties about the finances, but they decided to go ahead. During that year, Alan would develop his furniture making into a going income-producing concern and would do some outside consulting. Since Alan's work would be based at home, he would take on added responsibility for child care. In addition, they found a college student who would do housework and child care in exchange for room and board.

The first year, Alan invested $1,000 in improving his woodworking shop and took on a young apprentice to help him. He did some consulting in planning and started to buy up old homes for renovation and ultimate sale. He has already been successful enough for a city bank to approach him to look at a problem property for possible redevelopment. He has taught one course at a local university. Financially, he has done very nicely, and they have hardly dipped into their savings at all.

In looking over the year, Alan was pleased:

I wouldn't have done anything differently. It has been an adjustment to be at home all day with the children. There are many more interruptions. I realize that I often set bigger work goals for myself in the course of a day than I could possibly accomplish. It has been a useful training experience in managing my time. On the whole, I am enjoying being a househusband. I think it has been good for the kids. My youngest son has shaped up nicely under my firmer and more even discipline. All the children are now seeing broader sex roles for us as parents. Jill has found a good job she enjoys, although she misses not having as much time to cook and sew. Now, when she is with the kids over the weekends, she is more relaxed and enjoys being with them.

In retrospect, Alan finds that his goals and values have changed. His avocations and vocation have merged. He does work longer hours and is more jealous of giving up his time to volunteer civic activities. He does less journal reading, but enjoys the fact that he is now translating research and theory in his field into action. He says,

I have a greater belief in individual initiative than before. People too often take the easy way out and let others make their life decisions for them. People could rely on their own capabilities more. I find that there is a tremendous reward in being able to make my own decisions.

Alan and Jill's success in their new venture can be traced, at least in part, to their joint planning. They took a lot of time to talk through their decision. It was not one-sided, but had potential rewards for each partner as an individual as well as for the family unit as a whole. Neither was asked to make sacrifices without some compensatory gains. This kind of joint planning seems to have been quite common among the most successful of the career changers we talked to. Without it, a positive outcome is much less likely.

The men were asked to describe their wives' reactions to their career change. Enthusiastic reactions were reported by 60; 16 reported that their wives did not take the change easily but adjusted, and four reported that their wives did not adjust well to the change. In at least three cases, the disagreement was over money. These wives resented the fact that their husbands had traded the family's financial security for their own personal ego trips. Eleven did not respond. In a number of cases, the men told us that their wives had been

urging them to change for some time before they actually did
so.

Howard was one of those men. At 50, he was a CPA and
vice-president and treasurer of a large firm. He made a good
salary and, with investments, was financially secure. The job
involved long hours and heavy pressures. His wife really
pushed him to leave. She became concerned about his
health, and insisted that the money was not worth it—she
had no desire to be a rich widow.

Howard had always been intrigued with the idea of
teaching. When he was young and had just finished his
MBA, he had taught a few courses at night school. He contacted a number of graduate business schools to see if they
might be interested. Unfortunately, they preferred men with
doctorates. He then looked into undergraduate teaching at
the local college. While they were talking about a possible
job, an opening arose as treasurer of the college. He was
asked if he would take it, and he accepted. He has still not
had the opportunity to teach, but hopes to be able to do so.

According to Howard,

I have had to make a big adjustment to get used to the academic
environment and the decision-making process that goes on here,
which is very different from that in business. There are few clear-
cut decisions; I find that I have to be a real salesman to get my point
across.

He has had a substantial cut in pay, but is still comfortable.
His wife is much happier now that he has changed. He no
longer works evenings or Saturdays, and they are able to
travel fairly often. He now plays tennis three or four times a
week, and his blood pressure is down.

FINANCIAL RISK

The men were asked to rank the degree of financial risk
they took in order to accomplish their change; 54 reported
that the risk was high, 21 reported a moderate risk, and 12 a

low risk; 4 did not comment. However, one man who reported a high risk commented that he really had not worried about it. He said, "In this country, they don't let you starve. I knew that if my new business failed, I could pick up the pieces and do something else to earn a living." He was the only one to express these sentiments clearly, but they were implicit in the actions of many of the others. After all, these men were reasonably successful and could have found something else to do if their new career failed. Most of them came from middle-class families and had always lived in relative comfort. Their life experiences had been mostly successful, so they had no reason to doubt their own ability to do well.

We did not ask actual salary figures, but a number of the men did volunteer that information. More than half took substantial pay cuts in order to change careers. But, again, the majority of them did start out with a sizable financial cushion, such as savings, investments, equity in a house, or an inheritance.

Most of the men who changed careers had family responsibilities; only three, as we have said, were unmarried at the time of the change. Twenty had no children at home; 16 had one, 21 had two, 21 had three, 10 had four, and 3 had five children. Twenty-four had one child in college, 5 had two children in college, and 2 courageous men had three children in college at the time of their career change.

WORKING WIVES

Working wives were a helpful factor for some of the men. Sixteen of the wives were working full time, 18 were working part time, and 51 were not employed outside the home. Although the wives' incomes did ease the financial burden somewhat, in no case was the wife's income high enough to allow the family to depend totally upon her for support for a period of time during the husband's transition. Except for a few teachers, none of the wives was a manager or professional.

This group of men was from a generation and social class in which most wives tended to follow traditional patterns, with their lives centered primarily in the home rather than in a career. Actually, in several cases, the wife was forced to go back to work to help support the family, and she resented it. These women worked as secretaries or held other positions that were not very gratifying, and they would have preferred to be at home with their children or doing volunteer work in the community. The wives who were unskilled and could not hope to bring in much income were often more hesitant about the financial risks involved in the career change than their husbands.

Alan and Jill, the couple described earlier in the chapter, are, perhaps, forerunners of many more couples in the next generation. First, Jill has more skills and training and therefore more earning ability than many of the older wives. She is able to find interesting, gratifying work and thinks of herself as equally responsible for earning the family living. Alan, on the other hand, enjoys caring for their children, and doesn't find the role of "househusband" demeaning. Their relationship is more equal than that of many older career-change couples; they are willing to be quite flexible in their roles. There are many indications that the pattern Alan and Jill are following will become more common.

The changes brought about by the women's movement are important in this context. The proportion of women in the labor force has risen dramatically and is continuing to rise. Women in the generation born before World War II expected to work only a few years before marriage or the advent of children. Many have found themselves returning to work when the children grew up, but without the skills and training to earn a sizable income.

Women born after World War II have been taught to think of work as much more central in their lives. Since 1970, women have entered graduate and professional schools and formerly male occupations in increasing numbers. The proportion of women in many medical and law schools is now a third or more. Many of these women will build their lives around their work rather than consider work a time filler before or after children or a means of supplementing their husbands' incomes.

More and more married women, even those with children in the home, are working. In 1948, 26 percent of married women with school-age children were in the labor force; in 1976, the percentage had risen to 53.7. Even for women with children under six years of age the percentages are growing. In 1948, 10.8 percent of such women were in the labor force; in 1975, it was 37.4 percent.[1] The family in which both husband and wife work is now the norm in the United States. In 1975, only about 38 percent of all husband–wife families had just one worker. The wives' attachment to the labor force was neither temporary nor capricious; 72 percent were employed at full-time jobs.[2]

The result of the increased participation of women in the labor force has been a dramatic change in how couples view careers. Previously, the man's career needs were central and determined the family's life. Now there is much more joint planning. In recent years, in my counseling with college students, it has become increasingly common for an engaged or newly married couple to come in together for career counseling. It is not unusual to hear a story like this:

Jane and I plan to be married right after graduation. She will be going to medical school in Philadelphia. I plan to get a job there to support us and get some experience in business while she is in school. When she graduates, I will go back to school for my M.B.A. We will try to find a city where she could do her residency and I could find a top-flight business school.

Another couple I know, Jim and Betty, who are in their early thirties, have developed a similar sharing approach to

[1] U.S. Department of Labor, *Employment and Training Report of the President* (Washington, D.C.: U.S. Government Printing Office, 1977), p 194.

[2] Howard Hayghe, "Families and the Rise of Working Wives—An Overview," U.S. Department of Labor, Special Labor Force Report 189 (Washington, D.C.: U.S. Government Printing Office, 1976), p. 16.

their careers. When they were first married, Betty was not especially career minded. She held a variety of jobs while Jim worked on his Ph.D. When he graduated, they moved from California to Illinois so that he could accept a job offer there. By this time, Betty had moved up to higher level jobs, and was beginning to develop a career. Her employer in Illinois urged her to go for a master's degree, which she did on a part-time basis. She began to carve out a reputation for herself in a newly developing field. Her career success brought an excellent job offer from an employer in Connecticut. As a result, Jim and Betty both left their jobs in Illinois and moved to Connecticut, despite the fact that Jim did not have a job. Fortunately, he was able to find one in his field within a month of their arrival. They both share jointly in household duties and in the care of their son.

The increase in the number of working wives, in the importance of career to married women, and in joint husband-and-wife career planning has important implications for the prevalence of career change in the future. If there is always at least one paycheck coming in, it is easier for the other spouse to take time off to return to school, to gamble on starting a new business, or to take a substantial pay cut in order to start out in a new field. Couples have more leeway to plan their lives. For example, a young couple just starting out might decide they both should work at full capacity to save for the purchase of a home and a nest egg before having children.

Of course, much of the increase in the proportion of wives who work and in the possibility for such joint career planning is a direct result of the advent of reliable means of birth control. When children do arrive, both parents might work less or on a more flexible time schedule so that they can share in parenting. Later, as college expenses loom heavily, they may both decide to work at full capacity again. Then, as financial burdens ease, one or the other might wish to return to school or change careers. Such a scenario will be easier to follow in the future.

FAMILY INCOME

There is no question that many of the men we interviewed were well off. They had been able to finance their career change without any appreciable change in their lifestyle. Some had made money in business; others had family inheritances. But still others had modest life-styles and had obviously made great sacrifices in order to change careers.

This study suggests some interesting questions for economists who deal with family income. It was quite clear that hardly any of the men had changed careers to earn more money. Although specific income-level questions were not asked, it often came out in the interview that the family income level had declined as a result of the career change. However, neither the men nor their families seemed to be bothered by this, because they were still able to live in comfort. No one was forced to go on welfare, although a number incurred debts. The other benefits—career satisfaction, enhanced life-style, time spent with the family, and reduction of tensions—far outweighed the financial loss.

This was not true for three of the men—two clergymen and a kindergarten teacher. These three did not earn enough to provide for the normal needs of a middle-class family with children to educate. As a result, there were family stresses. One wife returned to work, but unwillingly. The study suggests that a family in the United States needs to earn a certain level of income in order to live without stress in comfortable middle-class circumstances. Beyond that level, more money does not necessarily bring happiness; but below it, family stresses do emerge. Of course, the Labor Department does publish regular statistics on the income level needed to sustain families in various parts of the country, but the experiences of the men we interviewed suggest that there is a psychological as well as a purely economic level, provided a minimum middle-class economic level is maintained.

Our final conclusions regarding the men we studied and their relationships to marriage, family, and life-style were very different from what we thought we would find when we started. In many ways, they are parallel to the findings of Mary Jo Bane, the author of *Here to Stay: American Families in the Twentieth Century.* She began a study of demographic indicators of family life in contemporary America to see if the family was in a state of imminent decline, as so many have suggested. As she says,

. . . as I delved further into the data that describes what Americans do and how they live, I became less sure that the family was in trouble. Surprising stabilities showed up, and surprising evidence of the persistence of commitments to family life.

She found that ". . . there may be more personal commitment to family today than ever before in America's history."

Our findings among the 91 men who changed careers would back up her suppositions. Not only was there very little divorce as a result of career change, but we found, instead, what seemed to be a strengthening of the marital bond in a joint partnership toward a new goal. A significant number of the men changed careers to improve their life-styles. Many consciously chose the new career so that they could spend more time with their families; others discovered that more time with their families was an unexpected and rewarding dividend of their career change. In a number of cases, higher financial rewards were rejected in favor of closer family ties. Some evidence could be seen of a trend to more egalitarian, sharing kinds of marriages among the career changers and their wives.

6

The Role of
Higher Education

Postsecondary education can be helpful as a mechanism for handling several of the discontinuities of life in a dignified and useful way—reentry into the labor force, retirement, a sharp break in life status. Education can play a role in the development of new patterns of life, new rhythms of life mixing education, work, and leisure.[1]

ADULTS AND HIGHER LEARNING

Malcolm S. Knowles, a leader of the adult education movement, likes to quote Alfred North Whitehead regarding the nature and purpose of education. According to Whitehead, for most of history, until the present century, the time span needed for major cultural change to take place was longer than the life span of any one individual. Events and changes occurred slowly. Therefore, education was seen as a means whereby culture and knowledge could be transmitted

[1] Carnegie Commission on Higher Education, *Toward a Learning Society: Alternative Channels to Life, Work, and Service* (New York: McGraw-Hill, 1973), p. 12.

to the young. What they learned in childhood would suffice throughout their lives without major modification.

But today, as Whitehead pointed out in a commencement address he gave at Harvard University in 1930:

We are living in the first period of human history for which this assumption is false. . . . Today this time-span is considerably shorter than that of human life, and accordingly our training must prepare individuals to face a novelty of conditions.[2]

As a result, the nature and purpose of education have changed. It must be a way for young people to learn how to learn, and people must be prepared to continue learning throughout their lives.

More recently, Alvin Toffler, in his best-selling book, *Future Shock*, made us all uncomfortably aware of the accelerating pace of change and the exponential growth of knowledge and technology. As a result of this growing awareness, more and more people are realizing that education must be a lifelong process, that individuals will have to continue learning both by studying on their own and by returning to the classroom periodically throughout their lives as they need further knowledge and skills.

American higher education has slowly begun to respond to this new recognition. There has been a long history of programs for adults in American colleges and universities, but they have tended to lack both funding and prestige in comparison with the "regular" programs geared to the traditional 18- to 22-year-old student.

The first formal university program for adults was set up when William Rainey Harper became the first president of the University of Chicago in 1892; he established a Division of University Extension as one of the branches of the university. This was followed in 1903 by a similar extension pro-

---

[2] Quoted by Malcolm S. Knowles, "Toward a Model of Lifelong Learning," in Forbes Bottomly (ed.), *Peak Use of Peak Years* (Washington, D.C.: U.S. Office of Education, 1975), p. 35.

gram set up by Charles R. Van Hise at the University of Wisconsin. In 1914, Congress passed the Smith-Lever Act which established the Cooperative Extension Service of the U.S. Department of Agriculture; it administers programs of adult education through the state land-grant universities.

University extension programs for adults grew slowly but steadily over the years. A major boost for adult education came when the returning veterans of World War II, subsidized by the GI Bill, enrolled in unprecedented numbers in the nation's colleges and universities. As a group they were highly motivated and eager students; they showed up the traditional 18- to 22-year-old group. The ex-GIs made educators realize that, in general, adults make good students, because they know what they want. They are not in school because someone else has told them to go. Therefore they tend to work hard and get good grades.

However, despite the good showing of the GIs, postsecondary education for adults remained the stepchild of higher education until the last decade. Adults who wanted to return to school had to jump many hurdles. There was first of all, the unwritten but very real barrier of admission

In Dale Hiestand's study of men and women who returned to school in order to change careers, he found that most of the colleges and universities he investigated had policies that tended to restrict the opportunities for older applicants, even though their catalogs avoided making formal statements to that effect. In general, an adult had second priority over a younger student, and his background and motivation came in for extensive questioning.

Many adults have old transcripts that may be poor—reflecting a carefree youth when education was unimportant to them. In addition, test-taking skills become rusty over the years, so adults may not perform as well on standardized tests as youngsters who are used to taking them in high school. Adults also encounter financial barriers to furthering their education. Until very recently, colleges and universities did not award scholarships or loans to part-time students, and most adults cannot afford to leave their jobs to attend school full time. Even those who were able to go to class on a full-time basis were given a low priority for scarce funds; younger applicants came first. Then there are the difficulties of time and scheduling of classes. When you have a job and family, it is usually impossible to take classes during the 8-to-4 schedule of most full-time college programs.

Geographic location is another barrier for many adults who cannot pick up and move their families hundreds of miles away to attend school. If a degree means a hundred-mile round trip several times a week, the sacrifice may be too great, especially if the parking facilities at the college are inadequate and the student must walk another half-mile once he reaches campus. On top of these are the psychological barriers of feeling different with your gray hairs among all those kids, not wanting to sit in the campus soda shop to drink your cup of coffee, and wondering if maybe you are too old to learn after all.

Colleges and universities first began to pay real attention to adult students and to make concessions to their needs during the 1960s. Growing numbers of women who had raised families and now wanted to complete their education and gain skills with which to enter the job market enrolled in colleges throughout the country. They began to request and receive special assistance.

Counseling programs were set up to help women find out what courses were available and how they would fit into their vocational goals. Group sessions were organized so that they could relearn study skills and talk through their fear of failure and their self-consciousness. Classes were scheduled at more convenient hours—either from 9 to 3, when the children would be in school, or in the evening, when fathers were home to babysit. These programs worked well and began to spread to colleges across the country.

The numbers of adults returning to school increased rapidly. The percentage of the population between the ages of 25 and 35 enrolled in higher education tripled between 1950 and 1970. From 1965 to 1975 the proportion of adults participating in some type of classroom education increased from one in thirteen to one in eight. Surveys show that even larger numbers of adults are interested in obtaining further education.

A survey done by the Commission on Non-Traditional Study, showed that 77 percent of a large group of adults between the ages of 18 and 60 was interested in enrolling in further classroom study if the obstacles of time and money could be overcome, and a third of them actually did enroll. Highest on their list of priorities for study were subjects related to their employment. Another large survey of adults, done earlier, showed similar results.

These studies indicate that the typical adult learner is likely to be under 40 (although more and more older students are seeking higher education, especially at the increasing number of schools that waive tuition for senior citizens), relatively affluent, and self-motivated. Usually he or she will have some previous college experience. In fact, the more education one has, the more likely one is to return for additional education. The typical adult student is employed in a professional or managerial capacity and is seeking to improve his or her occupational status by investing in further education.

During the late 1960s and early 1970s events and circumstances converged to bring about a growing attention to the needs of adults in higher education. Many professional groups began to call for formalized updating of knowledge and skills in order to maintain licensure; their members are required to attend classes for a specified number of hours each year. Then, as a result of the upheavals in higher education caused by the civil rights movement and the anti-Vietnam War protests, colleges and universities began a long process of self-examination and change. A number of formal study groups and commissions were established to look at the state of American higher education and recommend ways to improve it.

The most important of these was the Carnegie Commission on Higher Education, which, over the course of some five years, published a large number of volumes studying all aspects of higher education and making recommendations for policy changes. One of them looked at the role of colleges vis-à-vis the adult student. It was entitled *Toward a Learning Society: Alternative Channels to Life, Work, and Service.*

This influential book advocated a policy of lifelong education in the United States. The authors believed that early schooling should teach children the skills of learning. Men and women should be prepared to alternate periods of work and study, coming back to colleges and universities to learn specific subjects or skills throughout their lives whenever the requirements of job, family, community, or hobbies indicated the need for new learning. They sketched out a series of policy recommendations that would make lifelong learning feasible.

As a result of the recommendations of the Carnegie Commission and other groups, financial support from foundations and the federal Fund for the Improvement of Postsecondary Education, internal soul searching by colleges themselves, and the push of the increasing number of adult students coming to the campuses, a broad array of services is now offered by postsecondary institutions in support of lifelong learning.

Admissions policies and procedures have changed dramatically. Many schools have open admissions policies for adults. There is much less dependence on the high school or college transcript that is more than ten years old and much greater scrutiny of what the applicant has been doing with his life since he left school.

The College-Level Examination Program (CLEP), created by the College Entrance Examination Board and administered by the Educational Testing Service, has enabled hundreds of thousands of adults to take examinations in specific subject areas or in general information areas they know something about and gain college credit for the subjects if they can pass the exams. They have been able to use knowledge gained through individual reading or home study, educational television, or on-the-job training to shorten the requirements for a degree. The examinations are now accepted as evidence for credit at 1,800 colleges and universities and are endorsed by the American Council on Education.

The American Council on Education, in cooperation with the New York State Education Department, has assessed many learning programs offered by the military, business and industry, and other noncollegiate organizations so that those who have successfully completed such programs can apply them for credit toward a college degree. Many colleges now have programs whereby they grant degree credit for competencies acquired outside of formal courses through "credit for life experience."

In most cases, students demonstrate their knowledge through a written or oral examination or attend a workshop in which they are instructed on how to document their previous learning in what is known as a "portfolio" of their prior experiences. The completed portfolio is examined by a committee of faculty members who award varying amounts of credit, depending on how much learning has been documented. It is not unusual for a student with a broad and varied background to earn up to half the credits required for a degree.

Along with the easing of admissions criteria and new ways of earning college credit have come a whole array of nontraditional structures for learning, many designed specifically for the needs and learning styles of adult students. One of the first of these was the University of Oklahoma's College of Liberal Studies program, which began in the early 1960s. This has been followed by many other "University Without Walls" programs. Requirements are completed by a variety of means, sometimes including formal course work, but usually by individual off-campus study supervised in person or by mail by college faculty members.

Empire State College in New York has 25 regional offices throughout the state staffed by faculty "mentors" who help the students draw up "learning contracts"—agreements between the student and the mentor as to what the learning requirements are and how they will be met—through the completion of a course, a project, or a paper.

One innovative program is the Tunbridge Program at Lone Mountain College in San Francisco. It serves a mixed age group of students, ranging from high school seniors through traditional college-age students to adults. The central focus of the program is work in the community to explore potential career possibilities. Students begin with a two-week orientation session in which they analyze in depth their own interests and goals and pinpoint potential areas for exploration. They then consult a number of experts in the San Francisco Bay community who are knowledgeable about the student's area of interest. These experts are members of a "network" of some 350 professionals who have agreed to participate in the Tunbridge program by advising students.

The student goes through a process of defining one or more projects with the help of people from the network and a faculty advisor. The remainder of the semester is spent completing the projects with the assistance of one or more members of the network who have agreed to supervise. Before any proposal for a project is accepted, the terms are clearly defined, including the means to be used for evaluation. At the end of the semester, after the student has consulted frequently with the faculty advisor, his or her project is judged by a faculty–student panel, and appropriate credit is awarded, as well as a grade, if the student wants one. Projects have been done in a wide variety of areas, exploring such fields as veterinary medicine, television production, landscape design, and the writing of children's books.

Finances are still a problem for adult students, but federal loans are now available for part-time as well as full-time students who qualify by reason of family income level.

Time constraints are being met in a variety of innovative ways. More people attend colleges and universities part time than full time. More courses are being offered in late afternoon and evening hours. A new and apparently popular development is the "weekend college." A testament to the fact

that this idea has really caught on is the recent publication o
a guidebook to such programs. Students can live and eat on
campus at modest rates or may commute.

Some programs are intensive and will cover an entire
subject in a weekend. Others continue from one weekend to
the next, and students attend for a period of months. It is
possible to earn a master's degree in business administration
this way—a boon to the busy executive whose job requires a
great deal of travel from Monday through Friday. Some
weekend college programs combine learning with recrea
tion; students who are enrolled are entitled to use campus
recreational facilities.

A typical program for adult students is the ABLE pro
gram of Adelphi University. In a recent advertisement the
university offered the opportunity to earn either an associate
or a bachelor of arts degree. "The Program is designed to
minimize the pressures which have kept adults from the
classroom." Classes meet once a week for 13 weeks and are
offered days, evenings, and weekends at a variety of loca
tions both on and off campus throughout the New York met
ropolitan area. College credits earned at other institutions
may be transferred, and life experience is evaluated for
credit. Such services as financial aid, child care, course
counseling, and study skills workshops are available.

When the ad was written, some 1,400 students were
already enrolled, ranging in age from 22 to 70. Adelphi also
offers an M.B.A. that is given on two New York City commu
ter train lines during the morning and evening rush hours
days, evenings and weekends on campus, and at some 15
neighborhood centers.

John F. Kennedy University in Orinda, California, is an
accredited institution that offers courses at the upper divi
sion and graduate level, primarily to adults. The average age
of its students is about 40, and all classes are geared to the
time demands of adult students. Most of the students attend
part-time. The faculty, mostly practicing attorneys, busi
nessmen, or other professionals in the area, plus some full

time faculty from neighboring colleges and universities, is also at the school on a part-time basis. The university describes itself as being "designed specifically for people in their midlife passages." It offers strong support systems to adult students, many of whom are anxious about returning to the classroom after many years of absence.

Kennedy does not place much weight on traditional criteria for admission but, instead, interviews applicants and looks at previous work and volunteer experiences and the results of its own test in English proficiency. It offers a law degree, but does not place much weight on the standard Law School Admission Test. Its two top graduates in 1977 were women whose LSAT scores would not have gotten them admitted to most law schools. Many of Kennedy's students are adults who are making a midcareer change.

Much of the new activity in nontraditional programs is going on in the community colleges, which in many areas have taken the lead in providing for the learning needs of adults, up to and including senior citizens. In Connecticut, for example, the average age of community college students is over 30. Many four-year colleges have also initiated a variety of new programs. Graduate and professional education has been the slowest to change. A few graduate programs have provided external degrees, but they are still suspect in the educational community. Except for education, social work, and business, most graduate programs still require full-time attendance, and, even in those fields, a full-time degree is considered to be more prestigious.

How far all of the new programs for adults will go is still an open question, hinging upon the effectiveness with which these programs establish the right to certify their students. However, it is clear that adults now comprise a large segment of the educational market and are no longer being treated as second-class citizens by the nation's colleges and universities. One optimistic note came with the passage in 1976 of the Lifelong Learning Act by Congress, under the sponsorship of then-Senator Walter Mondale. Although it was short on funding, it did establish the principle of federal interest in and concern with the area of adult education and set up procedures for further research and coordination of programs.

COLLEGE COUNSELING SERVICES FOR ADULTS

Concurrently with the educational programs described above, colleges and universities increasingly provide career and educational counseling services to adults in the communities they serve. A few agencies were set up after World War II to assist returning veterans, but the real beginning of this movement occurred in the early 1960s, when women returned to school in growing numbers.

One of the earliest pioneers of this movement was the Radcliffe Institute for Independent Study, which provided a small stipend, a place to study and exchange ideas with others, and the opportunity for women with academic potential but family responsibilities to return to graduate study. Along with the opportunity for continuing education, a counseling service was set up for women in the community to discuss their career and educational aspirations in groups led by a trained counselor or in individual sessions. It also published a directory of part-time work and study opportunities for women in the Greater Boston area. The interest and response were overwhelming, and the institute is still going strong, approaching its twentieth anniversary.

Other pioneers in such programs were Sarah Lawrence College and the University of Minnesota. Similar programs for women were gradually set up throughout the country and are now available in many universities, colleges, and community colleges, as well as through YMCAs and other community organizations.

In the 1970s, as the numbers of adults who want to return to school have grown to the point where the post-college-age student is becoming the major consumer of educational services at postsecondary institutions, a new

novement has emerged. It is an outgrowth of the earlier
development of counseling centers for women, and, indeed,
ncludes many of them. However, it has other elements as
vell, most notably the presence of men.

I can remember the director of one of the older and more
successful women's centers describing to me how the husband of one of its satisfied clients called her on the phone
one day. He said, "Your program has done wonders for my
vife. She's a new woman since she took your counseling
program and has gone back to school. But what about me?
'm working for the same company I started with 15 years
ago, and I'm in a rut. I need help."

The newer agencies are called educational brokers.
Their function is to serve as middlemen between potential
adult learners and educational institutions and resources.
They offer counseling about career and educational opportunities, they give courses and workshops, and they refer
clients to other programs or to colleges and universities offering the kinds of courses these clients need to reach their
goals. Often they serve as advocates on behalf of their clients
to arrange for cutting red tape, waiving requirements, or
creating special programs when necessary. They are also
sources of information about the myriad numbers of programs available in many metropolitan areas.

One distinctive quality of brokering agencies is that they aim to
present adults with the complete range of educational and career
alternatives and help them to choose those most appropriate to
their individual needs. Brokering agencies are neutral towards the
choices made; conventional educational institutions usually aim to
increase their own clientele or student bodies.[3]

Brokering agencies perform a number of functions for
their adult clients. First they help them to define their objectives by exploring personal values, skills and abilities,
and possible occupational goals. Then they help them to dis-

[3] James M. Heffernan, Francis U. Macy, and Donn F. Vickers, *Educational Brokering, A New Service for Adult Learners* (Syracuse, New York:
National Center for Educational Brokering, 1976).

cover the best means to achieve their goals. This often means further education, but other kinds of learning experiences may be more appropriate. They can tell their clients about the wide variety of educational programs available to them and help the clients identify the courses or programs most suitable for their needs. Finally, brokers help the adults get through the admissions process. In some cases, brokers become advocates for their clients, attempting to change institutional policy when it seems to offer an obstacle to the learning needs of adult students.

Some agencies simply serve as a clearinghouse for information about educational resources and career preparation for adults. Examples are the Life-Long Learning Center in New York City and the statewide computerized Oregon Career Information Service. The latter has terminals in all the colleges in the state and in many social agencies. Some simply publish directories of programs, such as the METRODOC Directory in Toronto. The Educational Exchange of Greater Boston, founded in 1891, has published an annual catalog of learning opportunities in Greater Boston for years; it also provides other information and counseling.

Other educational brokerages are independent agencies and are not attached to any institution. Examples of these are the Regional Learning Service of Central New York in Syracuse, the statewide Regional Educational Opportunity Centers in Massachusetts, and the Career Education Project in Providence, Rhode Island. In several states, brokering agencies or networks—such as the Community College of Vermont in Montpelier and the Hudson Community College Commission in Jersey City—have been set up within the existing state college or community college system.

Brokering agencies have also been set up by consortia of colleges, such as the Regional Continuing Education for Women Program in Philadelphia. Some are independent units of existing colleges, where students may be referred to other institutions; examples are the School for New Learning at DePaul University and the Continuum Center of Oakland University in Rochester, Michigan.

A number of brokering agencies teach courses or give workshops besides offering counseling services. Usually, the courses will be in areas closely related to the needs of their clients. A refresher mathematics course, for example, may enable students to prepare for entrance examinations.

Many of the educational brokering agencies have provided useful assistance to people considering a change in their careers. A few programs have been set up specifically for these people. From 1963 to 1968, the Ford Foundation funded the New Careers Program at Columbia University under the direction of Alan Entine. It helped some 50 people obtain the counseling and education they needed in order to change careers. Hundreds of other people inquired about the program but had to be turned away.

Many colleges and universities offer courses for adults who want to change careers. Stanley Hyman has successfully conducted a career transition course at Catholic University in Washington, D.C., for a number of years. The enrollment has already included several thousand students, many of them retiring members of the armed forces.

One of the men we interviewed took Hyman's course and found it very helpful in his transition from the Air Force, where he had served as an officer using his training as a meteorologist. Stuart had become increasingly dissatisfied with the Air Force. He was then stationed in Washington, D.C., but his next assignment would probably be in a location with a school system that would be unsatisfactory for the education of his teenage son and the employment of his wife, a teacher. He had been soured by Vietnam. He was unlikely to make the next promotion, to full colonel, and he was not even sure he wanted it.

I would be an oddball, a radical; it would strain my integrity. I saw that the civilian job market was getting tighter, and I wasn't getting any younger. I could have stayed on for another six years, but I felt that I should make the move then, when I was 42, to give myself time to become established in a civilian career. I thought seriously about leaving for a year, and I began to prepare myself. First, I took a speed-reading course. I had a long talk with my immediate superior about my future in the Air Force; he advised me to retire. I also talked to some friends in the Air Force and discussed it at great length with my wife.

I saw an ad for a career transition course in an Air Force publication and decided to take it. It was taught by Stanley Hyman at Catholic University and was designed for military people. It met twice a week for three months and was quite intensive. There were 40 people in the class, almost all military. The course began with a battery of tests and a session with a psychologist. I learned how to translate my military background to civilian terms. We did a lot of role playing of interviews. We were given a lot of good job-hunting techniques and learned how to write a resume.

Stuart took the course in the spring semester. He filled out his retirement papers early in July, received his present job offer in the middle of August, and was out of the Air Force September 1. He felt that the course had been of invaluable help in enabling him to make a smooth transition from the security of the Air Force to civilian employment.

Alan Entine, who ran the Columbia University career change program mentioned above, is now director of a program at the State University of New York at Stony Brook, on Long Island. Part of the program is a Mid-Career Counseling Center, which provides vocational and educational counseling both in a group setting and individually to several hundred adults each year. In addition, Entine has set up a Mid-Life Assessment Program, which offers graduate-level courses to professionals who work with adults in counseling, training, and employment as well as to lay people interested in the issues of midlife. At present, six courses are offered, but it is anticipated that eventually the offerings will lead to a master of arts degree in adult development.

CAREER CHANGERS WHO RETURNED TO SCHOOL

Of the 91 men we studied, 40 went back to school in order to change careers. Two of the men took only one course and five took several courses but were not working toward a degree. (Some of them needed the courses for teacher certification.) Ten of the men earned a master's degree, eight studied for a doctorate, and fifteen earned a professional degree in theology, law, medicine, or optometry.

We found that men with a high personal desire to change careers were more likely to obtain additional schooling than men who were forced into the career change by external circumstances. Younger men and those motivated by a desire to find more meaningful work also figured largely in the back-to-school movement. Men whose career change was influenced primarily by a desire to move to a better locality were less likely to back to school; probably for these men life-style and family were more important than advancement in their work.

Almost all the men we spoke to already had a bachelor's degree and therefore returned for graduate education. In an unofficial survey of graduate divinity, law, and medical schools, Seymour Sarason found that between 12 and 20 percent of their applicants appeared to be seeking a career change.

The career changers who returned to school seemed to have no difficulties with admissions offices because of age. Law schools, particularly, appeared to be quite receptive, and encouraged older students; one of the men in our study returned when he was in his early fifties. Many people, of course, go to law school to gain the discipline of legal training and never intend to practice as attorneys. As a result, law-school admissions officers have never seen themselves as playing the role of gatekeepers in the same way as medical-school admissions officers do. The bar exam becomes the final screen, although older legal graduates will have trouble finding jobs with the prestigious large law firms.

Also, from a purely economic point of view, legal education is relatively inexpensive for a university to provide. No costly laboratories or other facilities, except for a good library, are needed. Classes are usually taught in large lecture sections rather than the small tutorials of other graduate and professional schools; these can easily be expanded to accommodate more students. Legal education is elastic in that programs can be expanded and new schools started in a relatively short time. This happened during the 1970s in response to a drastically increased number of applicants to law schools. Many new schools started up, and others added or expanded their part-time evening programs.

One of our career changers, a dentist, went back to school part-time at night for a law degree when he became restless in the routine of the dental office. He felt very confined by having to stay in his office all day long. He can now gratify his wanderlust by traveling all over the world as a forensic dentist, testifying in court cases and acting as a consultant. He has combined both professions to establish a most rewarding career, both intrinsically and financially; he is only one of a handful of such men in the world.

Graduate schools of social work, business, theology, and education have always welcomed older students. More mature people often do better in those fields because of their greater life experience. Harvard Business School, for instance, seldom will accept a student directly out of college.

In addition, many of these graduate schools offer classes on a part-time basis, so it is possible to complete their programs while still employed. An example is the Columbia University Graduate School of Business master's degree program for executives, which begins with an intensive one-week program in residence, and holds the remaining classes every Friday. In fact, many graduate classes are designed for professionals already in the field who want to update their credentials. However, full-time attendance is still considered better, and the most prestigious schools usually have only full-time programs.

Many medical schools are not interested in students over 30 or, at most, 35, both because of the physically arduous and demanding curriculum and long hours required and because of the great competition for admission. Unlike the programs in law schools, medical and dental school programs are not easily expanded. Each student must be provided with thousands of dollars' worth of laboratory equipment and materials. Space limitations do not permit the easy addition of a dozen more students to a class. The cost of building a new medical school facility is so great that the decision becomes a matter of hotly debated public policy; most of the 32 medical schools built since 1955 are state supported through tax dollars. A few medical schools occasionally accept an older student, and I personally know of several students who successfully completed their medical education when they were in their late thirties or early forties. But the strain is great, and marriages often suffer.

An experiment that has been watched with great interest is the University of Miami's program for people who hold a Ph.D. in the natural, physical, or engineering sciences and want to earn an M.D. Begun in 1971, the program had graduated 86 people by 1977. The age range at admission has been from 23 to 39. The number of applicants to the program each year is high, up to 1,000, from which only 75 are chosen. Naturally, those who gain admission are a highly qualified group of successful scientists, who are well able to take the pace of the accelerated 24-month program. The cost of tuition alone is $5,600 a year, so most of the graduates find they have sizable loans to repay when they are finished. About half the students are married, which may help if spouses are able to work to support the student member of the family.

One of the career changers we interviewed is in a similar kind of program, given by the Massachusetts College of Optometry for people with Ph.D.s in related fields, such as physics (optics) or psychology (perception). Ten or twelve students are admitted each year to the very intensive 24-month program. Ages of the students range up to 50.

One of the three men in our study who went to medical school was the only one of the 40 going back for more education who had any real difficulty with admission. Sam was a civil engineer with a Ph.D., whose specialty was stress; he had become a project director for a small research-oriented firm. His career change really started in 1967, when research money began drying up. He did not want to work on defense contracts, and by accident he found profitable work in medically related areas dealing with the structure of the human back and the effects of physical stress, doing the technology for physicians involved in research at a medical school.

After several years, Sam reached a point in his career where it was clear that he had to decide whether he should stay in a laboratory doing research, become an administrator, or go into business for himself. He came to the conclusion that he didn't want to continue doing the technical work for someone else who would ultimately receive the rewards for the project. So he decided to prepare for medical school by taking biology courses at a local university. His company allowed him extra time off to attend classes and even provided some tuition reimbursement. He was not very sophisticated about application procedures the first time around and was not accepted. The next year he applied to more schools and found one that was particularly interested in older students. He was accepted at the age of 35.

Sam had been divorced and had no dependents, so he was able to live off savings the first year. Later, he earned money by working as an assistant on a research project at the medical school. He didn't enjoy the experience.

I found medical school a humiliating, degrading experience. It was hard for me to play the obsequious student role. Being much older than most of the other students, I didn't share many of their concerns. I had to come to grips with being alone, and I had to focus on my ultimate goals. I slept a lot. There were satisfactions and a sense of accomplishment in dealing with patients.

He is now in a residency program in orthopedics, preparing for his ultimate goal of forming his own company to do research in orthopedic technology. He still thinks of himself as a researcher and scientist, superior to clinicians.

Hiestand's conclusions about the people he interviewed who returned to school in order to change careers, was that

. . . the general picture these respondents present is one of considerable success as students, a minimum of difficulty in reentering school and employment, considerable satisfaction about their past, and optimism about their future.

This was true for the men we talked to also. Most of those who went to school full time found that they enjoyed returning to higher education, and they all seem to have done well academically. In fact, several reported that they were much better students than they had been 20 years before as undergraduates. One, who had majored in sports and girls as an undergraduate and gotten by with barely passing grades, ranked first in his class at graduation from a seminary.

One man, who went to law school, looked back on his experience from the vantage point of his third year.

I knew it would be hard, but not that hard! My study skills were very rusty. The first year was very difficult. I was constantly trying to revise my methods, and there was no feedback until the exams at the end of the first semester. Ironically, six weeks after I began law school I had a serious ear infection that temporarily affected my hearing. Then, five days before that crucial first exam, I went to the hospital with appendicitis. I made out all right, but it was touch-and-go there for a while. The first year was very emotional, very exciting. I loved every minute of it, but I had enormous feelings of inadequacy. I was uncomfortable being graded. And the time commitment was very heavy. The second year was much easier.

Another man who returned to law school said,

It was a very smooth transition; I enjoyed it immensely. I fit in quite easily with the younger students and, in fact, made many meaningful relationships. That was something I hadn't expected. I knew another man who had made a similar change and returned to law school at about my age, although he had gone at night. It was helpful to talk to him.

Going back to school became the means to attaining a personal identity and independence for one man who had dutifully gone into the family business after graduation from college. He said.

After six or eight years in the business, I began to wonder "who am I?" I took some accounting courses in order to improve my skills for the business. I enjoyed them so much and did so well that I went on to earn a second bachelor's degree in accounting. I then continued on for an MBA, graduating first in my class. They asked me to do some part-time teaching there, which I did, and I enjoyed it.

The family business was not going well, and Tom disagreed with his father over the management. He walked out after a particularly heated argument, and applied and was accepted for a doctorate in business.

I began to realize I was not the "klutz" I had thought I was. We lived off savings and borrowed $5,000. My wife went back to work, and also had a fellowship. We moved to a smaller house and reduced our standard of living. But it took me two years to stop being ashamed of being a full-time student. I didn't want the neighbors to see me at home during the day when I was studying. I had the feeling that going to school was too pleasurable, too much fun, and I felt guilty. Somehow, I thought I should be going out to some regular 9-to-5 job.

Tom says that, in retrospect, his return to school was very healthy for the family. It brought him much closer to his wife and children. He got to know his kids better. Now that he is established in his teaching career, the next plan is for his wife, who has been a schoolteacher, to go to law school.

A number of the men went back to school in order to teach at the community college level. Ben had majored in history as an undergraduate in the late 1930s and had done so well that his professors had urged him to go on to graduate school. He had been accepted at Columbia, but the war intervened. When it was over, he was needed in the family business, which was undergoing a crucial transition, so he did not go on to graduate school. The business prospered, and after his father's death, he and his brother became partners.

When Ben was in his late forties he began to question his involvement with the business and felt bored with it. He got no intellectual stimulation from it and was frustrated by increasing federal regulations. His wife encouraged him to leave, and his brother willingly bought out his share of the partnership.

I had always read a great deal and continued my love for history. I was active in the local historical society as well as other community organizations. Through one of these, I got to know the president of the local community college well. He knew of my interests, and asked me to come and teach there. I started on an M.A. in history at the state university that summer and began to teach at the community college in the fall.

Ben is generally satisfied with his present life. However, he is worried that inflation is eroding his capital, and college expenses for his children are a big drain. He is also dissatisfied with the intellectual quality of community college students and their lack of responsiveness. Ideally, he would like to write a textbook and do research. He regrets that he does not have a Ph.D.

John, another person who earned a master's degree in order to teach, was a graduate of Annapolis and had spent 20 years as an officer in the navy. During this time he had had several opportunities to teach, and he enjoyed it. He decided that he was unlikely to become an admiral, so he began to plan for retirement at the end of his 20 years. He was assigned to a post in Washington, D.C., for two years, and he took courses toward a master's degree in mathematics at one of the universities there. When he finished, he was easily able to find a teaching position at a community college. He has worked his way up quickly to a tenured position, and enjoys teaching.

From the experience of the men who returned to higher education to change careers and from what we know about new trends in higher adult education, the advice to someone thinking about returning to school is "do it." Most of the men we interviewed found going back to school a stimulating and enjoyable experience. None of them had any regrets.

Most adults need not be afraid of being rebuffed by admissions officers or of not being able to find the right kind of program, unless they live in an isolated area. Because of the contracting demand for higher education and the imminent decrease in the population of 17- to 22-year-olds, colleges and universities are now eager for tuition-paying students, and they have realized that adults comprise a new market that may make the difference for their hard-pressed budgets.

Look around and talk to representatives of a number of institutions to see what they have to offer you. If possible, consult with a brokering agency or try to get a complete listing of colleges and universities in your area to see what is available before you commit yourself to any one program. If you don't see exactly what you want listed in the catalog, talk to the dean to see if special arrangements can be made to tailor a program to your needs, perhaps with the addition of one or two courses from another institution. If time constraints are a problem, look into a University Without Walls program that can be followed at your own pace, primarily at home.

Remember that colleges and universities are providing a service to you for which they are charging a lot of money. Be a discriminating consumer, and complain if you aren't getting what you want. It is now a buyer's market in higher education, and you should be able to find what you want and need.

But you *should* think out carefully what you need to learn beforehand, so that you are not going to college with just a vague idea of obtaining an education. The more clearly defined your goals, the more satisfied you should be with the outcome. In addition, if you are specific about what you want to learn, you will be much less likely to be put into a formatted program with generalized prescribed courses; instead, you should be able to choose a course of study that is meaningful for you. In the next chapter, we will discuss ways to go about defining your goals.

7

Planning a Change in Careers

TIME TO PLAN CHANGE

One of the most interesting aspects of changing careers in midlife is the process the men used. Some of the methods they stumbled on may be useful to you if you are considering a career change. What has been learned about them may help you to evaluate yourself and the process you are using.

Most significant is that they took a *long time* to change careers. The men were asked how long it took from the time they first began to consider the possibility of a career change until they actually left their jobs. Eight took only one month or less; 21 took one to six months; 21 took seven to twelve months; 33 took one to five years, and 6 took five years or more. In many cases, the time until they began their new careers was much longer, since some of them left their jobs to attend school full time before going on to these new careers.

As might have been anticipated, younger men tended to take longer to plan their career changes than the older men. In addition, those who were forced to leave their former jobs changed careers faster than men whose career change was entirely voluntary.

The lesson to be learned is not to expect a major change in career to happen quickly. Plan to spend at least a year thinking about it, researching the possibilities, and making plans. There is no statistically significant correlation between the length of time these men took to change careers and their stated outcome, but our interviews did leave us with the distinct impression that many of those who took longer to plan their moves ended up happier with the outcome.

This is only logical. Our work roles are very important to us; what we do for a living is the single most important badge of who we are—our social status. It seems reasonable to assume that we would have problems maintaining our emotional balance and self-identity while radically and suddenly changing that badge. We need to ask questions, explore roles, and, if possible, try out the roles on a test basis. We need time to look at the new image of ourselves, to day dream about it, to talk to other people who have the same occupation, to see how our friends and loved ones react to it. In short, it should and does take a long time to change careers.

METHODS TO USE

Many people put the cart before the horse when they try to find a new job or a new career. They start with the jobs that are out there and not with themselves and their skills, interests, knowledge, and abilities. This is the wrong approach. Granted, with luck, many people do find jobs by starting this way, but are they always the best, most satisfying jobs for them? It has been estimated that only about 20 percent of the total job market is covered by newspaper advertisements and employment agencies. The rest can be uncovered—but only through thorough research by an individual who knows what he wants and knows that he is the right person for that job.

Let me illustrate my point with the story of a client I saw several years ago who was not in the career change study. Dave was a good-looking young man of 29. Until just before he came to my office for help his life had been very successful. He had won a scholarship to a selective college, where he had majored in classics, graduating Phi Beta Kappa. He was accepted for graduate work at a top-ranking university and, in due course, he received his Ph.D. in classics.

Dave and his new wife spent a glorious postdoctoral year in Athens. When they returned, he took a one-year teaching appointment at a midwestern college, filling in for a professor who was on sabbatical. After that, the bottom fell out. Colleges across the country were cutting back on classics departments, and the growing glut of Ph.D.s meant that there were more applicants than jobs. Dave estimated that there were perhaps ten positions available for classics instructors throughout the country and 50 applicants, and he lost out in the competition.

Needless to say, Dave was a pretty discouraged young man when he came into my office. Nor did it help that his wife, an elementary school teacher, also found herself unemployed. It was quite a blow for Dave to have to stand in the unemployment line and apply for his first check.

After listening to his story, I agreed to work with Dave, but warned him that it would probably be a hard and lengthy process. I told him that we would start with him and not with the jobs out there. He agreed that the one thing he had plenty of at that point was time, and he might just as well fill it that way. He began by writing a lengthy autobiography of all of his work experiences, starting with the part-time jobs he had held during high school. We spent several hours trying to analyze his experiences, picking out things that he liked and didn't like, what he did well and what he didn't do well, the kinds of environments that turned him on and those that turned him off. We talked about his values and life-style, the way he and his wife lived, and the things they liked to do in their spare time.

After many hours of work, Dave came to some conclusions. He was particularly good at working with people in small groups and teaching and counseling them on a one-to-one basis. He also was a good writer and enjoyed expository writing; he could see himself becoming a journalist. His values were such that he preferred to stay in education or a helping field; he couldn't see himself selling soap. Above all, however, he and his wife had decided that they really wanted to go back to Greece to work for at least a few years, even if it meant a reduction in income.

Having analyzed himself and arrived at a firm goal, Dave's next step was to begin to research the job market out there. He began with the Greek consulate; Greek–American trade organizations, and the Greek offices of American newspapers, wire services, and magazines. Everyone was thoroughly discouraging. They all said that Greek law prohibited foreigners from obtaining employment; it was impossible to find a job overseas without a personal interview in that country; there just weren't any jobs for Americans in Greece. Discouraged but undeterred, Dave kept at it. He spent several hours in the library researching organizations dealing with Greece, Greek products sold in America, and so on. He talked to a lot of people.

One of the organizations he contacted was an educational tour agency that planned six-month stays in Greece for student groups. The week before, their Greek director had resigned. Dave was the answer to their prayers. In a month, he and his wife left for Greece, where he was employed as a combination tour guide, dean of students, and publicity director for the agency.

Maybe Dave would have landed this job without having gone through the long process beforehand. However, the fact that he had learned so much about himself and had convinced himself of his own skills and abilities made it easy for him to convince the president of the tour agency that he was the right man for the job. Moreover, this job had never been advertised. In fact, it had become available just a few days before Dave walked in. It probably would never have been advertised. The president of the agency didn't have time to go through that process. He had a new group of students arriving in a month and would have had to take some immediate action. If necessary, he would have gone to Greece himself.

Because Dave had done such a thorough job of researching the organizations that might have job possibilities for him, he had turned up the name of the tour agency. Since he was determined to do a systematic series of interviews with all possible organizations, it was inevitable that he would walk through the tour agency's doors. Although it was luck that made the previous Greek director resign the week before Dave was interviewed by the president, Dave's thorough preparation had enabled him to capitalize on that luck. A final happy note was the fact that the salary was higher than that for Dave's previous teaching job.

SELF-ASSESSMENT

The first step is self-assessment. If you don't know who you are, what you can do well, what you like and don't like, and where you want to work, you are not going to be able to find a new career that will really satisfy you. And you can't just carry all these things in your head. You must be able to sit down and make lists, and then be able to explain the lists in a meaningful fashion to someone else—friend, spouse, or anyone else. If you can't do this, how can you possibly explain what you want to a potential employer?

One of the best ways to start is the way Dave did. Write down your complete work history, starting with the first paying job you ever held and including community activities and volunteer positions. Don't list just titles and dates; describe each job, your responsibilities, functions, daily routine. After you have finished, analyze each job and decide what you liked and didn't like about it, what you were good at and what you didn't do so well. Try to think about each of the jobs you filled and how you did the work. Every job has specific requirements, but every person tends to do his job slightly differently, emphasizing the things he enjoys most and is best at, and downplaying or de-emphasizing those aspects he likes least.

Is there some common theme that runs through all your past experiences? For example, one person might always be looking for ways to improve his efficiency on the job. John, as a young lad, inherits his older brother's newspaper route which took an hour to complete. After a few weeks on the job, he discovers a shortcut and is able to complete the route in 45 minutes. As a young man, he wins $500 for putting a tip into the company suggestion box on ways to do a certain job faster and better. John is a natural for the kind of job in which one of the central tasks is to analyze a situation for efficiency. He should make an excellent time-and-motion study engineer. John is probably not suited for a job in which the emphasis is on maintaining the status quo and not rocking the boat. Another person always seems to be the one others come to for advice and help. His new direction should be one in which listening to and counseling others is central.

Continuing to use your work history, take a sheet of paper with columns for each job listing the skills used, knowledge gained, enjoyable features, and disagreeable features. You may also wish to add a column called "values." It could contain comments like "Working for this large, impersonal firm made me realize that I would only really be happy in a job in a small organization," "Working alone made me realize that I need the stimulation of colleagues in any future job," "I need the challenge of a fast-paced city organization with something new going on every minute," or "I want to live in a rural area and work at my own pace."

After you have made your lists, look them over and try to rank them in order of importance. For example, in your list of skills, which is the most significant or most marketable or most unusual, or which is your best skill? In your value list, which ones would be nice to have in a future job but are expendable, and which ones are absolutely non negotiable? When you are finished, if you have done a thorough job, you should have a fairly detailed outline of who you are occupationally—what your skills, abilities, knowledge, personal needs, and values are.

Another useful method, developed by Bernard Haldane, is his System for Identifying Motivated Skills. You make a list of 10 to 20 achievements in your life. These don't have to be accomplishments that made the papers or netted you rewards. They should just be things in your life that you did well, that made you proud of yourself, and that you enjoyed doing.

One man listed having built a tree house in the backyard with his three sons. A young woman planned a successful surprise twenty-fifth wedding anniversary party for her parents, inviting many of their old friends, decorating the room, baking and decorating the cake, and cooking all the food. More directly work-related achievements might include raising sales in a company branch by over 50 percent in the course of a year, designing a new system for dealing with a recurrent office problem, or getting the shiest child in the classroom to feel comfortable about making an oral presentation.

Everyone has achievements. Do not make excuses, and say you can't think of any. How are you going to convince a prospective employer to hire you if you can't convince yourself of your abilities? Be careful, in naming your achievements, to be specific and concrete. "Being a good parent" is far too global, but "devoted every Saturday afternoon to sports activities with my children, which helped them develop their coordination and led to better understanding between us" might be appropriate. Again, "being well organized" is not very helpful, but "devised a new system in the office to control and distribute orders to avoid peaks and valleys in the work" is concrete enough to be of value. Make sure that your list taps all facets of your life and is not just taken from work-related areas.

After you have made a list of 15 or 20 achievements, narrow them down to the half dozen or so that seem most important and most representative. Then try to analyze them for the kinds of skills involved. What should emerge is a pattern of a group of skills you have and you enjoy using.

These are your *transferable skills*. Ideally, they should be central components of any future job if you are to enjoy it and do well in it. For example, our friend who built the tree house might have found the following transferable skills when analyzing his accomplishments: planning a project, including measuring, ordering materials, and making blueprints; doing carpentry; teaching others how to do things with their hands; supervising others. The transferable skills used in the anniversary party include planning and organization, budgeting, ordering supplies, artistic and decorating skills, coordination, and cooking.

It is just common sense that you will enjoy a job that requires you to do things you do well and you like doing. The previous exercise has demonstrated to you by examples from your past experience what your transferable skills are. For a more complete description of the System for Investigating Motivated Skills, read Bernard Haldane's book, *Career Satisfaction and Success: A Guide to Job Freedom.* Howard Figler's *PATH: A Career Workbook for Liberal Arts Students* is designed for college students but may also be helpful.

Make sure that you have thought about all aspects of your life and understand where your preferences and abilities lie. You must force yourself to answer a great many questions. You need to find out if you work better or worse under pressure. Is a deadline necessary to get you going, or does it make you too anxious to function properly? Do you take in information best by reading, by listening, or by watching others?

Other questions to ask yourself: Where do you want to live? What kinds of people do you like to work with? What kinds of activities do you like? What are the working and living conditions that matter to you? What are your ideal job specifications? What are the business ethics you care about? What values do you hold to be important and beyond compromise? What are your major interests? What kinds of issues do you want to help solve? In what ways do you want to use your creativity? What do you need to care for your family?

Planning for the future brings up still more questions. What do you envision as your future life-style, and what is your loved ones' place in it? What are your immediate and long-range money needs and wants? How central is money to you? How do you want to develop your skills and knowledge? What alternatives do you always want to have at hand? You must find answers to these and other questions if you are going to be effective in defining the kind of job for which you are best suited.

For descriptions of other techniques you can use for self-assessment, plus other helpful hints, get Richard N. Bolles' *What Color Is Your Parachute?* This is revised periodically, so make sure the bookstore or library has the most up-to-date edition. If you don't read anything else, read this. It is the bible of career changers and contains a wealth of information, including a complete bibliography. Bolles has also put out a good, simple, and inexpensive workbook called *The Quick Job Hunting Map,* which may be obtained separately, or as part of *What Color Is Your Parachute?* A longer and much more complete workbook is *Where Do I Go From Here With My Life?* by Bolles and Crystal. Although it certainly has everything a career changer might need to go through the process, I frankly believe it requires a counselor or teacher as a guide. I think it is simply too overwhelming for most people to follow on their own. But see for yourself.

DEFINING YOUR OCCUPATIONAL GOAL

At the end of the self-assessment process one should have a list of skills, abilities, knowledge, interests, likes, dislikes, and values. The next step is to translate the list into an occupational goal. This is the point at which many people flounder, and where you are most likely to need help.

In my course for career changers, I have them work in groups of threes; if possible, people from similar backgrounds are separated. I ask them to bounce their lists off each other and do some brainstorming about the possible goals for someone with their particular configuration of skills. If you are working on your own, try your list out on friends, particularly those who have a broad acquaintance with the world of work. If you have some general idea of what area might interest you, talk to someone in that field about what kinds of opportunities might be available for someone with your particular profile of abilities and needs.

Tom, one of the men in the career change study, tackled this stage very effectively, I thought. He was a highly paid vice-president of an international construction firm. He traveled widely in the course of his job. In his early forties he came to a turning point for a variety of reasons. He realized that he had probably risen as high as was possible in his firm; several of the men senior to him were his age and younger, and it just didn't seem to be in the cards for him to get to the top.

In addition, Tom began to wonder if that was what he really wanted. His wife and college-age children had become very much involved in civil rights and anti-Vietnam War activities, and he began to be interested himself. He went through a period of intense soul-searching in which he questioned the value of what he was doing and wondered whether he would be satisfied to continue in his firm simply making money for a large corporation. One day he announced to the stunned president of his company that he planned to leave the firm one year from that date. He was telling them in advance so that there would be plenty of time for them to choose a successor and for him to train the person who would take over his job.

Tom then spent most of that year trying to decide what to do next. He had determined that his next job would probably be in a nonprofit area and that the most important criterion for him was that the job be one in which he was clearly doing something useful to help solve society's problems. He was a Harvard Business School graduate, and through classmates and business associates over the years, he had established a broad network of friends and acquaintances. He systematically interviewed a large number of men in positions of knowledge and authority, asking them for their suggestions as to how he might best use his talents. Many of these men were busy, highly placed, and important people, yet they were often quite interested in Tom's problem. Even I was surprised at the names of the prominent people who willingly gave Tom an hour of their time to discuss his future with him. During the course of the year, he received several job offers. He finally accepted a position in which his knowledge of construction and land acquisition was used in the redevelopment of his city.

Granted, everyone doesn't have the highly placed friends Tom had. But we all know people or can get the names of people working in the field we are considering. Most people are flattered to be asked for advice and are usually quite willing to help someone by offering information about their job or company. Start by talking to someone you know pretty well; ask that person for the names of several other people who might help you. Before long, you should have developed a sizable list of contacts and learned a good deal about the field you are considering. You may encounter some dead ends. A field that initially held promise might turn out to be all wrong when you investigate it further. Try something else, until you find the field or fields that are right for you.

In your information-gathering interviews, ask such questions as: What do you think the opportunities are in your field for someone with my background and interests? Do you see this business growing, and in what areas? How did you prepare for your present job? What do you see as some of the problems in your area or company that need to be tackled? What do you see as the positive and negative factors about work in this field/company? What salary level can I reasonably expect to earn if I get into this kind of job? How might someone with my background prepare for a job in this field/company?

In addition to talking to people and getting information

about potential fields, you can do some exercises to try to pinpoint your goals. Try to write some sample newspaper ads for the kinds of jobs you might want. That will force you to describe your requirements in words. It will also make you keep in mind the employer's point of view, rather than think only in terms of what *you* want to fulfull your needs. You will start to think in terms of tasks to be performed and problems to be solved.

Another useful exercise is to project yourself into the future. Write a description of a workday and a holiday some time between six months and five years in the future. Describe your activities in detail. This will help you to focus in on the kind of job you are looking for and the environment in which you want to live and work.

In these exercises, try to be as specific as possible. For example, before I became Director of Career Counseling at Trinity College, I had determined that I wanted to work as a counselor in the placement office of a co-ed liberal arts college or university within 150 miles of Boston. When the job opened up, six people called me about it. It took eleven months of looking, but when the job was available, it was a perfect match between job description and my requirements.

DECISION MAKING

Over and over again, when interviewing the men who changed careers, I heard the comment, "The hardest part of my career change was deciding to do it. The rest was easy." Working with people who are considering changing careers, I have found that it is relatively easy, given the time and motivation, for most people to assess their skills, knowledge, and values. Where they get stuck is on the actual decision making. If that's the spot you are in, it might help to spend some time analyzing your decision-making habits. You can do this by looking at how you have made important decisions in the past.

First of all, you must firmly believe that you do have

control over your life and its direction. Of course, we all recognize that much of what happens to us in life occurs by chance—the family into which we were born, the town we grew up in, our financial status, the educational opportunities we were given, the people we happened to meet. However, in everyone's life there are opportunities to do something with the raw material of experience that is thrust our way. We can shape it to meet our goals.

It is important at this stage of your life to look back at those past decisions. If the process you used is not what it should have been, this is an opportunity to change it. Looking at your choice of education, spouse, jobs, home, you may be surprised to find that you actually made very few decisions, that many things happened to you through inaction or default.

You may discover that many of your decisions were based on improper or insufficient information; you did not make the effort to discover all the facts and options first. Timing may have been off; you made decisions too quickly, only to regret them later, or too slowly, missing out on valuable options. You may find that you were too afraid to take risks that would have led you in desired directions. On the other hand, you may have taken too many risks or risks that were too great, with disastrous results.

List some of the important decisions you have made. Do not focus on the outcome, but think about the process you used to arrive at those decisions. Ask yourself the following questions: Did you take enough time to define the issues clearly and completely? If you didn't ask the right questions, you probably didn't get the right answers. Did you look at all possible alternatives? Did you use the advice and help of friends and family or professionals as fully as you could, still making the final decision completely your own? Did you take reasonable risks, or was your behavior too timid or too daredevil? What about your timing? Did you miss out on opportunities because of procrastination or rush into a decision without taking enough time? Have you been willing to assume the full responsibility for the outcome of your deci-

sions? Have your past decisions truly reflected the values
you wish to live by?

After asking yourself these questions, you may conclude
that you are not pleased with the way you have made deci
sions in the past. You now have a golden opportunity to
change your style and to try to apply some of the things you
have learned to the problem at hand—to your career. You
can modify your behavior so that this decision, at least, will
be right for you.

RESUMES

When you have finally narrowed your focus and determined on a specific career goal or goals, it is time to write
your resume, if the kind of position you are seeking warrants
one. Obviously there are situations, such as starting your
own business, for which a resume is unnecessary. Even in
this case, though, you may want to have a brief summary of
your background to give to potential customers or suppliers.

The most important part of a resume is the job objective.
This should be near the top, immediately following your
name, address, and telephone number. It should be stated
simply, in one sentence. Work and rework the wording of the
objective until you are sure that it expresses exactly what
you are looking for. It should be stated from an employer's
point of view; that is, it should emphasize what you can
offer, not what you want. It should include some idea of the
kind of environment you prefer, such as the type of firm,
size, and location—"a small firm in the Northeast," "a community college in an urban area."

The resume should also list the skills, abilities, and
knowledge in which you excel—"a position building on my
ten years of successful marketing experience and my
thorough knowledge of microprocessors," "a teaching position in a graduate school of business administration utilizing
the knowledge gained in over 20 years of experience in labor
relations, personnel, and training." If possible, it should in-

dicate to prospective employers the kinds of problems you can solve for them.

Sometimes you have more than one definitive job object-ive. Write more than one resume, tailoring the contents to complement the job objective and to illustrate how your past experience qualifies you to fill the position you are seeking. You cannot change the facts of your life, but you can play different aspects up or down to enhance the point you are trying to make and eliminate irrelevant data.

The *chronological resume* is the most common type. In this form, you list your jobs first. In most cases, you begin with a description of your previous job experiences, then add educational background and such optional categories as military service, community activities, honors, publications or patents, and personal information. If you are applying for an academic position or have a specialty for which academic credentials are necessary, you might put educational background before work experiences. Then again, if your work experience is more impressive than your educational background, or if your educational background is not all it should be for the kind of position you desire, keep your work experiences first. You might also want to follow this order if your degree(s) were earned a long time ago.

A *functional resume* is a good idea when you want to emphasize particular skills or abilities. This might be espe-cially true for someone who is trying to change fields and wishes to de-emphasize previous jobs. In this type of re-sume, you would only highlight certain aspects of the work, the skills you want to use in your new career.

A resume is written in a concise style without the use of the personal pronoun. The wording should always be posi-tive. Point up all your concrete accomplishments and omit negatives and excuses. Describe responsibilities and ac-complishments for each job you list. But keep your resume as brief as possible. Even if you've had many jobs or many years of experience, your resume should not cover more than two or three single-spaced typewritten pages. Form and spacing are very important, and judicious use should be made of blank space to make the resume easy to read.

Many books give instructions on and examples of resume writing. One that I find particularly helpful is J. I. Biegeleisen's *Job Resumes*. A good example of a chronological versus functional resume can be found in Richard K. Irish's *Go Hire Yourself an Employer*. Other helpful guides are Richard Lathrop's *Who's Hiring Who?* and Burdette E. Bostwick's *Resume Writing: A Comprehensive How-to-Do-It Guide*.

The final step is to locate the person or organization that has the position you want. Again, you will need to do the kind of research you did before, when you were narrowing your goal. You must talk to as many people as possible who know about your field. Spend time in your local library researching the firms or organizations that have your kind of job. Consult the reference librarian for suggestions. Begin with such reference works as Standard & Poor's, Dun and Bradstreet, Chamber of Commerce directories, state industrial guides, directories of educational institutions, and United Fund directories of where to find helping agencies, depending on your field.

Having made a list of possible organizations, do some detective work to find out the names of the people in those organizations who would be in a position to hire you. One very easy way is to call up the firm and ask the switchboard operator for the name of the director of the computer center, the head of marketing, or whomever you would want to contact. Or go to the office and read the directory of names in the lobby or ask the receptionist for the names you want.

You will then want to arrange interviews with those people to persuade them to hire you. Several of the books listed above give helpful suggestions on interviewing techniques. In addition, read B. Greco's *How to Get the Job That's Right for You*, R. J. Jameson's *The Professional Job Changing System*, and Burdette E. Bostwick's *Finding the Job You've Always Wanted*. If you are nervous, practice role playing. Conduct an interview with a friend or spouse. In my class, students do practice interviews that are videotaped and then rerun for critiques.

If your goal is to go into business for yourself, you still need to do the same kind of detective work. Several men in the study started with the Small Business Administration, which gives helpful, if rather elementary and general, information. Check with trade or professional organizations in your field; their names and addresses are listed in the *Encyclopedia of Associations,* which is available in most public libraries. You may also be lucky enough to find a course on how to start your own business at a local community college or business school. A helpful book is Gardiner G. Greene's *How to Start and Manage Your Own Business.*

Jack, one of the men in the study, went through this stage of the process very effectively. He was a successful advertising executive in New York City, tired of commuting and yearning for a job in a rural area that would give him more time with his young family. His wife was an artistic type of person and an excellent cook. They decided—as so many other people have, but only in their dreams—that what they really wanted to do was to run a small country inn.

Jack and his wife spent the better part of a year doing their research. Whenever they could get away, they spent a day or two at a different inn in New England and upstate New York. They tried to go at times that weren't too busy, so that they could spend several hours talking to the managers of the inns about the pitfalls and problems. They also arranged to meet the author of *Country Inns and Back Roads,* who was thoroughly discouraging.

However, when an opportunity to buy into an existing inn came along, they were well prepared to make an educated decision. They sold their house in Westchester and used the proceeds for a downpayment on the inn. When Jack was interviewed, the couple had been in business for several years, had gotten over the early start-up problems, and were beginning to show a small profit.

Whether you are planning to open your own business or are looking for a position with an established organization, you must do a thorough job of research if you want to find the job that is right for you.

WHAT ABOUT HELP?

It is entirely possible to change your career on your own; most of the men we studied did. But many people find they need professional help along the way. It can be very useful to get needed ego support, access to information, an objective analysis of your strengths and weaknesses, and assistance in developing strategies. The process of deciding to change careers and then preparing for the change is one that will make even the most self-confident person begin to question himself, his competence, and his sanity.

You develop a career identity over a period of many years. It becomes almost part of you, and discarding it in favor of a new and unfamiliar role is the psychological equivalent of cutting off an arm and growing a new one. Being assured by a professional person that you aren't crazy and that your goals are sensible and reachable is very helpful. Being in a group with other people thinking of changing careers can also be very useful. These other people all seem to be sensible, rational people, yet they are going through the same agonies as you.

Since most career changers know a great deal about their old career fields, but not too much about the ones they're going into, professional help or group experience can be invaluable, as is the opportunity to sound out one's strategies with someone who has had the experience in differentiating between what will work and what won't. Last, a structured program forces you to do helpful exercises you probably wouldn't have done on your own, unless you are a very well-disciplined person.

In general, I feel strongly that psychotherapy is not what a career changer needs. If your problems encompass more than the career issue or if you need personal adjustment counseling, that is another matter altogether, and should be dealt with separately. The process of changing careers and readjusting one's self-concept is threatening enough without analyzing and changing one's psyche at the same time. Also, most psychotherapists are not trained for career counseling.

They know very little about the world of work, and will generally distract from the task at hand.

Psychotherapy deals with changing you and the way you behave in relation to other people. If you want to change careers, you're looking to change your environment—your workplace, not you. The process should take you as you are, emphasizing your strengths and minimizing your weaknesses. It should help you find an environment that is the best fit for who you are and what you have to offer. What happens in psychotherapy is quite different. On the other hand, of course, a good career counselor should have enough professional training to be able to recognize an individual whose problems are primarily emotional and to refer that person to appropriate help.

CASE HISTORY

Reverend Ralph Schmidt is a 61-year-old Lutheran minister who came to see me for counseling. He has tired of his pastoral duties and would like to retire early next year. In good physical health, he would like to pursue a second career. Although Reverend Schmidt is older than the other career changers I've discussed, the process he followed is exactly the same one a career changer of any age might follow.

First, I asked him to write an autobiography. A copy, in outline form, follows. You will note that in our counseling session Reverend Schmidt and I went through the outline and underlined words representing the themes and patterns that seemed to emerge from his life: travel, languages, leader, music, printing, writing, radio, preaching, teaching, planning, raising money. He also made a list of his accomplishments, some of which are listed below.

During the course of our interview, some additional facts emerged. Reverend Schmidt's wife is a social worker, and they have often worked together effectively as a team; they would like to continue to do this. Although he was effective in the past as a fund raiser, he has lost his taste for this activity.

After going over the autobiography and list of achievements with me, Reverend Schmidt decided to consider and look into the following potential careers:

1. Teaching conversational German, music appreciation, or religious subjects in an adult education program.
2. Leading tour groups and planning itineraries—for example, to the Holy Land or places in Europe that are significant in terms of religious history, or throughout the United States, where he has traveled extensively.
3. Working with his wife to conduct preretirement training. The two of them would be free to travel to other cities. He would do the planning and lecturing, and she would carry out the counseling aspects.

Reverend Schmidt wrote both a chronological resume and a functional one. As you can see, the chronological resume highlights his many years of experience as a clergyman. But being a member of the clergy is not especially relevant for any of his proposed careers. In the functional resume, he was able to extract from his past experience the skills, abilities, and achievements that relate directly to the career he would like to establish. With his functional resume in hand, he is interviewing a number of people and organizations who are likely to need the services of a preretirement trainer.

Autobiography

Main memories from late grade school and high school years in Milwaukee. During high school summers traveled much with parents—including lake vacations, especially *travel* in West (early 1930s)—kept diary (travelogue)

At prep. school in Chicago—*liked languages*—good at this
Minor sports activities—instead, much walking
Considered self a *leader* (not always acknowledged by profs, but peers)
Main activities: glee club (president); school paper (editor, final year)

Summer of 1936: *traveled* with brother, by train, to Mexico (with tour group)
Seminary: interest in choir *music* kept me going (three different choirs)

1937: Summer work: gas station—drove panel truck to make deliveries, erect highway signs (unsupervised labor, simply took order and route sheet, and then on my own)

1937–1938: Seminary: broadened friendships horizons
Interest in printing develops (as assistant seminary mimeographer)
Typed class notes; mimeo work, collating, etc.
Choir *music* still chief interest—also social contacts

1938: Summer: ten-week tour of Europe with brother (by ship with tour group)
Extra *travel*—began work on "roots" which brother carried on

1938–1939: Vicarage (internship) in Pittsburgh, Pa.
Unhappy with placement—not enough direction
Served pretty much as flunkie—wasted time—not good learning experience

Father became sick in spring of 1939—meaningful visit to him in Denver (*By train—thrill!*)—much talk with him
Felt internship a dud—except for social experience
Bitterness over people, city, work—depression years
Chief enjoyments: (1) *preaching*; (2) *teaching adults*; (3) *planning events*
Early during vicarage the feeling developed as to inadequacy for this calling; but realized what was expected of me by parents et al.
In spite of disappointments, work generally above average
Now recognize that feeling of inadequacy compensated for by "aloofness," proud bearing, etc.

1939–1940: Senior yr. at seminary: minimal studying yet above average grades
Very active in choir *music* and social life
Much time spent as *mimeographer* (now "head mimeographer")
Leadership position in general slipped—except among close friends
May 1940 (two weeks before graduation): father died—and just prior to that broke up with girl friend
Very bitter—practically agnostic
Took finals privately after funeral—little study, passed honorably
Few positions for new pastors available: in our class of 120, only one received a position—the rest of us simply went home

Immediately after graduation (day after) went on choir *tour* thru
   Midwest, West, and along coast of California from Long Beach to
   Seattle
Not officially a *leader*, but in time took lead in various chores:
   writing diary, etc.—later *editing* this

Summer of 1940: returned home to pack father's books, clean desk
   and office
Completed father's church records—found all kinds of father's
   notes
In August contacted for temporary teaching position in Minneapolis

Fall of 1940: started *teaching* at small college, as assistant professor
Taught high school subjects: algebra, geometry, ancient history
   (frustrating subjects after nine years of theology)
Enjoyed teaching—worked hard for classes—liked by students
   (young and old)
Because for first two months I was only a few pages ahead of stu-
   dents in textbooks, *real challenge*—very enjoyable
After "getting ahead" enough for classes, much reading (too much
   fiction)
Wasted time—could have gone to school—but no inclination
Then assigned *management* of college store
(This raised my salary from $40/mo to $60/mo)
Worked with student manager: orders, schedules, etc.
Good contacts with students, especially older ones
Not much social life in first year—
Worked hard for classes—*liked teaching*—accepted and approved

Summer of 1941: left right after close of school to go on fishing
   vacation with oldest brother—highlight in memory
Returned home to Milwaukee to live with mother
Worked: printing company—10 weeks, 7 days/week
No brains required—plain labor—in 4 weeks worked self into easier
   position—much overtime: to make money
No social life—lonely but covered with hard work
Some preaching in Milwaukee—money the chief motive

Fall of 1941: return to Minneapolis: happy year—good classes
Classes did not require as much preparation—religion course
   added
Wasted much time—social life began with vengeance

After Xmas began going with future wife—many dates (4–5 per week) but no definite commitment

April 1942: "call" to small town in Illinois—visited—planned to begin in June

To (first parish) **June 1942:**
Soon recognized inadequacy of training (or my inattention) for routines of daily work—hit-miss experimentation—enjoyed
Parish split before I came there—made no special effort to bind up
Seemed to heal itself as I did routine, positive work
Did not do much official calling (didn't know how)
(Never did enjoy visiting members purely for contacts)
(Evangelism calls—"doorbell pushing" not strong suit)
Chief work: *sermons, service, and project planning—teaching adults* (At first teaching children enjoyable—later frustrating)

Became engaged **June 1942;** married **February 1943**
Honeymoon to West Va.—*enjoyed planning,* surprising wife
Rest of years 1st parish; 3 children, help with housework, garden, etc.
Worked at *preaching, planning* (cf. Xmas, VJ Day, VE Day, etc.)
Good results—Good responses
Brought *financial position* of *congregation* to leadership in district
Brought congregation to decision to build new church—*raised money* for this
In general: see now that I wasted time in busy work—enjoyed *printing*
Much *planning for vacations*
Accepted call to Chicago September 1947—happy to move there
Much work in neglected parish: (3 funerals before even installed)
Enjoyed work (now almost routine) under pressure: sick, *preaching, teaching*—good response to work
Remodeling program instigated and promoted: successful—new organ
Very *good results with financial campaigns* for home and church-at-large
New parsonage purchased—enjoyed pleasant new home
Active as *adviser to* outside groups. of church people
Lead *in campaign for new building*
Good social life here with special friends—good vacations

May 1954: to California—*thrilled at prospect of moving West*
Gained *reputation as preacher*—also on *radio*

Adult classes successful (no work gathering people)

Financial program again necessary—*good success*

Real and devastating (personal) problems developed with Sunday school

Enjoyed heavy pressure of work, routine and special (instigated by me)

Accepted in church-at-large as *leader:* on high school board; district board director

Had sympathy of leaders and peers in district for problems at church

Good friends—social group

Enjoyed mountain *travel*—never enough

Led preaching missions

Preaching and teaching—plus *training lay leaders*

Purchased trailer—highlight: *trip* in 1969 to Midwest (extensive)

1960 to Kansas: high spot of ministry

Mainly management type of people

Pressures very great in every field—kept high level—successful

Preaching—good reputation

Too much counseling—soon learned to refer

Financial—raised lots of money—enjoyed this phase of work

Worked 14–15 hr/day, 6½ days/week—practically every evening

Purchased home—first love

Acre and home a constant challenge—met with love

Good social life—friends

Prized limited time for family life—family weddings, social gatherings

Very active in church-at-large:

Radio board, district board director, social service groups

Enjoyed outside contacts, with minimal work, as diversion from church

Excellent *music* program in church—promoted and got new pipe organ

Planned many fine programs, celebrations, processions, banners, etc.

Not many routine "house calls"—legitimate excuse for my not liking them

Kept "rednecks" and "superconservatives" under control —but difficult

Had good staff help—2 excellent assistants for staff of 23

Learned "group" work—*delegating*

Supervised seminary "field workers" in practical *parish training*
Some wonderful *vacations:* Europe (1967); eastern U.S. (1965);
  et al.
But pressure of work finally affecting me physically
Sought way out—to smaller parish, less responsibility

1970 to Massachusetts:
May have been *"wanderlust,"* but legitimately began recognizing
  physical limitations
Best of intentions to serve as "pastor"
With lot of successful experience
Did not anticipate New England mindset
Beautiful parsonage—and upkeep—meaningful from start
Relished abundance of free evenings
Hi-fi *music,* recordings, etc.
Worked hard on preaching, programs, etc.—but people indifferent
Combination of: former pastor, times, type of people—very difficult
After 3 yrs, chance to leave for another church
Good leadership surfaced—became friends—change in attitude
Preaching still enjoyable (feel it's better than ever)
But miss reaction, comments—programs accepted indifferently
Now reached point where not working very hard—"get by"
Visit sick, teach, main duties—few meetings as possible
Accepted in area as *leader*
Chairman of clergy association
In district: *vice-president* until resigned in church controversy
Respected—also because of *planning* social gatherings
Plus increasing influence of wife in community, etc.
When national church problems developed some dissent in local
  church but negatives gradually leaving—closer unity developing
Feel soon it's time for younger man to step in with enthusiasm

ACCOMPLISHMENTS

1. Held first congregation together during war—planned special
   events and collections of thanksgiving, culminating in decision
   to build new church.
2. Planned extensive remodeling of church, plus new organ, with
   sound financial support. Included extensive property changes;
   eliminated old parsonage and purchased new.
3. Organized lay group to stage citywide rally for all churches.
4. Conducted extensive financial campaign with fund raiser for

liquidating debt on new church. Planned extensive property changes, and upgraded music program.

5. Planned and led two citywide celebrations, which included 95 congregations. This included a formal youth service; mass choir and audience music festival; mass celebration with drama music, worship, symphony orchestra, and a capella choir.

6. Supervised seminary field work students; especially proud of group processes in discussion.

7. Managed and MC'd a religious radio program weekly for several years. Had good radio voice. Wrote and directed several religious TV productions.

8. Throughout career enjoyed and was good at teaching adults both religious and secular subjects.

RESUME—CHRONOLOGICAL

RALPH P. SCHMIDT   Concord Lutheran Church
127 Fourth Street   69 Third Street
Concord, MA 01742   Concord, MA 01742
Phone: 617-742-6951   Phone: 617-742-5768

Career Objective: Teaching and consulting for preretirement planning

Education: Martin Luther College, Alton, Illinois, B.A., 1936
Lutheran Theological Seminary, Alton, Illinois, M.T.S., 1939

Special Training:
SMART (Senior Member and Retiree Training), one-week intensive course, 1977, Aid Association for Lutherans
Transactional Analysis (teaching), series of courses, 1971–1973 Lutheran Service Association of New England
Pastoral Conferences–semiannually, 1940 to date—seminars and training in parish leadership and pastoral counseling
Fund raising—Wells, Inc., Church Fund Raisers, 3-day seminar, 1969

Present Employment:
1970 to date
Parish pastor, Concord Lutheran Church, Concord, Massachusetts
500 members
Supervise church secretary and volunteer help

Parish activities include: preaching, teaching, visiting (sick and others), general administration

Previous Employment:

1960–1970

Head pastor, Bethlehem Lutheran Church, Kansas City, Kansas
2,200 members—Parochial School (K–8)—Budget $284,000/yr.
Supervised staff of 23, including pastoral assistants, school-teachers, secretaries, custodians, cooks, bus drivers
Supervised "seminary field workers" from Lutheran Theological Seminary
Activities included: general administration, most preaching, most teaching of adults, sick visits

1955–1960

Head pastor, Concordia Lutheran Church, San Francisco, California
1,900 members, Parochial School (K–8)
Supervised staff of 18, including pastoral assistant, pastoral intern, schoolteachers, secretaries
General pastoral activities: administration, preaching

1947–1955

Pastor, Trinity Lutheran Church, Chicago, Illinois
1,000 members—Parochial School (K–8)
Staff of 9, including 5 teachers
General pastoral activities
Directed renovation program, including new pipe organ

1942–1947

Pastor, St. Paul Lutheran Church, Milwaukee, Wisconsin
400 members
No staff—directed all-volunteer help
All pastoral duties

1940–1942

Assistant professor at Martin Luther College, Alton, Illinois
Subjects: History, Mathematics, Religion
Managed college store

Additional Experiences

Directed and MC'd weekly religious radio program on WXJR, Chicago, Illinois, 1952–1955
Directed, wrote, and participated in special religious TV productions, WXJR-TV, Chicago, Illinois, 1950–1955
Taught many adult classes, religious and secular subjects
Transactional Analysis (enrichment groups within the church)

Bethel Bible Class Series

Preretirement Training

Church fund raising (for volunteer solicitors)

Planned and supervised mass festivals

Chicago: Lutheran Hour Rally for whole city

San Francisco: Citywide (100 churches) festivals, including mass choirs, San Francisco Symphony, etc.

Led tour group through "Luther Land" of East Germany (1967)

Spoke on historical significance

Used skill in German language

Offices Held

Member, Board of Directors, California District, Lutheran Church–Missouri Synod, 1956–1960

Member, Board of Directors, Kansas District, Lutheran Church–Missouri Synod, 1963–1970

Member, Board of Directors, New England District, Lutheran Church–Missouri Synod, 1971–1977

Vice-president, New England District, Lutheran Church–Missouri Synod, 1972–1977

Board of Directors, Lutheran High School Association, San Francisco, California, 1955–1960

Board of Directors, Lutheran High School Association, Kansas City, Kansas, 1962–1970

Board of Directors, Radio Station WJBZ, Kansas City, Kansas, 1964–1970

Board of Directors, Lutheran Service Association of New England, 1972–

Chairman, Clergy Association of Concord, Massachusetts, 1977

Personal

Married to the former Viola Weingarten; four children, six grandchildren

Wife is a social worker at Concord General Hospital

Date of birth: September 16, 1916

RESUME—FUNCTIONAL

RALPH P. SCHMIDT
127 Fourth Street
Concord, MA 01742
Phone: 617-742-6951

Concord Lutheran Church
69 Third Street
Concord, MA 01742
Phone: 617-742-5768

Career Objective: Teaching and consulting for preretirement planning.

Education: Martin Luther College, Alton, Illinois, B.A., 1936
Lutheran Theological Seminary, Alton, Illinois, M.T.S., 1939

Special Training:
SMART (Senior Member and Retiree Training), one-week intensive course, 1977, Aid Association for Lutherans
Transactional Analysis (teaching), series of courses, 1971–1973 Lutheran Service Association of New England
Pastoral conferences—semiannually, 1940 to date—seminars and training in parish leadership and pastoral counseling
Fund raising—Wells, Inc., Church Fund Raisers, 3-day seminar, 1969

Skills:
PUBLIC SPEAKING: 37 years of preaching to small and large groups while pastor of the following churches, having memberships of 400 to 2,200:
Concord Lutheran Church, Concord, Massachusetts (1970 to date)
Bethlehem Lutheran Church, Kansas City, Kansas (1960–1970)
Concordia Lutheran Church, San Francisco, California (1955–1960)
Trinity Lutheran Church, Chicago, Illinois (1947–1955)
St. Paul Lutheran Church, Milwaukee, Wisconsin (1942–1947)
Directed and MC'd weekly religious radio program on WXJR, Chicago, Illinois, 1952–1955

TEACHING: on elementary, high school, college, and adult levels
Junior high school classes from 1947–1970 while responsible for directing parochial schools in Chicago, San Francisco, and Kansas City
Adult groups (classes of 3–150)
SMART—preretirement training classes at the Concord Lutheran Church (taught jointly with my wife, Viola Schmidt, M.S.W.)
Transactional Analysis personal enrichment classes (also taught jointly with my wife)—five classes, 1974–1977
Supervised "seminary field workers" from Lutheran Theological Seminary and conducted group discussions, 1965–1970
Trained parochial-school teachers in variety of subjects.

Bible class discussions and formal religious teaching

Assistant professor at Martin Luther College, Alton, Illinois, 1940–1942

Taught history, mathematics, and religion

COUNSELING: routine pastoral counseling and group discussions

During 37 years as a pastor, learned effective referral techniques, incorporated new methods learned in training groups

PROGRAM PLANNING:

Planned extensive remodeling of Chicago church, including new organ, with sound financial support. Included extensive property changes.

In San Francisco, planned and led two citywide celebrations which included 95 congregations. Consisted of a formal youth service, mass choir and audience music festival; mass celebration with drama, music, worship, symphony orchestra, and a capella choir

Directed, wrote, and participated in special religious TV productions, WXJR-TV, Chicago, Illinois, 1950–1955

Held many offices in regional and local religious associations

Special Knowledge:

Music—good acquaintance with classics, especially J.S. Bach and sacred choral music

Language—conversational German

Travel—widely traveled in United States and Europe, especially able in German and Reformation history

Led tour group through "Luther Land" of East Germany (1967)

Personal:

Married to the former Viola Weingarten; four children, six grandchildren

Wife is a social worker at Concord General Hospital

Date of birth: September 16, 1916

8

Where to Go
for Help

WHAT kind of help should you look for? The number of agencies and organizations offering help to career changers has grown tremendously in the last decade or two, and the techniques they use have improved considerably. However, as in any field that is as much an art as a science, there are charlatans and incompetents. New agencies start up, then are gone in a year or two. In addition, the assistance you find that is just what you need may be entirely inappropriate for your next-door neighbor, who also wants to change careers. Don't be afraid to be a comparison shopper, and ask specifically what the program has to offer. Try to be as exact as possible in describing your needs. Steer clear of any organization that promises to give you the right job and look for one that will help you find the career you want.

There are no comprehensive listings or evaluations of services available. The *Directory of Counseling Services*, published by the American Personnel and Guidance Association, is available in most libraries, but it is not by any means a comprehensive listing of resources, although it provides a reliable beginning list of accredited agencies. Richard Bolles' *What Color Is Your Parachute?* contains a listing of

counseling services by states without evaluation of quality
or type of service, and, again, it is not complete.

The need for comprehensive surveys of programs that
assist people to prepare for possible career change has begun
to receive national attention. Two federally funded projects
are being conducted (1977–1978) to gather information on
programs available, and, more important, to evaluate their
effectiveness. One of the projects, conducted by the Technical Education Research Centers in Cambridge, Massachusetts, is surveying 1,500 postsecondary educational institutions and 800 manufacturing and service corporations
in the United States to develop an overview of career-change
programs currently operated by employers and educational
institutions. It will then select a representative sample of
these programs for in-depth study and comparison. The
other project, at the University of California, Berkeley,[1] is
evaluating the effectiveness of a number of multi-
institutional programs offered by institutions of higher education, particularly for adults concerned with career change
or reentry into the labor market. These include both courses
and counseling.

Given the lack of any comprehensive guide, how should
you go about finding help? If you are lucky, you may be able
to receive assistance from the personnel division of your
present employer. Check there to begin with; if the personnel officer doesn't provide such services, he or she may well
know of community agencies to which you can be referred.

More and more colleges and universities are offering
career and educational counseling services as well as
courses, as was discussed in Chapter 5. Your next step
should be to inquire at a nearby college. The yellow pages of
your telephone directory will also list services, under the

---

[1] James G. Paltridge and Mary C. Regan, *Mid-Career Change: An
Evaluative Study of Diverse Models of Multi-Institutional Programs of Con-
tinuing Education for Persons Seeking Mid-Career Employment Change* (
University of California, Berkeley, study funded by the Special Community
Service and Continuing Education Project, Bureau of Post-Secondary Edu-
cation, U.S. Office of Education, 1976–1978).

eading of "Vocational and Career Guidance." In all cases,
owever, be a comparison shopper and investigate carefully
efore investing in any services. Some of the organizations
isted in the phone book may be primarily employment
gencies, and therefore not suitable for the career changer
who doesn't know what he wants and needs help in sorting
ut his priorities. Employment agencies work primarily in
ehalf of the employer, to fill vacancies of existing jobs.
areer consulting services, on the other hand, view the job
eeker as the client. They aim to make the best use of his
alents by helping to determine how he can link his career
eeds with the realities of the job market.

If you are a college graduate and live near that institu-
on, make use of the services of the college career counsel-
ig and placement office. Such services are ordinarily free to
lumni. The offices usually have an extensive library of
naterials relating to jobs as well as directories of employers
nd other useful resources. You will be able to obtain a copy
f *The College Placement Annual,* a directory listing a large
umber of employers in a broad range of fields who hire
ollege graduates. This is updated annually and contains
ames, addresses, and brief descriptions of the firms.

Although the jobs that placement offices have are ordi-
arily geared for entry-level college graduates, the coun-
elors usually have some knowledge of kinds of oppor-
unities available. If you are applying for a position in a field,
uch as education, that requires letters of recommendation,
ie counselors can help you compile a dossier of such let-
rs, and see that they are sent out to prospective employers.

The remainder of this chapter will be devoted to a de-
cription of the various kinds of help potential career chang-
s can find. The specific agencies that were contacted were
ostly in the Northeast, and the list is by no means exhaus-
ve. However, it should give you a fairly good idea of the
nds of possibilities available. Similar agencies should be
vailable to you if you live in or near a large population
enter.

COUNSELING HELP OFFERED BY BUSINESS
AND INDUSTRY

A number of large companies have developed interna
career-planning programs for their employees. Walter L
Storey, manager of Career Planning and Organization De
velopment for the General Electric Company, expresses hi
company's reasons for setting up such a program:

1) For individuals, to stimulate and guide them to grow within thei
interest and abilities while contributing to the needs and aims c
the organization; and 2) for the employing organization, t
humanize its attempts to deal with the needs of its members withi
operating realities in order to maintain its own survival an
growth.

General Electric has found that the benefits of it
career-planning program have included improved fitting c
jobs to people, higher quality of data for manpower reviews
development of a framework for affirmative action, and bet
ter allocation of funds for employee education. A forma
program helps managers to conduct career-related discus
sions with their employees by providing a structured vehicl
for doing so.

Few studies have been conducted to determine the "bot
tom line" effect of internal career-planning programs, bu
most companies that have ongoing programs seem to fee
that the contribution to employee morale and the possibilit
for removing unhappy and unproductive employees fror
jobs they don't like and transferring them to positions tha
will suit them better are worth the cost. Many companie:
particularly those employing large numbers of engineers c
other professionals with highly technical training, are ver
much concerned with the problem of professional obsoles
cence and stagnation. They see career planning an
continuing-education programs as a good investment t
keep their employees growing and learning.

Crocker National Bank in San Francisco, which has a one-to-one career-counseling program that has helped over 200 employees at all levels, has been able to document actual financial savings as a result of its program. Karen Kobrosky, staff planning officer, reports reduced employee turnover, improved employee attitude and performance, and increased employee participation in training programs and further education as a result of career counseling. Crocker is about to institute a group program as well.

The General Electric program consists of a family of four self-study workbooks, the first two for use by the individual, and the third and fourth by the individual's manager and the employee relations or training and development people. The workbooks include exercises the individual does on his own to help him to assess his career and his skills and interests and to plan for next steps. The concepts and nomenclature in the workbooks are appropriate for a variety of businesses.[2]

The Lawrence Livermore Laboratory, one of three research and development laboratories of the University of California, sponsors a career planning program for its employees, many of whom are in highly technical professions. The program consists of group workshops of 18 employees, open to any worker who is interested. The workshops are conducted on company time and consist of exercises in self-assessment and career assessment and exploration of interests, values, and goals. Each participant ends up with a personal career and life-strategy plan. The workshops seem to stimulate employee interest in further learning. In general the laboratory is pleased with the results of the program.[3]

For many years, the Polaroid Corporation has had an internal program of career counseling. It was one of the pioneers, over 20 years ago, in the concept of open job post-

[2] The workbooks may be purchased from General Electric's Management Development Institute. Write to Career Dimensions, General Electric Company (Crotonville), P.O. Box 368, Croton-on-Hudson, New York 10520.

[3] *Bulletin* (Syracuse, New York: National Center for Educational Brokering, November 1976), p. 2.

ing, in which all job vacancies are advertised within the company before being advertised outside. Employees are encouraged to apply, even for positions in totally different areas of the firm. If they are unsuccessful in obtaining the job for which they applied, opportunities are made available for counseling and training so that the worker can prepare for the next similar opening, if that is his or her goal. Along with open job posting, Polaroid developed a group counseling workshop in which employees participate in exercises designed to help them clarify their skills, interests, values, and goals and come up with a career plan. Groups consist of hourly employees in addition to managers and professionals.

Another company offering programs of life planning and career development is the London Life Insurance Company in Canada; close to half their 1,500 home-office employees have participated in the program. The program is conducted during regular office hours in two stages. It is a combination of a half-day seminar for life planning and, at a later date, a one-day seminar for career development; they are scheduled periodically throughout the year. The group is limited to 25 employees at a time. The company has an open job-posting system, and it believes that the career development program will help employees to make more realistic plans concerning their future career growth.

The Connecticut General Life Insurance Company has developed a more comprehensive approach to career development, one that is part of the whole scheme of the management of its human resources. It consists of annual performance and development appraisals with an employee sign-off, supported by open job postings for positions up to the $20,000 level; "people brokering" by a personnel network for jobs beyond that level; job and career counseling available to individuals; therapeutic counseling for employees with emotional problems; and rehabilitation counseling for people with physical handicaps. The development appraisal focuses on the person's career future and provides the opportunity for him or her to develop a career plan and strategies for implementation. Corporate and division personnel staff are available for consultation by those who want to move from one area of the company to another.

What a Connecticut General employee can expect is illustrated by the story of one man who had been employed for about five years in its mortgage and real estate department. Peter, a graduate of Annapolis with an M.B.A. from Columbia, had done well in his department, but was getting itchy in his job. During the annual development appraisal he expressed his feelings to his boss, saying that he felt very insulated from the mainstream of the rest of the company and would like to move. His feelings were conveyed to the division's personnel director. A phone call was put in to corporate personnel staff, who arranged for Peter to have a chat with personnel people in various divisions. As a result, specific positions were identified, and he interviewed for them.

Peter chose one of the positions he was offered, a managerial job in the property and casualty subsidiary of the company. His new job was totally unrelated to what he had been doing before. Now that he was supervising eight people, he had an opportunity to test his managerial skill. In his former position, he had been working on his own and had no managerial responsibility. Peter's reaction was very positive. He reported that "It was the most exciting experience of my life, and gave me a chance to explore a variety of other options for my career."

At Connecticut General, if appropriate internal help is not enough, professional external counselors are made available at company expense to people who need the additional career counseling. The company permits and encourages not only job changes that are seen as upwardly mobile, but lateral and downward moves as well, if they fit the individual's present needs. Individuals who must or want to leave the company are assisted with counseling and company-paid out-placement services. According to William R. Stanley, director of personnel planning and development, it is not unusual for a person who decides that a

career change outside of the company is in his or her bes
interest to be helped by this process.

The measure of the effectiveness of company-sponsorec
career development programs is the degree to which the\
permit and encourage employees to make career plans o\
their own and follow through on them. Too often, the pro
grams are paternalistic in nature, with the employer de
veloping the employee and encouraging a passive accep
tance of whatever is offered. Some of the programs, too, ar\
tacked on and peripheral to what actually goes on in th\
company. They are good window dressing, but do not actu
ally make much difference in the everyday operation of th\
company. Some programs help identify needs, but without \
process to implement them, they only lead to frustration
However, all the blame cannot be placed on management. I
is often much easier for an employee to sink into passiv\
acceptance of whatever happens than to take responsibilit\
for the control of his career.

NONPROFIT COUNSELING AGENCIES

There is a broad variety of nonprofit counseling agen
cies available, with at least one or two in any major city
Many are attached to colleges or universities and are dis
cussed in Chapter 5. The granddaddy of them all are th\
counseling centers of the YMCA. They are usually staffed b\
accredited psychologists and offer a diagnostic battery o
testing and several interview sessions for a nominal fee. Al
though many are changing and incorporating new tech
niques and group workshops, they mainly tend to rely on th\
traditional model of diagnosis by means of interest and abil
ity tests and interviews to tell you, the client, what occupa
tional choices might be appropriate for you. They will hel\
you in a few sessions to brush up on your resume and giv\
you some suggestions about further training or educatior
and where to go looking for a job. This may be enough fo\

you, or you may not be able to afford more. The Jewish Vocational Service in major cities offers similar services. Both agencies are more appropriate for younger people or those with limited options; they may not be sophisticated enough for the midcareer changer.

For those who cannot afford a large fee, group career workshops are often very helpful. One that has been quite successful is Life Work Planning, developed by Arthur and Marie Kirn.[4] The Kirns have adapted techniques from a variety of sources, including encounter groups, problem solving, and other management tools, to come up with a workbook, which they have published.[5]

The Kirns have trained a wide network of psychologists, educators, and personnel officers (who are listed in the workbook) to be group leaders of Life Work Planning sessions. Their only profit is through sale of the workbooks. The groups are offered across the country whenever a trained leader wants to give one; a schedule of forthcoming sessions is published twice a year. The cost for a 30-hour workshop is less than $100. Sessions can be arranged either as a marathon over a whole weekend or at weekly intervals.

The advantages of Life Work Planning are that the workbook forces an individual to go through exercises that will help him to analyze himself, clarify his goals, and set priorities, and then develop an action plan for getting there. The other members of the group help to provide reinforcement and keep the participant on the track. The main advantage of Life Work Planning is its emphasis on taking personal responsibility for your own life.

One of the drawbacks of Life Work Planning is lack of follow-up. You may end a weekend session fired with enthusiasm to go out and accomplish your goals, but by the time the next weekend arrives, you may already have run out of steam. Life Work Planning is not specifically designed for

[4] RFD 1, Wilton Center, New Hampshire 03086.
[5] Arthur Kirn and Marie Kirn, *Life Work Planning* (New York: McGraw-Hill, 1977).

career planning, but it can be used to deal with any aspect of your life, including your career.

An unusual resource for career counseling is self-help groups. Among these are the Forty Plus organizations for people who find themselves unemployed and the victims of age discrimination. One of these self-help groups was established as a result of the sharp and drastic decline of technical employment among the space-related industries of the Route 128 belt in Massachusetts in the early 1970s. A group of unemployed engineers and other technical workers and those concerned with their plight established the Association for Technical Professionals (ATP) as a self-help and lobbying group.

ATP's nonprofit arm, the ATP Education Fund, is concerned with the social, economic, and political aspects of science and technology. Today, the ATP Education Fund functions in three areas, providing (1) business services, (2) human services, and (3) services relating to technology and society. It has been funded by grants from the Massachusetts Department of Commerce and Development and the Economic Development Administration of the U.S. Department of Commerce.

The activities of ATP are quite varied. Career changers would be interested in the following services: It provides consultation and guidance to major corporations in addressing their layoff problems and technical and business guidance to small businesses. A member of the staff provides individual job counseling to any technical professionals and other nonclerical white-collar workers who want it. ATP has co-sponsored employment workshops in which hundreds of professionals and semiprofessionals who are seeking new work opportunities have developed skills. As a nonprofit agency with minimal fees, its services are, of course, rather basic, but they have been helpful to many, including several of the career changers described in the preceding chapters.

Another program that was started in part as a response to the sharp decline in aerospace jobs in the early 1970s is the only state-supported program we know of in the United

States. This is Career Change, a program of the Employment Security Department of the State of Washington, which was initially supported by a combination of state funding and federal CETA funds, and is now completely supported by state funds totaling over a million dollars. It was the brainchild of its present director, Rev. John L. F. Slee, who faced a career change himself as a result of a heart attack suffered in 1972. Since then, although he is now in his fifties, he has earned three degrees and sparkplugged the Washington program.

Career Change is open to all people who have been unemployed for 30 days or who know that a career change is imperative for health, technological, or economic reasons; that is, if their occupation is in a decline or has an excessive supply of workers or if their skills have been made obsolete by new techniques. The program has no restrictions because of income. It is targeted to help a broad spectrum of clients, including middle-income people who have been stable employees but suddenly need help. It is hoped that the program can be preventative by making people self-reliant and able to handle change, thus helping to keep them from experiencing a severe personal or family crisis.

The program starts with an analysis of the client's personal and family situation, skills, work history, and disabilities. This includes a series of diagnostic tests. The client and counselor then agree on an individual plan of service. Supportive services are provided, and if necessary for income maintenance, temporary jobs are found. Clients make use of self-directed support groups in which eight to ten program participants meet regularly to discuss problems, provide support, and share job contacts. The client learns job search techniques, interviewing, and resume writing. Vocational or academic training is provided as needed. The goal of the program is placement in a new career within nine months. The program is still quite new, so follow-up and evaluation have not been reported as yet.

Each region of the country has counseling services specifically set up for clergy who wish to reassess their calling; most of these are not open to the general public. One that is, however, and that offers a variety of services, is the Mid-Atlantic Career Center, Inc., located in Washington D.C. Church professionals comprise about 50 percent of their clients; the remainder are men and women from all walks of life, most heavily professionals and people from the government and the military, as well as from local businesses and service organizations.

Thirty percent of the clients are women, divided roughly into three groups—housewives entering or reentering the job market, women who are seriously underemployed or misemployed, and highly successful women who are experiencing an unofficial ceiling to their advancement, as seemingly less talented men are promoted past them. Ages range from college into retirement, although the great bulk of adults are in their thirties and forties. Thus midcareer change, with its midlife issues, has become something of a specialty of the Mid-Atlantic Career Center. The staff consists of several counselors, all with academic training, and a number of consulting psychologists and a consulting physician.

Central to its programs, according to Director Barton Lloyd, is the "principle of empowerment" stressed by Richard Bolles in *What Color Is Your Parachute?* and embodied in the old folk adage, "Give me a fish and I will eat today. Teach me to fish and I will eat the rest of my days." Following this principle, its programs take people through a process they can learn and reuse on their own at any time in their lives. For this reason, psychological testing is kept to a minimum, and its findings are reviewed late in the program, after people have had several weeks to reflect on and analyze their own personal experiences. In that context, test findings "come alive" more easily and may be related more readily to the individual's self-understanding.

The Mid-Atlantic Career Center is extremely explicit in outlining what it offers the prospective client. Its Basic Career Consultation Program contains the following components and services: registration, eight hours of basic evalua-

ion and planning, one hour of follow-up counseling, two to
three hours of counselor preparation and a staff case confer-
nce, one optional hour of spouse participation, testing, a
psychologist's interview and assessment, evaluation of med-
cal history by a consulting physician, and a tape cassette of
est findings. In addition, clients are assigned written
homework between sessions. Folders of clients who go
through a career program are kept on file for five years for
follow-up as needed. Fees for this service are on a sliding
cale, based on income, but start at about $700. In addition to
he Basic Career Consultation Program, an eight-session
roup job-finding seminar is offered for $250. A variety of
ormats are offered, depending on the individual's needs.
Group programs are also sponsored; these usually are week-
ong and are scheduled at an overnight retreat.

The advantage of the Mid-Atlantic Career Center's pro-
ram is its comprehensiveness. Not only does it provide a
tructured and guided format for the individual to use to
dentify issues facing him, resources, and personal assets
nd to develop an action plan, but it assists in implementa-
ion of the plan and provides a support system for feedback
uring the job-search phase.

PROFIT-MAKING COUNSELING SERVICES

Although the services offered by profit-making career
ounseling agencies are generally more expensive than
hose available from nonprofit organizations, there are
egitimate reasons for using them. Because they are business
nterprises, they are more likely to have to demonstrate a
ertain degree of success; they depend for their profits on
word-of-mouth referrals and are often sent clients by com-
anies who pay their fees and therefore insist upon results.

The largest and oldest firm in the business is Bernard
Haldane Associates, founded in 1947, after Haldane's suc-
essful experience in counseling returning military officers
nd in helping to set up the placement service of Harvard

Business School. There are now licensed offices in 20 major
cities, and planning is under way for many more, including
an international operation. Haldane counselors do no
necessarily have academic credentials in social service pro
fessions; they come from a variety of backgrounds. Many o
them have changed careers themselves. They undergo a
rigorous two- to three-week orientation program in one o
the four regional training centers, then do counseling under
supervision for six months. There is an elaborate system o
staff monitoring and client feedback, so incompetent coun
selors don't last very long. Success criteria are well defined
and counselors are measured by the number of successfu
cases they have handled.

Since 1947, approximately 100,000 clients have been
seen in Haldane offices. In a recent month, one branch office
saw 49 job campaigns completed and 56 new clients en
rolled. Most of the clients have professional and manage
ment backgrounds. About 20 percent of the clients are
women. They range in age from 25 to 65, but tend to cluster
in their thirties and early forties. Roughly 45 percent of the
clients seek and achieve career changes.

The Haldane program is highly structured and does no
rely heavily upon psychological testing. In the first phase
data are gathered, reviewed, and evaluated during four
counseling sessions and 15 to 20 hours of homework as
signments to identify and document areas of the client's
achievements. Among the tools used are Bernard Haldane's
copyrighted Success Factor Analysis. Each case is discussed
in a staff conference, and the counselor's handling is moni
tored by a team of regional counseling directors, headed by
the national director of client services; if a client is dis
satisfied with a counselor, there is a structured opportunity
to air problems or dissatisfactions.

A career objective is defined and then a resume is pre
pared by the client, with advice and critiques from the coun
selor. One of the key factors of the Haldane approach is the
system of teaching clients to develop a network of contacts
with individuals in the field in which they hope to find a job

The client is encouraged to set up advice- and information-seeking interviews with such people. An all-day "market campaign" seminar provides an opportunity for practicing interviewing, negotiation, and follow-up techniques.

During the job campaign, the client remains in close contact with the counselor and returns for sessions to monitor progress and results. The average job campaign lasts 12 to 13 weeks. Problem-solving workshops, scheduled twice a week, provide support from others in the same situation and exchange of information during the campaign. After a job offer is accepted, a plan for the future is worked out. Clients maintain contact with their counselors as needed over the five-year period covered by their initial agreement assuring continued career-evaluation progress.

The Haldane program is not inexpensive. Fees are based on a sliding scale reflecting both current and projected earnings and start at about $1,000. However, the program is well established, has a proven track record, and is carefully monitored for quality control. It takes the client through a disciplined process, including career follow-up and advancement.

Another long-time operation is Life Management Services, Inc., of McLean, Virginia, founded almost 20 years ago by John C. Crystal who, along with Bernard Haldane, has been one of the prime idea men of the career counseling field. Crystal was an important source for Richard Bolles in formulating his book, *What Color Is Your Parachute?*, and together the two men wrote the workbook, *Where Do I Go From Here With My Life?*, which details the method used by Crystal.

The basic course offered by Life Management Services consists of 10 three and a half hour sessions given over a period of 12 weeks. An optional graduate course of four additional three and a half hour sessions is offered for those who wish to continue. In addition to its office in Virginia, Life Management Services has a branch in Manhasset, New York. Week-long intensive courses are given periodically at resorts in various locations. Specially tailored programs are arranged for government agencies, corporations, and other institutions. Crystal gives frequent lectures and workshops across the country.

Mainstream Associates in New York City was started almost ten years ago by a minister as a counseling center for other clergy who were leaving. Mainstream continues to work with clergy, but has expanded its service. The majority of its clients now are professionals—educators, artists, people in social service, and people with business-oriented backgrounds. Most are college educated and almost half have advanced degrees. The clients tend to be in their thirties; 50 percent are women. They tend to come in because they have found themselves on a professional career track leading nowhere. Mainstream's specialty is helping people such as this, with largely liberal arts backgrounds, to find positions—often in business and industry. Its approach is a humanistic one.

Everyone on the staff of Mainstream has made at least one career change himself or herself. The members of the staff are not therapists and come from a wide variety of backgrounds. The process begins with a written inventory battery offering a broad overview of a client's abilities and interests and some of the personality factors involved in achieving successful career placement. The client then works with a consultant in a series of meetings to define this overview further. Between sessions clients complete homework assignments, including keeping a personal journal and doing exercises aimed at assessing skills and goals.

The process is task and action oriented, and is designed to bring out the best in a person rather than change him. The duration of the process from the outset to job relocation is generally about six months, but Mainstream's contractual agreement is to stay with a client until he is satisfactorily relocated. Fees are variable, according to the amount of work needed by the client, but start at about $1,100.

People Management, Inc., of Simsbury, Connecticut, is a consulting firm with a national clientele of major corporations in such areas as space, chemicals, insurance, gas, and petroleum. Founded 17 years ago, it is run by two men,

Arthur Miller, Jr., and James Cunningham, both of whom have had extensive experience in business management in a variety of industries. They met when they both worked for the Haldane organization, Cunningham as vice-president.

The firm specializes in internal evaluation of employees, and helps companies by advising them how best to use their human resources. It also does out-placement and executive search and has branched out to do some counseling of hard-core unemployed, college students, and housewives returning to the work world. A few clients come in on their own through word-of-mouth referral, and a one-day group Career Guidance Workshop is held once a month at a cost of $50, but the great majority of its individual clients are referred by their employers, who pay their fee. People Management spends approximately 25 hours in analyzing each client's background and 15 to 22 hours assisting him or her with the job search.

Central to the work of People Management is the concept of its System for Identifying Motivated Abilities (which has many parallels to Bernard Haldane's System to Identify Motivated Skills). The client is asked to describe achievements he recalls enjoying and doing well in detail. Then a tape-recorded interview is conducted in which the client is asked to describe these experiences in detail again.

According to People Management, these achievements, when analyzed, reveal a consistent, recurring pattern of strengths and motivations, which is unchanging throughout a person's life. It finds that people will always try to perform work in accordance with their motivational pattern—for example, an innovator will change things, an overcomer will find or make things to overcome, a doer will continue to take care of the details, regardless of what the job description is or what the boss wants or what is needed in that situation.

As a result, for career success, a person must be placed in a job that requires the kind of motivational pattern he has. People Management estimates that only one out of every three people is really well suited for his job. Therefore, it tries to identify people's motivational patterns and help them to look for the right jobs to fulfill them. When it works for employers, it helps them to analyze job requirements and to find the person whose pattern best fits the needs of the job. Approximately 40 percent of the clients it sees end up by making a substantial career change.

Executive Progress, Inc., of New York City works very closely with companies and does a great deal of "out-counseling"; almost a third of its fees are paid by client companies. Its clients are primarily businessmen, professionals of all types, although it is getting an increasing number of educators and clergy; a quarter of its clients are women. A full-time psychologist who administers a battery of tests, including projective tests, is on the staff.

A client meets for several hours with the psychologist. The purpose is to help the client retrace and isolate his or her positive and negative life influences. In this way, and with counseling and guidance, the person is able to select and achieve the career pattern that is really his own choice.

The client is then referred to the business consultant, who helps him to plan a personal marketing strategy. A three-year follow-up guarantee is established; clients may come back for remarketing if jobs don't work out, unless they have taken a position against the recommendations of the counselor. This is a relatively rare occurrence. The process usually takes two to five months, depending on the individual's capacity for work and commitment. Unemployed people usually relocate faster. Older people and those in a higher income bracket take longer. Thirty to 40 percent of its clients change careers. The fees are about $500 for evaluation and assessment; $1,000 plus for the job campaign phase.

EPI does not dictate what a client should do. The EPI staff acts only as professional facilitators, helping clients to use the life experiences, preferences, and aptitudes they already possess to attain their goals. One of the gratifying results of the program is the increased self-awareness and confidence developed by the client. In fact, many clients state that this is the most valuable asset of the program.

WHICH TO CHOOSE?

Among college placement offices and career-change courses or educational brokers, YMCA and Jewish Vocational Service, company-sponsored programs, Life Work Planning, and other group workshops, and individual counseling through private agencies, there are many alternatives for a potential career changer to choose from. I repeat my warning from the beginning of the chapter. Be a wise consumer and do some comparison shopping to find out which service is best for you before you commit your time and money to any one program.

What service do you actually need? Help in sorting out what it is you would like to do? Information about educational programs that will help you reach your goal? Help in planning a job-hunting campaign? Help in sorting out the various aspects of your life to integrate career and family or leisure pursuits better? Some agencies will be more helpful in meeting certain needs than others. You must decide if the agency you are investigating has the capacity to help you to solve your particular problem.

There are distinctions between programs with regard to their basic philosophies and points of view. Does it seem as if they will test you and find out about your background, make a diagnosis as to your best course of action, then write a resume for you and play your job campaign? Is this what you really want? If so, go ahead and buy into such a program. My own feeling, however, is that you would be making a mistake. It may seem easier to commit yourself to the hands of an "expert" who will solve your problems for you. But, as the economists say, "There's no such thing as a free lunch." Just as one cannot buy happiness, one cannot buy a life plan. You have to do the work.

A career counseling agency or group program can provide a framework, can give you moral support along the way, and can demonstrate proven techniques. But you must do the work; you must agonize over the choices available and see if they are comfortable for you. In the long run, such a program makes much more sense for several reasons.

First of all, the final goal you reach is more likely to be one that you can live with happily because *you* have made all the decisions along the way. By analyzing your own strengths and weaknesses, needs and values, you have been able to discard goals that are unrealistic. By doing your own market survey of what kinds of jobs are out there in the field to which you aspire, you can set realistic, attainable goals for yourself.

Almost equally as important, you will have learned a technique that you should be able to apply in the future to other career-choice situations as well as other transitions in your life. The techniques are equally applicable to the kinds of decisions that must be made at retirement, for example, in choosing where to live, how to allocate limited financial resources, and how to spend one's time.

A final warning. None of this can be done overnight. A substantial change of career is going to take time. But if you are willing to invest the time and effort, chances are that it will be worth it.

9

Career Change
and the Future

IN an interview with *Psychology Today* editor Mary Harrington Hall some years ago, Peter Drucker made the following cogent remarks.

Drucker: The real career crisis is the extension of the working-life span. In the time of our grandparents, man's working life was over at 45. By then, few people were physically or mentally capable of working. It was a rural civilization and the pre-industrial farmer was either worn out or had been killed by an accident by age 45. The Chinese or Irish who built our railroads had a five-year working life. Within five years they were gone—by liquor, or syphilis, or accident, or hard work.

Now suddenly you have people reaching the age of 65 in the prime of physical and mental health. This is due partly to the movement of people from the farm to the city—accidents occur on the farm with about ten times the frequency of that in the most dangerous industrial employment—and partly to scientific management taking the toil out of labor. We have pushed up education to compensate for this.

Hall: What possible solution is there other than a continual increasing of life-long education programs?

Drucker: I am absolutely convinced that one of the greatest needs is the systematic creation of second careers. At 45, after having been a market research man, or a professor of English or psychology, or an officer in the armed services for 20 years, a man is spent. At least he thinks so. But he is mentally, biologically, and physically sound. His kids are grown up and the mortgage is paid off and he has plenty to contribute to society.

You know, one of the most thrilling things that has happened in the last 20 years is the new careers for the crop of military officers who are being axed by the military services at age 47. They've reached lieutenant colonel or lieutenant commander, gone as far as they can go, and they're out.

Hall: What does one do after 20 years as an officer?

Drucker: That's exactly what they want to know. They are absolutely sure there is nothing they can do. They are terribly conscious that they have been in an insulated, artificial environment.

Hall: I should think they'd be scared to death.

Drucker: They are, scared out of their wits. Most of them think they need a graduate degree or some kind of guidance. All they need is for someone to say: "Look, Jack, there's nothing wrong with you." They can apply to one of the big downtown law firms for a job as office manager. These have 99 people who know nothing but law, and they need someone to organize them. There are jobs as business managers of law firms or accounting firms or small colleges. All kinds of good jobs.

Hall: It would be like starting life all over again.

Drucker: Six months after these former servicemen have taken on their new jobs, they are 20 years younger. They have recovered enthusiasm, they are growing, they have ideas. Their wives are enchanted. They are exciting again.

Hall: Not everybody would be a success as an office manager. Are there any other jobs that are especially suited to second careers?

Drucker: Indeed there are. The older professions are best suited to become second careers. Middle age is really the best time to switch to being the lawyer, the teacher, the priest, the doctor—I shocked you—and the social worker. Twenty years from now, we'll have few young men in these fields.

By this time, the reader is probably in agreement with Peter Drucker in his enthusiasm for midlife career change. The majority of men who changed careers in midlife reported a good outcome. They experienced an increase in job satisfaction, feelings of autonomy and control over their own lives, and a rejuvenation in their outlooks. The benefits have spilled over to have a positive effect on their wives and families. Not only has career change not brought on an increase in divorce; it seems to have helped to strengthen some marriages.

Seymour Sarason reports on a research project of one of his students who was investigating the career satisfaction of teachers. He discovered that the higest levels of job satisfaction were among those who had had one or more previous careers before teaching. Sarason also did a systematic study of the lives of men listed in *Who's Who* for the years 1934–1935, 1950–1951, and 1974–1975. He found that for each year, the overall frequency of career change among the people listed was approximately 40 percent. Although he was unwilling to commit himself to saying that the data suggest that career change is characteristic of successful people, he did feel that the findings were an indication of the frequency of career change, particularly among people who have been characterized by others as being successful.

Most of the men we talked to were fortunate enough to have enough financial resources in the form of savings, inheritance, investments, equity in a home, or the income of a working wife to be able to absorb the financial risks most career changes are likely to involve. It was apparent that a majority probably ended up with a reduced level of income as a result of their career change, although some were able to return to previous income levels or go even higher. Nevertheless, the availability of a financial cushion is almost essential. Is there any way that people with more modest resources might also experience the benefits that career change in midlife can offer?

CAREER CHANGE AND GOVERNMENT POLICY

It is quite clear that the advantages to the individual of career change are well worth the risk. What about the benefits to society as a whole? One would assume that these men's level of productivity probably increased as a result of their greater involvement in and pleasure derived from their new work. Many entered fields in which their direct service to other people was apparent. Two recent study groups have produced significant monographs that go into great detail on ways to improve the quality of work life. Both *Work in America*, written by James O'Toole and others and commissioned by the U.S. Department of Health, Education and Welfare, and *The Boundless Resource*, written by Willard Wirtz and the National Manpower Institute, advocate policies encouraging midcareer change as a social good.

James O'Toole and his associates propose a "Universal Worker Self-Renewal Program," providing a six-month sabbatical every seven years or a one-year sabbatical every 14 years to all workers. Moreover, they suggest that this proposal would not only benefit the workers but would probably justify itself on the grounds of economic efficiency. They believe that worker retraining should be considered a national capital investment.

O'Toole and the others argue convincingly in *Work in America* that career change is desirable for the improvement of society as a whole. In a dynamic economy such as ours, there is a constantly changing need for certain skill categories. Lack of worker mobility from occupations of oversupply to those of undersupply is one cause of inflation. Career stagnation or pressure for early retirement causes a serious inflationary effect on both slow-growth and fast-growth industries.

In industries that have slow growth or no growth at all,

workers continue to receive increases in pay because of seniority, although there is no increase in productivity. Such industries, in fact, may well be overstaffed. Thus, goods and services cost more than they should. In high-growth industries, salaries must be increased because of the competition for the few workers skilled in the desired fields. Sometimes untrained workers are all that can be found, decreasing productivity. Thus, the *Work in America* task force argues that it is economically desirable to offer incentives to workers to leave oversupplied industries and be retrained for jobs for which workers are in demand.

Secretary of Commerce Juanita Kreps is a manpower economist whose area of expertise is in the trade-offs among time, work, leisure, and income. She has suggested that one of the most acceptable ways both to increase the number of jobs and to lower the number of persons who are unemployed would be to create more part-time jobs and extend the possibility of education over the entire life span. Both of these alternatives might lead to career change. She believes that some sort of income scheme that would encourage the return to education would reduce both the short- and the long-run costs of unemployment.

Former Secretary of Labor Willard Wirtz and his associates at the National Manpower Institute point out that it is already clear that in our ever-changing technological society, most people will be forced to change jobs and careers anyway. They propose the following governmental policies to promote career change:

That the cash value of the unused portion of "twelve years of free education" be available for a broad range of learning opportunities to those who did not receive that education in their youth.

With a high school diploma now an essential prerequisite for almost any kind of job, this seems to be a modest proposal.

That the Unemployment Insurance system be adapted to provide income support for unemployed adults who pursue further education and training in order to make a job-market adjustment and extended for this purpose beyond normal duration periods.

It is absurd that in order to collect unemployment insurance an individual must swear that he or she has not attended school during the period of unemployment. In many cases, additional training may be exactly what is needed to make that person employable again. Naturally, provisions need to be made so that unemployment insurance is not used as a way to "free load," and that training undertaken is directly applicable to improving marketable skills.

That in order to reduce the barriers to job mobility, consideration be given to more flexible seniority systems, to the fuller vesting of pensions, and to removing unnecessarily restrictive occupational licensing practices.

Many people who have considered the idea of a career change have been forced, reluctantly, to give it up because the loss of financial security would be too great. With the possibility of portable pensions, these people would find a change of career more feasible.

That the principle of flexible work scheduling, especially for the purpose of dovetailing work with part-time educational opportunities, be applied as broadly as possible.

The popularity and success of flexitime in many firms and governmental agencies both in this country and abroad have shown that there is nothing sacrosanct about the traditional 8 to 4 or 9 to 5 work schedule. In addition to providing the opportunity for further education, flexitime is beneficial in reducing rush-hour traffic congestion, enabling parents who are both working to arrange their hours to provide for maximum child care, and simply allowing individuals to adjust their work schedules to their own diurnal rhythms. People who are "owls" can work late, and those who are "roosters" can work early in the day when they are most productive. Most companies are able to arrange their schedules so that a variation in hours worked does not cause undue confusion.

Congress has long provided income tax credits for education that furthers a person in a field in which he or she is already employed. This has been a difficult rule to interpret accurately. The present allowance for education is inconsistent and should be dropped altogether, and all education for the purpose of training for employment should be included. Parents have long pushed to make the cost of college education for their children tax deductible. If such a measure should pass, indicating Congress believes that education is such an important social good that it should be encouraged by means of tax credits, then education undertaken for the purpose of entering a new field should also be tax deductible.

Another recommendation of *The Boundless Resource* is

That thorough inquiry be instituted into ways and means of creating workable incentives to increase employer investment in training.

The amount of training provided by many large corporations in the United States, particularly those in high technology areas, has increased tremendously in recent years. IBM, for example, has a whole university campus and invests huge sums in training its employees in every conceivable area. Smaller firms, however, are at a disadvantage, and cannot afford the cost of extensive training programs for their employees. As an aid to small businesses tax credits or other incentives might be offered to smaller firms that provide training or permit their employees to study in formal educational programs.

CAREER CHANGE AND BUSINESS

Samuel R. Connor and John S. Fielden set up a lively debate several years ago in the *Harvard Business Review* by attacking what they termed the outmoded notion of "one company, one career, retirement at 65." They encouraged younger managers to anticipate and prepare for second careers in other organizations and fields. They advocated that companies should provide "educational green stamps" to help pay for training in new fields. If employees do not take advantage of such help and remain what they term "shelf-sitters," Connor and Fielden believe that the company can, in good conscience, insist upon demotion or early retirement for highly paid but unproductive managers.

Emmanuel Kay, in *The Crisis in Middle Management* reported a survey of a large group of middle managers who were members of the American Management Associations. Many of them were dissatisfied with their jobs and were considering changing careers. As a result of what he learned Kay urges companies to encourage midcareer managers who choose to do so to pursue second careers by providing the opportunity to work only half-time while preparing for the change, and by providing counseling, sabbaticals, and released time to attend classes.

Many more firms should offer the kind of career planning services we described in Chapter 8. They would find that it would help to motivate employees to take more responsibility for their own career development. Such services are likely to improve employee morale and help workers to move to jobs in which they are interested and likely to be competent. Those who are unhappy in their present positions would have the opportunity to investigate why and to look into alternatives either within or outside the company.

Such services should provide employees with guided instruction in how to test and assess their occupational interests, their educational and personal needs, and their skills and abilities. Feedback must be given by supervisors and personnel staff on employee performance, and a career planning interview should be a regularly scheduled aspect of the individual's employment.

Many companies are experimenting with sabbaticals for management staff. These provide an opportunity for employees to do something different or pursue a learning experience. In most cases, the employee is expected to come back, but it might provide an opportunity for some people to test out long dreamed-about second careers to see if they are what they really want. The Xerox Corporation has had a successful program of social service leaves for a number of years. This has enabled Xerox employees to work for non-profit agencies involved in community improvement. The sabbatical is seen as a rewarding opportunity for growth of the individual.

CAREER CHANGE AND OBSOLESCENCE

The rapid advance of technology during the last 25 years has brought with it a new concern with the problem of professional obsolescence. More and more professionals are finding it essential—even mandated by law—to continue formal learning throughout their careers. It is becoming increasingly necessary for those whose occupation depends on their command of a certain body of knowledge to update their knowledge and skills through frequent formal learning.

Work obsolescence can be measured by using the concept of *half-life*. The *half-life* is defined by Samuel S. Dubin as the period of time after completion of formal education when approximately half of what the professional has learned is no longer applicable. The half-life of knowledge in any profession depends on the rate of change and the addition of new data and knowledge. Dubin estimates that the half-life of medical knowledge is five years; in psychology it is ten years. For engineering, it was twelve years in 1940, but had shrunk to five years by 1970.

For many high-technology industries the problem of professional obsolescence is a significant one. The costs to the company of obsolete managers tend to be hidden. They are found in poor and untimely decisions and lack of innovation and creativity. It is generally agreed that keeping a person current depends more on motivation than on age. Most experts in the area of adult learning seem to concur; people who have a strong desire for growth and a feeling of optimism about the future are more likely to continue learning.

There does not seem to be a simple, clear-cut relationship between increasing age and obsolescence. H. G. Kaufman points out that the world seems to be divided into two populations, those who go downhill and become obsolete after they reach 40 and those who are able to overcome their "midlife crisis" and remain highly productive. Kaufman hypothesizes that if employees do not obtain career success their growth needs are frustrated. Then these higher-order needs may be replaced by the protective security needs.

Kaufman also points out that the length of time that has elapsed since a professional has completed his education is a much more crucial factor than mere age in susceptibility to obsolescence. Thus, someone who had returned to school for a higher degree is less likely to become obsolete than someone the same age who has not done so.

Employers can use a variety of strategies to keep their professional staff from becoming obsolete. Many companies invest heavily in continuing education programs, either holding them in-house or paying for those offered by colleges and universities or consulting firms. Work structure and job assignments can be changed to motivate employees to keep up to date; sabbaticals can be offered. However, some people simply won't keep up, for one reason or another. Kaufman and others suggest that in this case, the possibility of a career change should be offered, within the company or elsewhere. A flexible retirement policy and more portable pensions would encourage obsolescent professionals to leave the organization, since they could do so without losing their vesting rights.

CAREER CHANGE AND HIGHER EDUCATION

The final recommendation of the National Manpower Institute in *The Boundless Resource* is

That additional educational options be developed for adults, with particular attention to open universities, certification based on competence examinations, credit for experience, and a broader community base for the expanding community colleges.

In Chapter 6 we talked about some of the innovative programs now offered by colleges and universities to serve the educational needs of adults. This variety should be continued and expanded. No one type of program will fill the needs of all adults, and it is important that what former SUNY Chancellor Samuel Gould calls "diversity by design" be available.

It is important to maintain the educational quality of programs, but flexibility in terms of time and place are also important. The Carnegie Commission suggests that a network of "learning pavilions" be established to provide not only a library of books, but access to audio and video cassettes, computers, microfiche readers, and independent learning laboratories. These would be established so as to provide maximum access to large numbers of potential learners.

A major need is for more information and counseling resources to help adults choose their educational and career goals. These should be available at modest cost and at times convenient to adult clients, usually in the evening. Greater use should be made of public libraries, museums, and public schools as convenient neighborhood facilities in which information services could be provided.

Morris T. Keeton, director of the Council for the Advancement of Experiential Learning, paints an intriguing picture of the lifelong-learning society of the future. It would be linked through educational brokering agencies, where men and women would come to seek help in exploring their interests and career goals and to obtain information about available learning opportunities. Public libraries would be an important part of the network, interconnected through a central catalog and reference service system with daily delivery of materials from source to users.

There would be mutual cooperation among businesses, all levels of government, schools, libraries, and other community agencies, so that space for learning would be made

available wherever it was most convenient for students.
Employers would provide a certain portion of work time for
learning and upgrading of skills. Staff members of companies and government agencies who are competent would
be encouraged to join the pool of available teachers to provide instruction in their areas of knowledge. There would be
flexibility among learning programs so that a student could
choose the courses or learning experiences most relevant to
his or her needs from a variety of sources.

Instead of being locked into existing degree structures
and requirements, adults should be provided with opportunities to choose the learning they need. Documentation of
their studies should be provided in an easily accessible form
so that potential employers or other interested parties can
find out about their learning experiences quickly and easily.

A major stumbling block both for people and for communities in providing the kinds of lifelong-learning opportunities described is the matter of financing. A number of
people have suggested that government support of lifelong
learning be made in the form of subsidies to individual adult
students rather than directly to institutions. They would be
in the form of promissory notes or entitlements that would
obligate the government to provide a specific amount in the
way of scholarships or loans that the student could use to
participate in any accredited program of education or training. The GI Bill is given as a model of a system that worked
rather effectively in providing educational opportunities to a
great many people. Amounts of entitlements would vary according to financial need and other criteria.[1]

George Nolfi, who has worked in Massachusetts on establishing a network of regional counseling centers for
adults and an experimental selective entitlement voucher
system, says that a sound public policy with regard to
lifelong education would be composed of four elements: a
subsidy system for low-income adults who most need it, an
easily accessible system that would provide counseling and

---

[1] Norman D. Kurland (ed.) *Entitlement Papers* (Washington, D.C.: National Institute of Education Papers in Education and Work, No. 4, March
1977).

information to potential adult students, better coordination
among postsecondary educational institutions to encourage
cooperation and avoid duplication, and a better mechanism
to provide educational credentials to the adult students who
use the learning opportunities available.

CAREER CHANGE AND DEMOGRAPHIC TRENDS

It is clear to demographers that the United States is
headed for profound changes in its way of life as a result of
the low fertility and mortality rate of recent years, which
they predict will continue. The average age of the population will increase, and the nation will have a larger proportion of elderly people and a smaller population of children.
In addition, with improved medical care and health habits,
people will not only live longer, but for a greater part of their
lives they will be healthy and fit.

The implications of these population changes for the
prevalence of career change are fairly strong. Later marriage,
smaller families, and an increase in two-breadwinner
families have been brought on by both the lowered fertility
rate and the women's movement. Therefore, more people
will have the financial leeway to consider other alternatives
to keeping their nose to the grindstone in order to pay for the
family's food and shelter.

The average family now has two or three children who
leave the nest when the father is in his forties and still has
the time, money, and energy to return to school or in other
ways prepare for a new career. With more and more wives
working, it is possible for a man to take financial risks to
obtain his goals, knowing that some income will be available
for necessities even if he is not producing it.

Many more people are in good physical condition well
into their seventies. At the same time, the average age of
retirement is declining, so many men are now automatically
planning ahead to a second career to occupy them creatively
after their official retirement. Indeed, simple boredom may

well be a factor in many career changes of the future. In the past, few people lived to spend many years in retirement. They usually worked until they were physically unable to work any longer or until they died. The stretch of time in one occupation did not seem so long. Now, with a longer work span for most people, there is enough time and energy to have several different careers in one lifetime.

We have been reading dire predictions that the Social Security system is going to go bankrupt as the numbers of retired people increase to such a degree that the younger working population cannot support them with their contributions. The retirement age has already been raised. According to *The New York Times* reporter Jerry Flint,

But one way or the other, it appears that the mandatory retirement age will be lifted, for the elimination is part of the quiet revolution under way in the American work place. That revolution is of options: the option to early retirement after 30 years or 25 years or 20 years, to part-time work, to voluntary overtime, to flexible hours, shared jobs and four-day weeks. The right to keep working is another option.

A NEW CONCEPT OF LIFE STAGES

The career changers we studied represent a new trend. They are the advance wave of a movement gaining momentum to change the prevailing cycle of life from what Richard Bolles calls the Three Boxes Model—Education, Employment, Retirement, as symbolized by crib, diploma, gold watch, and coffin. It may be that we are seeing a trend for men remarkably similar to the one that has taken place for many women in our society, beginning in the early 1960s with Mary Bunting's plea to recognize that women's lives have several phases, and that they should be encouraged to make the necessary transitions between motherhood, education, and career in midlife. Now more men are seriously considering returning to school, either to improve their skill and knowledge in an existing occupation or to prepare for a change. Others are preparing for a more drastic change, to get off the ever accelerating escalator to "success" and find a more relaxed and personally rewarding life-style.

Fred Best and Barry Stern call the traditional model the "linear life plan." They recommend that an alternative, which they call the "cyclic life plan," be considered.

The basic idea of this alternative is that current time spent on education and retirement, as well as any further gains in non-work time, be redistributed to the center of life in the form of extended periods of leisure or education.

Some people might want a four-day workweek or an occasional two-month vacation.

Although the compression of work into the middle period of the life cycle is the culmination of a long historical trend which has basically healthy features (e.g., child labor laws and the possibility of retirement with a pension) there is evidence that the trend has gone too far. The "lock-step" is especially frustrating for youth and retirees, who both want more work, independence, and responsibility. . . . There is also evidence that a significantly large minority of prime age workers want more leisure without having to sacrifice too much in the way of economic security and job status to get it.

Many people argue that much of education is wasted on youth, who must stay in school well into their twenties "preparing" for life. If it were made easier for young people to find meaningful work experiences right after high school, they might be motivated to return to higher learning with a clearer idea of what they need and want to learn and with greater motivation.

Emerging from the findings of the study of career changers is a new assumption about the phases of men's career lives—at least for men of managerial or professional level. In the early career years, when motivation to succeed, to earn money, and to gain recognition in the eyes of the community are foremost in importance to the individual, the large bureaucracy is a most suitable workplace, since it is where such rewards as money and esteem are most likely to be found.

However, as middle age arrives, inner values and meanings become more important than the outer trappings of success. The bureaucracy may be a much less suitable environment in which to achieve one's desires at this stage in life. Efforts should be made to make it less difficult for middle-aged people to leave the corporation and begin more autonomous activities. Not only would such a move have value for them, but it would also provide places for younger, more eager and ambitious individuals to get ahead.

The second career phase will begin in the forties or fifties, as soon as the heavy financial demands of family rearing are ended. Self-employment and work in a helping profession or craft, where the rewards are smaller financially but greater in terms of personal satisfaction and autonomy, are popular choices. The second occupation will be more flexible in terms of hours and demands both of which could be arranged to allow a slow winding down as age advances and energy level declines. Thus, the sharp break between a 40-hour workweek and nothing to do, which has created such a crisis in the lives of many new retirees, will no longer be necessary.

The second career is more likely to call upon the stores of wisdom the older person has gained through rich life experience than upon technical expertise. Interspersed in both the primary and secondary work periods will be time for education or other forms of personal or professional renewal, so no one need fall into a rut. Seymour Sarason suggests that with the weakening of the cultural imperative for one life—one career and a change to a cyclical life plan, the concept of the midlife crisis as tied to a specific age interval will end. When the dynamics of change and growth become possible throughout the life span and values such as authenticity, autonomy, self-expression, and new experiences become dominant, a crisis will no longer be a prerequisite for changing direction.

THE CYCLIC LIFE PLAN AND CAREER EDUCATION

The cyclic life plan and its possibilities for change, learning, and growth throughout the life span have significant implications for the education of youth. The career education movement initiated by Sydney Marland is based upon the old-fashioned notion of one career life. It assumes that if school-age children are given enough information about the world of work when they are young, they will be able to make the "right choice" of career, and thus live happily ever after.

In my experience counseling college students, I have seen that this assumption is erroneous. Work is something that must be experienced. Like most important things in life, you really don't know what it's all about until you have done it yourself. The young person must have a variety of job experiences to test out how they fit his particular configuration of personality needs and abilities. In addition, as you age and as the world around you changes, your needs and requirements change. What is the right job for you when you are 25 is wrong when you are 40, and the one that is right at 40 may be inappropriate when you are 55 or 70. To quote Eli Ginzberg,

. . occupational choice is a lifelong process of decision-making, in which the individual constantly seeks to find the optimal fit between career goals and the realities of the world of work.

What we need to teach young people is how to learn and how to make choices and decisions. Instead of confronting them with the awful choice of "a career" at age 22, we should enable them to try out jobs, which will be a way of trying out the world of work to see what will fit. They must understand that there may be many changes in direction along the way, but if they are prepared to learn from them and use them to grow, the changes need not be perceived as crises.

Ginzberg has expressed the lifelong career process well

While I still believe that few individuals make occupational choices that satisfy all of their principal needs and desires, I now think that a more correct formulation is that of *optimization*. Men and women seek to find the best occupational fit between their changing desires and their changing circumstances. This search is a continuing one As long as they entertain the possibility of shifting their goals, they are constantly considering a new balance in which the potential gains are weighed against the probable costs.

The psychological and developmental needs of men and women, as well as the economic needs of society, will be served better if the time constraints of work life are broken down. People must be given the option of changing their direction and of creating the mix of work, learning, and leisure best suited to their own happiness and development No longer should education be only for the young, work only for the middle-aged, and leisure only for the elderly; all age groups must be able to create for themselves the synthesis of all three that most suits their particular needs at that particular phase of their lives.

Appendix A
Some College Programs
Specifically Designed
for Adults

THE following colleges offer specially designed programs for adult students. The list is no more than that. I am not evaluating the quality of the schools or making any promises of being complete or comprehensive. It was compiled from several sources. The best and most current source is an excellent guide for adults who want to return to college and is written by three experts in the field. It is *College Learning Anytime, Anywhere* by Ewald B. Nyquist, Jack N. Arbolino, and Gene R. Hawes (New York: Harcourt, Brace, Jovanovich, 1977). Additional names were obtained from James B. Maas et al., *The Yellow Pages of Undergraduate Innovations* (Ithaca, New York: The Cornell Center for Improvement in Undergraduate Education and *Change* Magazine, 1974) and from a listing of the colleges involved in programs of the Council for the Advancement of Experiential Learning.

I. **External Degree Institutions**

Regents External Degree Program of the University of the State of New York
99 Washington Avenue, Albany, New York 12230

Thomas A. Edison College
Forrestal Center, Forrestal Road, Princeton, New Jersey 08540

Board for State Academic Awards of the State of Connecticut
340 Capitol Avenue, Hartford, Connecticut, 06115

II. **University Without Walls Programs**

University of Alabama
New College, University, Alabama 35486

Antioch College/Philadelphia
1227 Walnut Street, Philadelphia, Pennsylvania 19107

Antioch College/West
3663 Sacramento Street, San Francisco, California 94118

Bard College
Annandale-on-Hudson, New York 12504

University Without Walls/Berkeley
2700 Bancroft Way, Berkeley, California 94704

Chicago State University
95th and King Drive, Chicago, Illinois 60628

University Without Walls/Flaming Rainbow
P.O. Box 154, Tahlequah, Oklahoma 74464

Florida International University/Miami Dade Community College
300 N.E. Second Avenue, Miami, Florida 33132

Friends World College
Plover Lane, Huntington, New York 11743

Goddard College
Plainfield, Vermont 05677

Hispanic International University
3602 Navigation, Houston, Texas 77003

Hofstra University
Hempstead, New York 11550

Johnston College
University of Redlands
Redlands, California 92373

Loretto Heights College
3001 S. Federal Boulevard, Denver, Colorado 80236

University of Massachusetts
Amherst, Massachusetts 01022

University of Minnesota
Minneapolis, Minnesota 55455

Morgan State College
Urban Regional Learning Center
Baltimore, Maryland 21212

Northeastern Illinois University
Bryn Mawr at St. Louis Avenue, Chicago, Illinois 60625

University of the Pacific
Stockton, California 95204

Pitzer College
Claremont, California 91711

Roger Williams College
35 Richmond Street, Providence, Rhode Island 02903

Shaw University
Raleigh, North Carolina 27602

Skidmore College
Saratoga Springs, New York 12866

Stephens College
Columbia, Missouri 65201

Universidad Boricua
1766 Church Street, Washington, D.C. 20036

Universidad de Campesinos Libres
841 W. Belmont Avenue, Fresno, California 93706

Westminster College
Fulton, Missouri 65621

University of Wisconsin at Green Bay
Green Bay, Wisconsin 54302

III. **Empire State College**
State University of New York
2 Union Avenue
Saratoga Springs, New York 12866

IV. **External Degree Programs of California State University and Colleges**
California State University, Chico
Chico, California 95926

California State University, Hayward
Hayward, California 94542

California State University, Sacramento
Sacramento, California 95819

San Francisco State University
San Francisco, California 94132

San Jose State University
San Jose, California 95192

Other CSUC institutions offering such programs (and the degrees to which their programs lead) include:

California State College, Dominguez Hills (B.A. or M.A. in the humanities)
Dominguez Hills, California 90747

California State University, Long Beach (M.A. in vocational education, offered for certified teachers)
Long Beach, California 90840

California State University, Sonoma (B.A. in the liberal arts)
Rohnert Park, California 94928

General information about these off-campus degree programs may be obtained from:
The Consortium of the California State University and Colleges, 5670 Wilshire Blvd., Los Angeles, California 90036.

V. University of Mid-America (consortium of five universities: Iowa State, Kansas State, University of Kansas, University of Missouri, and University of Nebraska)

University of Mid-America
P.O. Box 82006, Lincoln, Nebraska 68501

VI. Other Programs

College of Liberal Studies
University of Oklahoma
Norman, Oklahoma 73069

Adult Degree Program
Goddard College
Plainfield, Vermont 05667

Independent Study Programs of Syracuse University
Room 21, 610 East Fayette Street
Syracuse, New York 13203

Open University
University of Maryland/University College
College Park, Maryland 20742

Open University Program
University College, Rutgers, The State University
  of New Jersey
New Brunswick, New Jersey 08903

Open University Program
University of Houston
Houston, Texas 77004

TV College, City Colleges of Chicago Central Office
180 North Michigan Avenue, Chicago, Illinois 60601

External Degree Project
Roosevelt University
Chicago, Illinois 60605

Metropolitan State University
St. Paul, Minnesota 55101

Governors State University
Park Forest South, Illinois 60466

Coordinated Off-Campus Degree Program
Upper Iowa University
Fayette, Iowa 52142

"17-65"
Sacred Heart University
Bridgeport, Connecticut 06604

School for New Learning
DePaul University
Chicago, Illinois 60604

Chaminade College of Honolulu
Honolulu, Hawaii 96816

Board of Governors Degree, Bachelor of Liberal Studies
Western Illinois University
Macomb, Illinois 61455

Thomas More College
Fort Mitchell, Kentucky 41017

Aquinas College
Grand Rapids, Michigan 49506

College of New Rochelle
New Rochelle, New York 10801

Salem State College
Salem, Massachusetts 01970

Park College
Kansas City, Missouri 64152

College of Saint Rose
Albany, New York 12203

Elizabethtown College
Elizabethtown, Pennsylvania 17022

University of Pittsburgh
Pittsburgh, Pennsylvania 15206

Sarah Lawrence College
Bronxville, New York 10708

University of Wisconsin–Extension
Madison, Wisconsin 53706

St. Louis University
St. Louis, Missouri 63103

University of Arkansas
Little Rock, Arkansas 72204

Trinity College
Hartford, Connecticut 06106

Howard University
Washington, D.C. 20001

University of Northern Colorado
Greeley, Colorado 80631

Community College of Vermont
Montpelier, Vermont 05602

Johnston College
University of Redlands
Redlands, California 92375

LaGuardia Community College
City University of New York
Queens, New York 11101

Miami–Dade Community College
Miami, Florida 33176

Framingham State College
Framingham, Massachusetts 01701

Metropolitan State University
St. Paul, Minnesota 55101

Appendix B
National Directory
of Adult Counseling
Organizations*

IN the 1970s there has been dramatic growth in the number of educational services for people beyond traditional school and college ages. Instruction is now offered at new times and places to accommodate the schedules of busy adults. Noninstructional support services are now available to adults at a wide range of community sites in addition to schools and colleges.

The clientele of these services and adult surveys in the 1970s reveal widespread need for information on career opportunities, education requirements for careers, educational/training options, comparative costs, and financial assistance. In addition to information, many adults in transition want assistance in clarifying their values, planning life/career goals, overcoming lack of confidence, seeing beyond sex and age stereotypes, cutting through institutional red tape, gaining credit for prior learning, and deciding

*Reprinted from the National Center for Educational Brokering

among a confusing array of career and educational options. In response to these needs, impartial information and counseling services have multiplied in recent years. While some initially specialized either in educational or occupational opportunities, many have developed the capacity to assist clients in both areas because educational and occupational decisions are interdependent for a large number of adults.

These services act as intermediaries that link searching adults with the resources for learning and earnings that are most appropriate to their individual needs and goals. Because of their client-focused, in-between role, such services have been increasingly referred to as "educational brokering" services. The essential aspects of educational brokering are information, assessment, advisement, referral, and advocacy.

This Directory lists 215 sites in 41 states where information and advice on educational and career decisions are available to people not currently in educational institutions. Services are mainly sponsored by independent agencies, public libraries, community women's services, state/local government, and interinstitutional arrangements.

We have included in the Directory 44 nonprofit independent agencies engaged in educational brokering, as their entire service or as a part of their services, which are supported by a wide variety of public and private funding. Some of these cater especially to women returning to school and/or work and emphasize occupational information. We have so far identified 42 public libraries that have separate advisory services for adults, staffed by specially trained personnel, whose emphasis is usually on learning resources throughout the community. Brokering services are offered through 31 interinstitutional arrangements involving usually three or more colleges and sometimes a library or school system. Those in Illinois and Minnesota are supported by state appropriations and not only counsel adults but also arrange for cooperating institutions elsewhere in the state to offer courses locally in response to their clients' learning needs.

Programs at a few individual degree-granting institutions have been included in the Directory for special reasons. Eight have grants from the U.S. Office of Education to run Educational Opportunity Centers that appear to be neutral in their referrals to a wide range of educational opportunities. Several institutions have no faculty or courses of their own and facilitate the use by students of educational resources in other institutions or community facilities in fulfillment of degree requirements. The University of Wisconsin–Extension, Madison, operates the largest state educational brokering network, Community-Based Counseling for Adults, with trained community people working as educational counselors in Cooperative Extension Offices, libraries, and other agencies in 40 counties to refer clients to all public and private educational resources.

Our decisions on Directory entries were based on the returns from a mailing in spring 1977 of over 1,400 questionnaires to prospective sites and on-site visits and telephone interviews. Addresses of those chosen for inclusion were checked by mail in December 1977. All appear to be sources of information and advisement that experience no conflicts between serving the interests of a particular institution for enrollments and the interest of each client for objective and complete information or options. There are, no doubt, many more services that impartially facilitate career and educational decisions and actions. We hope to hear from them and include them in the 1979 Directory.

In the meantime, we wish to thank those who responded to our mailings; Nancy McQue at Syracuse University for preparation, mailing, and processing of the questionnaires; Carol Ryan at NCEB, Washington, for resourceful fact finding and meticulous preparation of the final text; the Council on Interinstitutional Leadership, for addresses of possible sites; the Catalyst Network of Women's Services and the College Entrance Examination Board's Library Project for Independent Adult Learners; and the staffs of the Carnegie Corporation of New York and the Fund for the Improvement of Postsecondary Education, for their encouragement and financial support of NCEB.

James M. Heffernan
Francis U. Macy
National Center for Educational Brokering
January 1978

ALABAMA

Interinstitutional Programs

Alabama Open Learning Program
P.O. Box 1487
Tuscaloosa, Alabama 35401
Contact: Paul Spell, Project Director, (205) 348–4505

For counseling sites located in Birmingham, Tuscaloosa, and rural
West Alabama, contact Paul Spell at above number.

Degree-Granting Institutions

North Alabama Educational Opportunity Center
2205 University Drive, N.W., Suite F
Huntsville, Alabama 35805
Contact: Dr. Harold Dickerson, Director, (205) 534–8403

Computer-Based and/or Telephone Information Services

Alabama Occupational Information System
901 Adams Avenue
Montgomery, Alabama 36130
Contact: Dr. Charles Graves, Director, (205) 832–5737

ALASKA

Degree-Granting Institutions

Educational Opportunity Center
University of Alaska at Anchorage
2533 Providence Avenue
Anchorage, Alaska 99504
Contact: Pat Reeves, Project Director, (907) 279–6622, X450

ARIZONA

Degree-Granting Institutions

Phoenix Educational Opportunity Center
34 West Monroe, Room 601
Phoenix, Arizona 85003
Contact: George Carrillo, (602) 965–7081

CALIFORNIA

Independent Brokering Services

ACCESS
Center for Education and Manpower Resource, Inc.
P.O. Box 112
Ukiahi, California 95482
Contact: Catherine Rolzinski, (707) 468–0238

Educational Opportunity Center
Fresno County Educational Guidance Project
1350 O Street, Room 303
P.O. Box 12507
Fresno, California 93778
Contact: Vincent Guerrero, Director, (209) 266–7757

Open Road/New Avenues
Citizen's Policy Center
1323 Anacapa Street
Santa Barbara, California 93101
Contact: Nancy Franco, Executive Director, (805) 966–2258

Library Programs

FIND
Fullerton Information Needs Directory
Fullerton Public Library
353 W. Commonwealth
Fullerton, California 92632
Contact: Florence Fitzgerald James, (714) 871–9440

Degree-Granting Institutions

Educational Opportunity Center
1100 S. Grand Street
Los Angeles, California 90015
Contact: Leon Wood, Director, (213) 748–9639

Educational Opportunity Center
UCLA Extension
318 S. Lincoln Boulevard, No. 19
Venice, California 90291
Contact: Richard Cheka Maddox, (213) 392–4527

Computer-Based and/or Telephone Information Services

EUREKA—The California Career Information System
Diablo Valley Community College
Pleasant Hill, California 94523
Contact: Leigh Robinson, Co-Director, (415) 237–8770

COLORADO

Interinstitutional Programs

Consortium for Coordinating Education for Adults in the Pikes
  Peak Region
Blanca 203
2200 Bott Avenue
Colorado Springs, Colorado 80904
Contact: Leary O'Gorman, Executive Director, (303) 471–7546

Library Programs

"On Your Own"
Denver Public Library
1357 Broadway
Denver, Colorado 80203
Contact: Thomas La Free, (303) 573–5152, X271

Degree-Granting Institutions

Educational Opportunity Center
1009 Grant Street
Denver, Colorado 80203
Contact: David Patterson, Director, (303) 893–8868, X277

Outreach Adult Counseling and Information Services
Colorado Mountain College
526 Pine Street
Glenwood Springs, Colorado 81601
Contact: David Beyer, (303) 945–9196

Computer-Based and/or Telephone Information Services

Colorado Career Information System
University of Colorado
Willard Administrative Center, Room 7
Boulder, Colorado 80302
Contact: Pauline Parish, Director, (303) 492–8932

CONNECTICUT

Independent Brokering Services

Career and Educational Counseling Center
Stamford YWCA
422 Summer Street
Stamford, Connecticut 06901
Contact: Mrs. Ruth Polster, (203) 348–7727

Planning for Education and Careers (PEAC)
30 Maple Avenue
Windsor, Connecticut 06095
Contact: Joan Gould, (203) 688–1098

Interinstitutional Programs

Regional Counseling Center of Southeastern Connecticut
76 Federal Street
Samuel Seabury Center
New London, Connecticut 06320
Contact: Margaret S. Atherton, Director, (203) 442–4556

Women's Services

Information and Counseling Service for Women
301 Crown Street, P.O. Box 5557
New Haven, Connecticut 06520
Contact: Mary Louise Rodell, Director, (203) 436–8242

DISTRICT OF COLUMBIA

Independent Brokering Services

Educational Opportunity Center
Alabama Avenue and Naylor Road, S.E.
Washington, D.C. 20020
Contact: Mrs. Mary P. Morgan, Director, (202) 581–2205

FLORIDA

Women's Services

Center for Continuing Education for Women, Inc.
P.O. Box 3028, 1 West Church Street, Valencia Community College
Orlando, Florida 32802
Contact: Beatrice B. Ettinger, Director, (305) 843–4260 or 423–4813

GEORGIA

Independent Brokering Services

Educational Opportunity Center
965 Hunter Street, N.W.
Atlanta, Georgia 30314
Contact: Samuel Johnson, Director, (404) 577–3990

Library Programs

Atlanta Public Library
126 Carnegie Way, N.W.
Atlanta, Georgia 30303
Contact: Paul Porterfield

Computer-Based and/or Telephone Information Services

Georgia Career Information System
Georgia Consortium
c/o Dr. Kay Crouch
Georgia State University
Atlanta, Georgia 30303
Contact: Dr. Kay Crouch, (404) 658–3016

HAWAII

Degree-Granting Institutions

Educational Opportunity Center
Maui Community College
310 Kaahumanu Avenue
Kahului, Hawaii 96732
Contact: Jane Lemont, Project Director, (808) 244–9181

ILLINOIS

Independent Brokering Services

The Education Network for Older Adults
36 South Wabash Avenue, Suite 714
Chicago, Illinois 60603
Contact: W. A. Buchmann, Executive Director, (312) 782–8967

Interinstitutional Programs

Educational Opportunity Center
4378 Lindell Street
St. Louis, Missouri 63108
Contact: George H. Brantley, Project Director, (314) 534–2700

Counseling Centers in Illinois (For additional centers, see Missouri
   listing)

   Alton Center
   Educational Opportunity Center
   1623 Washington
   Alton, Illinois 62002
   Contact; Josephine Beckwith, Counselor, (618) 462–9573

   Belleville Center
   Educational Opportunity Center
   415 East Main, 2nd Floor
   Belleville, Illinois 62220
   Contact: Berma Patrich, Counselor, (618) 235–1776

   East St. Louis Center
   Educational Opportunity Center
   411 East Broadway, 3rd floor
   East St. Louis, Illinois 62201
   Contact: Jessie Hawthorne, Counselor, (618) 271–2643

   Graduate Studies Center
   Millikin University
   Decatur, Illinois 62522
   Contact: Wm. D. Lewis, Director, (217) 424–6202

   Quad-Cities Graduate Study Center
   639 38th Street
   Rock Island, Illinois 61201
   Contact: Donald A. Johnson, Director, (309) 794–7476

   Rockford Regional Academic Center
   215 N. Wyman Street
   Rockford, Illinois 61101
   Contact: Ronald Hallstrom, (815) 968–0834

Women's Services

Counseling Service for Women
Applied Potential
Box 19
Highland Park, Illinois 60085
Contact: Carole A. Wilk, President, (312) 432–0620

Women's, Inc.
15 Spinning Wheel Road
Hinsdale, Illinois 60521
Contact: Marge Rossman, Executive Director, (312) 325–9770

INDIANA

Interinstitutional Programs

Adult Education Information Center, Inc.
Consortium for Urban Education
155 E. Market Street, Room 809
Indianapolis, Indiana 46204
Contact: Marcy Hertz, Project Director, (317) 264–3463, or Michael
    Dean, Counselor

Postsecondary Adult Student Services
School of Continuing Studies
Indiana University
Bloomington, Indiana 47401
Contact: Nancy C. Seltz, (812) 337–1684

Women's Services

Woman Alive!, Inc.
YWCA
229 Ogden Street, Box 1121
Hammond, Indiana 46305
Contact: Gloria Gray, (219) 931–2922

IOWA

Women's Services

Community Career Planning Center for Women
Drake University
1158 27th Street
Des Moines, Iowa 50311
Contact: Elizabeth Burmeister, Director, (515) 271–2916

Women's Supportive Services
YWCA
717 Grand Avenue
Des Moines, Iowa 50309
Contact: Maxine Wilson, (515) 244–8461

Computer-Based and/or Telephone Information Services

Career Information System of Iowa
Department of Public Instruction
Grimes State Office Building
Des Moines, Iowa 50319
Contact: Erik Eriksen, Supervisor, (515) 281–5501

KANSAS

Computer Based and/or Telephone Information Services

FIRST (For Information/Referral Services Toll-Free)
The University of Kansas
Division of Continuing Education
Adult Life Resource Center
Lawrence, Kansas 66045
Contact: Gary Davis, Coordinator, (800) 532–6772

KENTUCKY

Interinstitutional Programs

Kentuckiana Metroversity's Educational Opportunity Center
1018 South 7th Street
Louisville, Kentucky 40203
Contact: Norman Gershon, Project Director, (502) 584–0475

LOUISIANA

WYES-TV Channel 12
P.O. Box 24026
New Orleans, Louisiana 70184
Contact: Sharon Litwin, (504) 486–5511

MAINE

Library Programs

Learners Advisory Service
Portland Public Library
619 Congress Street
Portland, Maine 04101
Contact: Barbara Smith, (207) 773–4761

Women's Services

Women's Resource Center
Telmar Woods, 23B
Orono, Maine 04473
Contact: J. Tolmasoff, Director, (207) 942–2092

MARYLAND

Independent Brokering Services

World Education Services, Inc.
P.O. Box 8643
Baltimore/Washington International Airport, Maryland 21240
Contact: James S. Frey, Executive Director, (301) 788–3783

Library Programs

College Learner's Advisory Service (CLAS)
Enoch Pratt Free Library
400 Cathedral Street
Baltimore, Maryland 21201
Contact: Emily W. Reed, Coordinator of Adult Services,
   (301) 396–5470

Women's Services

Baltimore New Directions for Women, Inc.
2517 N. Charles Street
Baltimore, Maryland 21218
Contact: Marian Goetze, Coordinator, (301) 366–8570

MASSACHUSETTS

Independent Brokering Services

Educational Exchange of Greater Boston
17 Dunster Street
Cambridge, Massachusetts 02138
Contact: Zelda Lions, Executive Director, (617) 876–3080

Educational Opportunity Center
YMCA
140 Clarendon Street
Boston, Massachusetts 02116
Contact: Bessie L. Davis, (617) 539–7940, X34

Educational Opportunity Center
38 Center Street
Chicopee, Massachusetts 01013
Contact: Jane Baatz, Director

Interinstitutional Programs

Educational Opportunity Center
Rodman House
106 Spring Street
New Bedford, Massachusetts 02740
Contact: Mrs. Doris K. Harriman, Director, (617) 996–3147

Regional Educational Opportunity Center
Worcester Consortium for Higher Education, Inc.
819 Main Street
Worcester, Massachusetts 01610
Contact: Diane Moorhead, (617) 755–2592

Women's Services

Career and Vocational Advisory Service
Civic Center and Clearinghouse, Inc.
14 Beacon Street
Boston, Massachusetts 02180
Contact: Sandra Kahn, Phyllis Adelberg, (617) 227–1762

WINNERS—Women's Inner-City Education Resources
  Service Center, Inc.
334 Warren Street
Roxbury, Massachusetts 02119
Contact: Marguerite Goodwin, Director, (617) 440–9150

Degree-Granting Institutions

Educational Opportunity Center
Central Square
Lynn, Massachusetts 01901
Contact: Kathleen S. Teehan, Director, (617) 592–0440

Computer-Based and/or Telephone Information Services

Massachusetts Occupational Information Service, Inc.
Wellesley Office Park
60 William Street
Wellesley Hills, Massachusetts 02181
Contact: Dr. Thomas Welch, President, (617) 237–2942

MICHIGAN

Library Programs

College Level Examination Program
Charles A. Ranson Public Library
180 S. Sherwood Avenue
Plainwell, Michigan 49080
Contact: Janice Park, (616) 685–8024

College Without Walls
St. Clair Shores Public Library
22500 Eleven Mile Road
St. Clair Shores, Michigan 48081
Contact: Frances Ceraudo, (313) 771–9020

Women's Services

Women's Resource Center
226 Bostwick, N.E.
Grand Rapids, Michigan 49503
Contact: Susan Ferrara, (616) 456–8571

Computer-Based and/or Telephone Information Services

Michigan Occupational Information System
P.O. Box 928
Lansing, Michigan 49804
Contact: Dr. Rod W. Durgin, (517) 373–0815

MINNESOTA

Independent Brokering Services

Community Career Center
Sonneyson Elementary School
3421 Bonn Avenue, N.
New Hope, Minnesota 55427
Contact: Betty Olsen, (612) 546–0466

Interinstitutional Programs

Iron Range Post-Secondary Education Center
Minnesota Higher Education Coordinating Board
Mesabi Community College, Room 150
Virginia, Minnesota 55792
Contact: Patrick Baudhuin, (218) 741–4210

Rochester Regional Center
Rochester Community College, Room A–102
Highway 14 E.
Rochester, Minnesota 55901
Contact: Wilbur Wakefield, Coordinator

Wadena Regional Center
11 Colfax Avenue, S.W.
Wadena, Minnesota 56482
Contact: Floyd Hansen

Library Programs

Learning Unlimited
Minneapolis Public Library
00 Nicollet Mall
Minneapolis, Minnesota 55401
Contact: Joseph Kimbrough, (612) 372–6500

Computer-Based and/or Telephone Information Services

Minnesota Occupational Information System
690 American Center Building
150 E. Kellogg Boulevard
St. Paul, Minnesota 55101
Contact: James R. Spensley, Executive Director, (612) 296–6962

MISSOURI

Interinstitutional Programs

Educational Opportunity Center
4378 Lindell Street
St. Louis, Missouri 63108
Contact: George Brantley, Project Director, (314) 534–2700

Counseling Centers in Missouri (For additional centers, see Illinois
   listing)

   Midtown Center
   Educational Opportunity Center
   1408 N. Kingshighway
   St. Louis, Missouri 63113
   Contact: Tyrone Taborn, Counselor, (314) 367–8100

   Montgomery-Hyde Park Center
   Educational Opportunity Center
   2240 St. Louis Avenue, Greeley Center
   St. Louis, Missouri 63106
   Contact: Deborah Patterson, Counselor, (314) 621–3434

   Northside Center
   Educational Opportunity Center
   414 S. Florissant
   Ferguson, Missouri 63135
   Contact: Walter Manning, Counselor, (314) 521–0030

   Skinker-Debaliviere Center
   Educational Opportunity Center
   6008 Kingsbury
   St. Louis, Missouri 63112
   Contact: Adele Levine, Counselor, (314) 725–4949

Southside Center
Educational Opportunity Center
822 Lafayette
St. Louis, Missouri 63104
Contact: Robert Deem, Counselor, (314) 621–4141

Library Programs

St. Louis Public Library
1301 Olive Street
St. Louis, Missouri 63103
Contact: A. James Lyons, (314) 241–2288

NEBRASKA

Computer-Based and/or Telephone Information Services

Nebraska Career Information System
Research Coordinating Unit
Box 33, Henzlik Hall
University of Nebraska
Lincoln, Nebraska 68588
Contact: Elton B. Mendenhall, (402) 472–3337

NEVADA

Independent Brokering Services

Educational Opportunity Center
495 Idaho Street, P.O. Box 177
Elko, Nevada 89801
Contact: Frank J. Joe, Director, (702) 738–7297

NEW HAMPSHIRE

Independent Brokering Services

Adult Tutorial Program
Carroll County Learning Center
124 Washington Street
Conway, New Hampshire 03818
Contact: Elizabeth Farrington, (603) 447–6650

The Learning Center, Inc.
Box 19
Lebanon, New Hampshire 03766
Contact: Ole Amundsen, Outreach Director, (603) 448–4303

Women's Services

Women for Higher Education
State Coordinating Office
RFD 4, Hackett Hill Road
Manchester, New Hampshire 03102
(603) 668–0700, X44

Counseling Sites

Concord/North County Regional Office
Women for Higher Education
Box 1255
20 South Main Street
Concord, New Hampshire 03301
Contact: Janet Waldron, Regional Director, (603) 228–0571

Durham/Seacoast Regional Office
Women for Higher Education
One Incinerator Road
Durham, New Hampshire 03824
Contact: Ellen Barnett, Regional Director, (603) 862–2350

Keene/Claremont Regional Office
Women for Higher Education
Keene State College
Elliott Hall
Keene, New Hampshire 03431
Contact: Diane Stradling, Regional Director, (603) 352–1909, X367

Manchester/Nashua Regional Office
Women for Higher Education
Merrimack Valley Branch
RFD 4, Hackett Hill Road
Manchester, New Hampshire 03102
Contact: Rose Leblanc, Regional Director,
   (603) 668–0700, X44

NEW JERSEY

Independent Brokering Services

New Jersey Education Consortium, Inc.
228 Alexander Road
Princeton, New Jersey 08540
Contact: Robert Steiner, Executive Director, (609) 921–2021

Library Programs

Learner's Advisory Service
Free Public Library of Woodbridge
George Frederick Plaza
Woodbridge, New Jersey 07095
Contact: Nancy White, Coordinator, (201) 634–4450

Women's Services

Adult Service Center
Montville School, Montville Township Community Education
12 Main Road
Montville, New Jersey 07045
Contact: Mrs. Donna M. Hains, Coordinator, (201) 335–4009 or
   335–4420

Degree-Granting Institutions

Thomas A. Edison College, Statewide Counseling Network
Forrestal Center
Forrestal Road
Princeton, New Jersey 08540
Contact: Jean A. Titterington, Director, Academic Counseling,
  (609) 452–2977

Counseling Sites

> Thomas A. Edison College
> Forrestal Center
> Forrestal Road
> Princeton, New Jersey 08540

> Thomas A. Edison College
> Montclair Public Library
> 50 South Fullerton Avenue
> Montclair, New Jersey 07042

> Thomas A. Edison College
> Labor and Industry Building
> 501 Landis Avenue
> Vineland, New Jersey 08360

Hudson County Community College
8511 Tonnelle Avenue
North Bergen, New Jersey 07047
Contact: Joseph F. Scott, (201) 854–3900, X17

NEW MEXICO

Degree-Granting Institutions

New Mexico Educational Opportunity Center
Northern New Mexico Community College
P.O. Box 250
Espanola, New Mexico 87532
Contact: Diane Bird, Director, (505) 753–6959 or 6962

Sites

New Mexico Educational Opportunity Center
P.O. Box 1100
Bernalillo, New Mexico 87004

New Mexico Educational Opportunity Center
P.O. Box 1052
Taos, New Mexico 87571

NEW YORK

Independent Brokering Services

Academic Advisory Center for Adults
Turf Avenue
Rye, New York 10580
Contact: Laura Kornfeld, Director, (914) 967–1653

Counseling Services
NYCTI's Education and Career Headquarters
225 Park Avenue South, Suite 505
New York, New York 10003
Contact: Bonita Davis, Director, (212) 677–3800

Regional Learning Service of Central New York
5 Oak Street
Syracuse, New York 13203
Contact: Jean Kordalewski, Director, (315) 425–5262

Interinstitutional Programs

Admissions Referral and Information Center (ARIC)
Commission on Independent Colleges and Universities
26 West 56th Street
New York, New York 10019
Contact: Floyd Weintraub, Director, (212) 541–4114

Education Consortium of Health Care Agencies of Northern
    New York
Box 552
Ogdensburg, New York 13669
Contact: Robert L. Wright, Executive Director, (315) 393–4440

Lifelong Learning Referral Service
Hudson Mohawk Association of Colleges and Universities
Council for the Advancement of Lifelong Learning (CALL)
Box 489, 849 New Loudon Road
Latham, New York 12110
Contact: Marc ˙S. Salisch, Executive Director, (518) 785–3219

Library Programs

Higher Education Library Advisory Services (HELAS)
University of the State of New York
99 Washington Avenue
Albany, New York 12230
Contact: Patricia Dyer, Project Director, (518) 382–3500

Sites

>   Schenectady Public Library
>   Liberty and Clinton Streets
>   Schenectady, New York 12305
>   Contact: Phyllis Ochs, HELAS Librarian, (518) 382–3500
>
>   Queens Borough Library
>   89-11 Merrick Boulevard
>   Jamaica, New York 11432
>   Contact: Edith Singer, HELAS Librarian
>
>   New York Public Library
>   8 East 40th Street, 4th floor
>   New York, New York 10016
>   Contact: Beth Wladis, HELAS Librarian
>
>   Corning Public Library
>   Civic Center Plaza
>   Corning, New York
>   Contact: Nancy Perrin, HELAS Librarian

Learner's Advisory Service
New York Public Library
Office of Adult Services
8 East 40th Street
New York, New York 10016
Contact: Pauline Lewis, (212) 790–6443

Advisement Centers

Manhattan

Mid-Manhattan Library
8 East 40th Street
New York, New York 10016
(212) 790–6589 and 6576

General Library for the Performing Arts at Lincoln Center
111 Amsterdam Avenue
New York, New York 10023
(212) 799–2200, X246

The Bronx

Fordham Library Center
2556 Bainbridge Avenue
Bronx, New York 10458
(212) 933–5200

Staten Island

St. George Library Center
10 Hyatt Street
Staten Island, New York 10301
(212) 442–8560

Learn Your Way
Brooklyn Public Library
Grand Army Plaza
Brooklyn, New York 11238
Contact: Philip Klingle, (212) 636–3132

Library Programs

Long Island Advisory Centers
Sponsored by Long Island Regional Advisory Council on Higher
    Education, Nassau and Suffolk Library Systems, and Nassau
    County Women's Service
1425 Old Country Road
Plainview, New York 11803
(516) 420–5101

Advisement sites are located in the following libraries. Telephone
    for appointment:

Smithtown	265–2072	Farmingdale	CH9–9090
Middle Country	585–9393	Glen Cove	OR6–2130
Mastic-Shirley	399–1511	Oceanside	RO6–2360
South Huntington	549–4411	West Islip	661–7080
Hempstead	IV1–6990	Riverhead	PA7–3228
Elmont	FL4–5280		

Nassau Library System
900 Jerusalem Avenue
Uniondale, New York 11553
Contact: Mrs. Estelle L. Goldstein

State-Supported Programs

Inmate College Advisory Project
University of the State of New York
99 Washington Street
Albany, New York 12230
Contact: Kate Gulliver, (518) 474–3703
For project locations, contact Kate Gulliver at above number

Regents Volunteer Advisors Network
99 Washington Avenue
Albany, New York 12230
Contact: Patricia S. Dyer, (518) 474–3703
For names and telephone numbers of over 150 educational advisors
   located throughout New York State, contact Patricia S. Dyer at
   above number

Women's Services

Nassau County Women's Services
1425 Old Country Road
Plainview, New York 11803
Contact: Lurana Tucker Campanaro, Director, (516) 420–5101

Putnam North Westchester County Women's Center, Mahopac
2 Mahopac Plaza
Mahopac, New York 10541
Contact: Susie Smithline, Director, (914) 628–9284

Women's Career Center, Inc.
121 North Fitzhugh Street
Rochester, New York 14614
Contact: Linda Cornell Weinstein, Executive Director,
   (716) 325–2274

Westchester County Women's Center, Mt. Vernon
W. 2nd Street and S. 6th Avenue
Mt. Vernon, New York 10550
Contact: Jane B. Wilson, (914) 664–7988

Westchester County Women's Center, White Plains
170 E. Post Road, Room 206
White Plains, New York 10601
Contact: Joyce Levine, Director, (914) 682–3410

Degree-Granting Institutions

Computer-Based Educational Opportunity Center
City University of New York
Office of Admissions Services
875 Avenue of the Americas
New York, New York 10001
Contact: Nathan F. Johns, Director, (212) 790–4652

Counseling Sites

   Educational Opportunity Center
   2090 Seventh Avenue
   New York, New York 10027

   Hostos Community College
   475 Grand Concourse
   Bronx, New York 10451

   Henry Street Settlement
   265 Henry Street
   New York, New York 10002

Evaluation and Placement Center for the Gifted
Child Study Center
Columbia University Teachers College
New York, New York 10027
Contact: Lynn Kurtz, Director, (212) 678–3880

Geneseo Migrant Center
State University College
Geneseo, New York 14454
Contact: Gloria Mattera, Director, (716) 245–5681

Mid-Career Counseling Program
Mid Life Assessment Program
111 Humanities
State University of New York, Stony Brook
Stony Brook, New York 11794
Contact: Dr. Alan D. Entine, (516) 246–3304

NORTH CAROLINA

Interinstitutional Programs

Adult Learning Information Center
Olivia Raney Library
104 Fayetteville Street
Raleigh, North Carolina 27601
Contact: Rosemary N. Jones, Counselor-Coordinator,
   (919) 833–1098

Library Programs

ACE (Adult Continuing Education)
Forsyth County Public Library
660 W. Fifth Street
Winston-Salem, North Carolina 27101
Contact: Ann Gehlen, (919) 727–2556

Lifetime Educational Opportunities
Greensboro Public Library
Drawer X-4
Greensboro, North Carolina 27402
Contact: Mrs. Karen Behm, (919) 373–2471

OHIO

Independent Brokering Services

Greater Cleveland External Degree Service
2422 Prospect Avenue
Cleveland, Ohio 44115
Contact: Allan F. Pfleger, Director

Interinstitutional Programs

Educational Opportunity Center
136 West Monument Avenue
Dayton, Ohio 45402
Contact: Stuart L. Fickler, (513) 223–5074

Women's Services

Project EVE
Cuyahoga Community College
2900 Community College Avenue
Cleveland, Ohio 44115
Contact: Evelyn Bonder, Director, (216) 241–5966, X209

Computer-Based and/or Telephone Information Services

Ohio Career Information System
145 S. Front Street
Columbus, Ohio 43216
Contact: Deborah Gorman, (614) 466–8987

OKLAHOMA

Library Programs

Adult Learner Advisory Service
Tulsa City County Library System
400 Civic Center
Tulsa, Oklahoma 74103
Contact: Suzanne Boles

Open Access-Satellite Education Services
Capital Hill Library
334 S.W. 26th
Oklahoma City, Oklahoma 73109
Contact: Sandy Ingraham, (405) 631–7649

OREGON

Computer-Based and/or Telephone Information Services

Oregon Career Information System
University of Oregon
271 Hendricks Hall
Eugene, Oregon 94703
Contact: Paul Franklin, Coordinator, Technical Assistance,
  (503) 686–3872

PENNSYLVANIA

Independent Brokering Services

Adult Career and Education Services (ACES)
1005 W. 3rd Street
Williamsport, Pennsylvania 17701
Contact: Linda Fenner, Coordinator, (717) 326–3761, X246

Interinstitutional Programs

RETURN: Regional Network for Adult Students
RETURN Sites

> RETURN
> Continuing Education for Mature Students
> Bucks County Community College
> Newtown, Pennsylvania 18940
> Contact: Susan Schuehler, Coordinator of Regional Network for
>   Adult Students, (215) 968–5861

RETURN
Adult Program
Temple University
207 Mitten Hall
Philadelphia, Pennsylvania 19122
Contact: Dorie Gilchrist, Acting Associate Director,
   (215) 787–7602

RETURN
Community College of Philadelphia
34 South 11th Street
Philadelphia, Pennsylvania 19107
Contact: Sandy Kunz, Counselor, (215) 972–7588

RETURN
Montgomery County Community College
340 DeKalb Pike
Blue Bell, Pennsylvania 19422
Contact: Cathy Pillar, Continuing Education Coordinator,
   (215) 643–6000, X403

RETURN
Opportunities/Adults
Delaware County Community College
Media, Pennsylvania 19063
Contact: Sue Staas, Coordinator, (215) 353–5400, X324

University Center at Harrisburg
2991 N. Front Street
Harrisburg, Pennsylvania 17110

Library Programs

Education Information Center
Carnegie Library of Pittsburgh
4400 Forbes Avenue
Pittsburgh, Pennsylvania 15213
Contact: Joseph F. Falgione, (412) 622–3127

Lifelong Learning Center
Free Library of Philadelphia
Logan Square
Philadelphia, Pennsylvania 19103
Contact: Marge Pacer, (215) 567–4353

Lifelong Learning Center
Reading Public Library
5th and Franklin Streets
Reading, Pennsylvania 19602
Contact: Maryann Haytmanek, (215) 376–6501

Women's Services

Options for Women, Inc.
8419 Germantown Avenue
Philadelphia, Pennsylvania 19118
Contact: Marcia Kleiman, Co-Director, (215) 242–4955

PUERTO RICO

Degree-Granting Institutions

Educational Opportunity Center
Inter American University–Arecibo Regional Colleges
P.O. Box 845
Arecibo, Puerto Rico 00612
Contact: Margarita González, Director, (809) 878–2830

RHODE ISLAND

Independent Brokering Services

Career Counseling Service
Ocean State Training Center
Quonset Point
North Kingston, Rhode Island 02819
Contact: Mildred Nichols, Director, (401) 272–0900

Interinstitutional Programs

Project CHOICE
Clearinghouse on Information on Continuing Education
Urban Education Center
830 Eddy Street
Providence, Rhode Island 02905
Contact: Brenda Dann-Messier, Project Coordinator,
 (401) 461–3990

TEXAS

Independent Brokering Services

Central Counseling and Placement Program
Vocational Guidance Service, Inc.
2525 San Jacinto
Houston, Texas 77002
Contact: Gaye Brown-Burke, Director, (713) 659–1800

Library Programs

Adult Basic Education
Memorial Library
317 Stilwell Boulevard
Port Arthur, Texas 77640
Contact: Helen B. Rethke, (713) 982–6491

Neighborhood Information Centers
Houston Public Library
500 McKinney Avenue
Houston, Texas 77002
Contact: Dianne Summar, (713) 224–5541, X206

Degree-Granting Institutions

Educational Opportunity Center
701 Elm Street, Room 303
Dallas, Texas 75202
Contact: Rita White, Director, (214) 746–2197

UTAH

Library Programs

Independent Study Program
Whitmore Library
Salt Lake County Library System
2197 East 7000 S.
Salt Lake City, Utah 84121
Contact: Ms. Pat Montgomery, (801) 943–7614, X213

Salt Lake City Public Library
209 E. 5th Street, S.
Salt Lake City, Utah 84111
Contact: Thomas Phelps

VERMONT

Degree-Granting Institutions

Community College of Vermont
P.O. Box 81
Montpelier, Vermont 05602
Contact: Peter Smith, President

Counseling Sites

Central Vermont
8 Langdon Street
Montpelier, Vermont 05602

Northwest Region
Jackson State College
Box A-14
Johnson, Vermont 05656

Northeast Region
Box 927
Lyndonville, Vermont 05851

Southeast Region
5 Canal Street
Bells Falls, Vermont 05101

VIRGINIA

Women's Services

FOCUS of Charlottesville
P.O. Box 3365, 214 Rugby Road
Charlottesville, Virginia 22903
Contact: Susan C. Bates or Barbara Durkee, Administrative Directors, (804) 293–2222

Northern Virginia Information and Counseling Center for Women
127 Park Street, N.E., Suite A
Vienna, Virginia 22180
Contact: Pat Warren, Director, (703) 281–2657

WASHINGTON

Independent Brokering Services

Educational Opportunity and Resource Center
515 South M Street, P.O. Box 165
Tacoma, Washington 98405
Contact: Ruth Russell, (206) 572–5960

Degree-Granting Institutions

Okanogan County Educational Brokerage Service
Wenatchee Valley College
Box 2058
Omak, Washington 98841
Contact: Ms. Wini Voelckers, (509) 826–4901

Computer-Based and/or Telephone Information Services

Washington Occupational Information Service
c/o The Evergreen State College, Sc. Lab II
Olympia, Washington 98505
Contact: Elton W. Chase, Executive Director, (206) 866–6740

WISCONSIN

Degree-Granting Institutions

Community-Based Counseling for Adults
University of Wisconsin–Extension
432 N. Lake Street
Madison, Wisconsin 53706
Contact: Carmen Thompson, Coordinator, Educational Counseling
    Services, (608) 263–2055
For address and telephone numbers of local counseling sites in 40
    counties, contact Carmen Thompson at above number

Computer-Based and/or Telephone Information Services

Higher Education Local Program (HELP)
1600 Van Hise Hall
1220 Linden Drive
Madison, Wisconsin 53706
Contact: Bobbi Hahn, Counselor, (608) 263–4567

Wisconsin Occupational Information System
Wisconsin Vocational Studies Center
321 Education Building
Madison, Wisconsin 53706
Contact: Roger Lambert, Executive Director, (608) 263–2704

Bibliography

Chris Argyris, *Personality and Organization* (New York: Harper & Row, 1957).

Lotte Bailyn, "Involvement and Accommodation in Technical Careers: An Inquiry into the Relation to Work at Mid-Career," in John Van Maanen (ed.), *Organizational Careers: Some New Perspectives* (London: John Wiley & Sons, 1977).

Mary Jo Bane, *Here to Stay, American Families in the Twentieth Century* (New York: Basic Books, 1976).

Richard Beckhard, "Managerial Careers in Transition; Dilemmas and Direction," in John Van Maanen (ed.), *Organizational Careers: Some New Perspectives* (London: John Wiley & Sons, 1977).

Fred Best and Barry Stern, "Lifetime Distribution of Education, Work and Leisure: Research Speculations and Policy Implications of Changing Life Patterns" (Washington, D.C.: Institute for Educational Leadership, December 1976).

J. I. Biegeleisen, *Job Resumes* (New York: Grosset & Dunlap, 1976).

Richard N. Bolles, *The Quick Job Hunting Map* (Berkeley, California: Ten Speed Press, 1976).

Richard N. Bolles, *The Three Boxes of Life* (Berkeley, California: Ten Speed Press, 1978).

Richard N. Bolles, *What Color Is Your Parachute?* (Berkeley, California: Ten Speed Press, 1977).

Richard N. Bolles and John C. Crystal, *Where Do I Go From Here With My Life?* (New York: The Seabury Press, 1974).

Burdette E. Bostwick, *Finding the Job You've Always Wanted* (New York: John Wiley, 1977).

Burdette E. Bostwick, *Resume Writing: A Comprehensive How-to-Do-It Guide* (New York: John Wiley, 1976).

Orville G. Brim, "Theories of the Male Mid-Life Crisis," *The Counseling Psychologist,* 1976, volume 6, pp. 2–9.

Charlotte Buhler, "The Curve of Life as Studied in Biographies," *Journal of Applied Psychology,* August 1935, pp. 406–409.

Carnegie Commission on Higher Education, *New Students and New Places* (New York: McGraw-Hill, 1971).

Carnegie Commission on Higher Education, *Toward a Learning Society: Alternative Channels to Life, Work and Service* (New York: McGraw-Hill, 1973).

Willard C. Clopton, *An Exploratory Study of Career Change in Middle Life* (Unpublished doctoral dissertation, University of Cincinnati, 1972).

John R. Coleman, *Blue-Collar Journal: A College President's Sabbatical* (New York: Lippincott, 1974).

The College Placement Annual (Bethlehem, Pennsylvania: The College Placement Council).

Samuel R. Connor and John S. Fielden, "Rx for Managerial 'Shelf-sitters' " *Harvard Business Review,* November–December 1973, pp. 113–116.

Wilbur Cross, *The Weekend Education Source Book* (New York: Harper's Magazine Press, 1976).

K. Patricia Cross, John R. Valley, and others, *Planning Non-Traditional Programs* (San Francisco: Jossey-Bass, 1974).

Samuel S. Dubin, "Obsolescence or Lifelong Education: A Choice for the Professional," *American Psychologist,* May 1972, p. 487.

Samuel S. Dubin, "Updating and Midcareer Development and Change," *Vocational Guidance Quarterly,* December 1974, p. 152.

Lee D. Dyer, "Implications of Job Displacement at Mid-Career," *Industrial Gerontology,* Spring 1973, pp. 38–46.

Erik H. Erikson, *Childhood and Society* (New York: W. W. Norton, 1950).

Howard Figler, *PATH: A Career Workbook for Liberal Arts Students* (Cranston, Rhode Island: Carroll Press, 1975).

Margaret Fisk and Mary W. Pair (eds.), *Encyclopedia of Associations* (Detroit: Gale Research Co., 1976).

Jerry Flint, "Mandatory Retirement: Division in the Work Force," *The New York Times,* August 11, 1977, p. 36.

Eli Ginzberg, *The Manpower Connection: Education and Work* (Cambridge, Massachusetts: Harvard University Press, 1975).

Ellen Goodman, "How About Major in Keeping Afloat?" *At Large, Boston Globe,* April 3, 1977.

Gary D. Gottfredson, *Career Stability and Redirection in Adulthood* (Baltimore, Maryland: The Johns Hopkins University Center for Social Organization of Schools, November 1976), Rept. 219.

Jay M. Gould, *The Technical Elite* (New York: Kelley, 1966).

Roger L. Gould, "The Phases of Adult Life: A Study in Developmental Psychology," *American Journal of Psychiatry,* November 1972, pp. 529–530.

B. Greco, *How to Get the Job That's Right for You* (Homewood, Illinois: Dow Jones-Irwin, Inc., 1975).

Gardiner G. Greene, *How to Start and Manage Your Own Business* (New York: McGraw-Hill, 1975).

Bernard Haldane, *Career Satisfaction and Success: A Guide to Job Freedom* (New York: AMACOM, 1974).

Douglas T. Hall, *Careers in Organizations* (Pacific Palisades, California: Goodyear, 1976).

Douglas T. Hall and Roger Mansfield, "Relationships of Age and Seniority with Career Variables of Engineers and Scientists," *Journal of Applied Psychology,* April 1975, pp. 201–210.

Robert J. Havighurst, *Developmental Tasks and Education* (New York: Longmans, Green, 1952).

James M. Heffernan, Francis U. Macy, and Donn F. Vickers, *Educational Brokering, A New Service for Adult Learners* (Syracuse, New York: National Center for Educational Brokering, 1976).

Margaret Hennig and Anne Jardim, *The Managerial Woman* (New York: Anchor Press/Doubleday, 1977).

Frederick Herzberg, Bernard Mausner, and Barbara B. Snyderman, *The Motivation to Work* (New York: John Wiley, 1959).

Dale L. Hiestand, *Changing Careers After Thirty-Five* (New York: Columbia University Press, 1971).

Charles M. Holloway, "Miami's Scientist-Physicians," *Change,* April 1977, pp. 21–22.

Everett C. Hughes, "Institutional Office and the Person," *American Journal of Sociology,* November 1937, p. 26.

Stanley D. Hyman, "Changing Careers in Midstream," *Manpower,* June 1975, pp. 22–26.

International Association of Counseling Services, *Directory of Counseling Services* (Washington, D.C. American Personnel & Guidance Association).

Interview with **Peter Drucker,** *Psychology Today,* March 1968, p. 21.

Richard K. Irish, *Go Hire Yourself an Employer* (Garden City, New York: Anchor Books, 1973).

R. J. Jameson, *The Professional Job Changing System* (New York: Performance Dynamics, Inc., 1976).

Elliott Jaques, "Death and the Mid-Life Crisis," *Work, Creativity and Social Justice* (New York: International Universities Press, 1970).

Walter C. Johnstone and Ramon J. Rivera, *Volunteers for Learning* (Chicago: Aldin, 1965).

Carl G. Jung, "The Stages of Life," in J. Campbell (ed.), *The Portable Jung* (New York: The Viking Press, 1971).

H. G. Kaufman, *Obsolescence and Professional Career Development* (New York: AMACOM, 1974).

Emmanuel Kay, *The Crisis in Middle Management* (New York: AMACOM, 1974).

Morris T. Keeton and others, *Experiential Learning* (San Francisco: Jossey-Bass, 1976).

Arthur Kirn and Marie Kirn, *Life Work Planning* (New York: McGraw-Hill, 1977).

Malcolm S. Knowles, "Toward a Model of Lifelong Learning" in Forbes Bottomly (ed.), *Peak Use of Peak Years,* 1975 Institute for Chief State School Officers (Washington, D.C.: U.S. Office of Education, 1975), p. 35.

Juanita Kreps, "Some Time Dimensions of Manpower Policy," in Eli Ginzberg (ed.), *Jobs for Americans* (Englewood Cliffs, N.J.: Prentice-Hall, 1976).

Norman D. Kurland (ed.), *Entitlement Papers* (Washington, D.C.: National Institute of Education Papers in Education and Work, No. 4, March 1977).

Richard Lathrop, *Who's Hiring Who* (Reston, Virginia: Reston Publishing Company, 1976).

Harvey C. Lehman, *Age and Achievement* (Princeton, New Jersey: Princeton University Press, 1953).

Daniel J. Levinson, "The Mid-life Transition: A Period in Adult Psychosocial Development," *Psychiatry,* May 1977, p. 100.

Daniel J. Levinson and others, *Seasons of a Man's Life* (New York: Knopf, 1978).

Jean Lipman-Blumen and Harold J. Leavitt, "Vicarious and Direct Achievement Patterns in Adulthood," *The Counseling Psychologist,* 1976, volume 6, p. 30.

Marjorie Fiske Lowenthal, M. Thurner, D. Chiriboga, and others, *Four Stages of Life: A Comparative Study of Women and Men Facing Transitions* (San Francisco: Jossey-Bass, 1976).

Michael Maccoby, *The Gamesmen* (New York: Simon and Schuster, 1976).

Abraham Maslow, *Motivation and Personality* (New York: Harper & Row, 1954).

John B. Miner, "Conformity Among University Professors and Business Executives," *Administrative Science Quarterly,* 1962, volume 7, pp. 108–109.

Bernice L. Neugarten, "Adaptation and the Life Cycle," *The Counseling Psychologist,* 1976, volume 6, p. 16.

The New York Sunday Times, The Week in Review, July 31, 1976, Section 4, p. 9.

George J. Nolfi, "The Case for Selective Entitlement Vouchers," Dyckman W. Vermilye (ed.), *Individualizing the System. 1976 Current Issues in Higher Education* (San Francisco: Jossey-Bass, 1976).

James O'Toole, *Work, Learning and the American Future* (San Francisco: Jossey-Bass, 1977).

James O'Toole and others, *Work in America* (Cambridge, Massachusetts: Massachusetts Institute of Technology Press, 1972).

James G. Paltridge and Mary C. Regan, *Mid-Career Change: An Evaluative Study of Diverse Models of Multi-Institutional Programs of Continuing Education for Persons Seeking Mid-Career Employment Change* (a University of California, Berkeley, study funded by the Special Community Service and Continuing Education Project, Bureau of Post-Secondary Education, U.S. Office of Education, 1976–1978).

George E. Parsons and James V. Wigtil, "Occupational Mobility as Measured by Holland's Theory of Career Selections," *Journal of Vocational Behavior,* 1974, pp. 321–330.

Anthony H. Pascal, *An Evaluation of Policy Related Research on Programs for Mid-Life Career Redirection,* Rand Corporation Report (R-1582/2-NSF), Santa Monica, California, February 1975 (NTIS No. PB-242 373/LL).

Robert C. Peck, "Psychosocial Developments in the Second Half of Life," in Bernice L. Neugarten (ed.), *Middle Age and Aging* (Chicago: University of Chicago Press, 1968).

Robert C. Peck and H. Berkowitz, "Personality and Adjustment in Middle Age," in Bernice L. Neugarten (ed.), *Personality in Middle and Late Life* (New York: Atherton Press, 1964).

Donald C. Pelz and F. M. Andrews, *Scientists in Organizations* (New York: John Wiley & Sons, 1966).

Robert Perrucci and Joel E. Gerstl, *The Engineers and the Social System* (New York: John Wiley, 1969).

Robert Reinhold, "New Population Trends Transforming U.S.," *New York Sunday Times,* February 6, 1977, p. 42.

Richard R. Ritti, *The Engineer in the Industrial Corporation* (New York: Columbia University Press, 1971).

Paula I. Robbins, *Career Change in Males in Middle Adulthood and Its Implications for Higher Education.* (Unpublished doctoral dissertation, University of Connecticut, 1977).

Betty H. Roberts, *Middle-aged Career Dropouts: An Exploration* (Unpublished doctoral dissertation, Brandeis University, 1974).

Seymour B. Sarason, *Work, Aging, and Social Change* (New York: The Free Press, 1977).

Theodore J. Shannon and Clarence A. Schoenfeld, *University Extension* (New York: The Center for Applied Research in Education, Inc., 1965).

Gail Sheehy, *Passages. Predictable Crises of Adult Life* (New York: E. P. Dutton, 1976).

Harold L. Sheppard, "The Emerging Pattern of Second Careers," *Vocational Guidance Quarterly,* December 1971, p. 89.

Harold L. Sheppard and Neal Q. Herrick, *Where Have All the Robots Gone? Worker Dissatisfaction in the 70's* (New York: The Free Press, 1972).

William A. Sievert, "A California Campus Where Adults Can Return to College 'on Their Own Terms,'" *The Chronicle of Higher Education,* December 12, 1977.

William A. Sievert, "Exploring Careers at Lone Mountain College," *The Chronicle of Higher Education,* January 19, 1976, p. 3.

Cyril Sofer, *Men in Mid-Career: A Study of British Managers and Technical Specialists* (Cambridge, England: Cambridge University Press, 1970).

Dixie Sommers and Alan Eck, "Occupational Mobility in the American Labor Force," *Monthly Labor Review*, January 1977, pp. 3–19.

Michèle Stimac, "A Model for Evaluation of Decision Passages: A Facet of Self-Assessment," *Personnel and Guidance Journal*, November 1977, pp. 158–163.

Walter D. Storey, "Self-Directed Career Planning at the General Electric Company" (Ossining, New York: General Electric Company, 1976).

Donald E. Super and Martin J. Bohn, Jr., *Occupational Psychology* (Monterey, California: Brooks-Cole, 1970).

Dale Tarnowieski, *The Changing Success Ethic* (New York: AMACOM, 1973).

Alvin Toffler, *Future Shock* (New York: Random House, 1970).

George E. Vaillant, *Adaptation to Life* (Boston, Massachusetts: Little, Brown, 1978).

George E. Vaillant and Charles C. McArthur, "Natural History of Male Psychological Health. I. The Adult Life Cycle from 18–50," *Seminars in Psychiatry*, 1972, volume 4, pp. 415–427.

John Van Maanen, "Introduction: The Promise of Career Studies," in John Van Maanen (ed.), *Organizational Careers: Some New Perspectives* (London: John Wiley & Sons, 1977).

Willard Wirtz and the National Manpower Institute, *The Boundless Resource: A Prospectus for an Education–Work Policy* (Washington, D.C.: New Republic, 1975).

Daniel Yankelovich. "Turbulence in the Working World—Angry Workers, Happy Grads," *Psychology Today*, December 1974, pp. 81–87.

Abraham Zaleznik, Gene W. Dalton, and Louis B. Barnes, *Orientation and Conflict in Career* (Cambridge, Massachusetts: Harvard University Press, 1970).

Index